WHO'S BETTER, WHO'S BEST

in

GOLF?

"Mr. Stats" Sets the Record Straight
on the Top 50 Golfers of All Time

ELLIOTT KALB

McGraw·Hill

New York   Chicago   San Francisco   Lisbon   London   Madrid   Mexico City
Milan   New Delhi   San Juan   Seoul   Singapore   Sydney   Toronto

The **McGraw·Hill** Companies

Library of Congress Cataloging-in-Publication Data

Kalb, Elliott.
      Who's better, who's best in golf? : "Mr. Stats" sets the record straight on the top 50 golfers of all
   time / Elliott Kalb.—1st ed.
         p.   cm.
      ISBN 0-07-146977-X (book : alk. paper)
        1. Golfers—Rating of—United States.   2. Golfers—United States—Biography.   I. Title.

  GV964.A1K35   2005
  796.352092—dc22   2005035205

Material in Chapters 1 and 11 is reprinted by permission of FOXSports.com

1 2 3 4 5 6 7 8 9 0   DOC/DOC   0 9 8 7 6

ISBN 0-07-146977-X

Interior design by Nick Panos

McGraw-Hill books are available at special quantity discounts to use as premiums and sales promotions, or
for use in corporate training programs. For more information, please write to the Director of Special Sales,
Professional Publishing, McGraw-Hill, Two Penn Plaza, New York, NY 10121-2298. Or contact your local
bookstore.

This book is printed on acid-free paper.

To my family: my mom and dad, my aunt Barbara and uncle James, my brother, David, and sister, Randi;

my children, Wyatt, Heath, Alissa, and Jordan;

and my wife, Amy—

You are all the loves of my life.

CONTENTS

FOREWORD
Brent Musburger

Who's the greatest golfer of all time? When my friend Elliott Kalb asked me that question, I answered that the greatest 18-hole showdown would be Jack Nicklaus and Ben Hogan in their prime. Man, that would be some match, wouldn't it?

I don't think you can ever look past what Jack accomplished over the years. I was at Augusta in 1986, getting ready for the presentation downstairs, when Nicklaus put on his charge. I have never heard a roar in Amen Corner like the one I heard that day nearly 20 years ago.

It's easy for my younger friends to talk about Tiger Woods and for me to wax on about Jack Nicklaus. But I stand in awe of what people say about Ben Hogan. He was a remarkable figure. He didn't do it on the best-conditioned courses or with the modern equipment. My goodness, just look at how the equipment has changed in the years since the Hogan blades.

Kalb forced me to think about the greats over the years. Sam Snead was one of the most agreeable men I've ever had the pleasure of talking to. I enjoyed his stories and wit. He had an unbelievable swing—very rhythmic.

Seve Ballesteros was a favorite of mine. In fact, at his peak he compares with Tiger Woods. Seve was great at trouble shots—recovery shots—the best I ever saw until Tiger came along. Ballesteros was remarkable in his ability to be off in the pines—well off the fairways—and hit great shots. Tiger is even better at getting out of trouble—he's a real artist with a wedge—and Seve is right behind him. It's a shame he couldn't keep it going over the last 10 years.

Jack and Ben were relentless machines in the fairways. They were the two greatest 1-iron players. The other thing that Nicklaus and Hogan shared is that they almost never made mental mistakes late.

There are so many great players throughout history. Lee Trevino gave Nicklaus all he could handle there for a while. And Raymond Floyd was another one. He was a great money player and one tough hombre.

When asked who the greatest putters of all time are, I generally answer with Tiger Woods and Arnold Palmer. In terms of sheer drama, can you name me a better putter with everything on the line than these two?

The other thing that Tiger shares with Arnold is that television ratings went up when either of them was in the hunt. Palmer had great sex appeal. He could flick a cigarette and people wanted to watch. He had that unusual powerful swing. It's a tribute to Jack—

who wasn't as popular as Palmer—that he hung with it, until Nicklaus eventually soared past Palmer.

I have the greatest respect for what Tiger Woods has accomplished. It's still debatable at this point if he's surpassed Nicklaus. Is Tiger up against more depth and better talent than Nicklaus was?

One thing I told Kalb was that Woods and Nicklaus and Hogan share a similar trait—an obsessive will to win. They came to bury their opponents. It is a mark they have in common with many great athletes in other sports.

That's what makes this book such a fine read. Kalb not only triggers memories but presents some arguments that sports fans will eat up. You know, one wouldn't be far off by ranking the top golfers of all time by merely listing the number of majors each one has. But Elliott resists that. He looks further and finds out, for example, the inequities with lesser playing fields of the 1940s and '50s British Opens. He argues that it's unfair to rank Nick Faldo, who has six majors, ahead of Billy Casper, the great golfer that no one ever talks about, who only won three. Kalb points out that Faldo entered 65 consecutive majors at one point. That's over 16 years of playing all four majors. But Casper played all four majors only from 1968 to 1972. How can Sam Snead's seven majors not be well ahead of Tom Watson's eight?

Kalb uses perspective to illuminate the numbers. He finds reasons—wartime service or injuries, for example—to explain gaps in a career. And he is one serious, passionate sports fan.

I've always enjoyed talking sports with Kalb, and his series of *Who's Better, Who's Best* books are like sitting down with him and shooting the breeze, remembering the great athletes of all time.

You don't have to agree with his choices—in fact, many people do not—but I guarantee you'll enjoy the read as he presents his choices.

ACKNOWLEDGMENTS

I've been very lucky in my life. I've worked with some of the most intelligent and interesting people—the greatest sports broadcasters and writers—in the nation. It makes my job the equivalent of a two-foot putt. You've heard of Bobby Jones's Grand Slam and Tiger Woods's Tiger Slam. Well, I was able to complete the "Television Grand Slam" in the preparation of this book. Brent Musburger shared with me his stories of covering the Masters. Dan Hicks did the same for me with his years covering the U.S. Open. Jim Nantz, the voice of CBS Sports, was also gracious with his time and eloquent in his words, answering so many of my questions, particularly about the different Masters and PGA Championships that he covered. TNT's Ernie Johnson Jr. was a wordsmith, e-mailing me a firsthand account of the particulars and feel of the British Open Championship. I'm knocked out by all of their talent, wit, and memories.

Other television analysts who assisted on this project include Johnny Miller and Lanny Wadkins, two of the greatest players of all time. Other former pros, including Peter Alliss, Brandel Chamblee, Gary Koch, Roger Maltbie, Dottie Pepper, and Bobby Casper, all graciously shared their time and opinions with me. Maltbie and I are living proof that 49ers fans and Raiders fans can be friends!

Then there are the sportswriters that I have to thank, including Dave Anderson at the *New York Times*, Tim Rosaforte of *Golf World* magazine, and Rick Reilly of *Sports Illustrated*.

NBC's magnificent golf producer, Tom Roy, has been a friend for 20 years. I'm extremely lucky that I could call on him for help on this project. Others at NBC that I am extremely grateful to are Dick Ebersol, Jon Miller, Kevin Monahan, Ricky Diamond, golf expert John Goldstein (who gives up his place to me in the tower each year at Lake Tahoe for the American Century Celebrity Golf Championship, for which I am eternally grateful), Gil Capps, and Joe Martin. Mark Mandel and Mike Pearl, from ABC Sports, need to be thanked as well.

The guys at foxsports.com (Ross Levinson, Jim McCurdie, and Tom Seeley) gave me a column and the support I need to write it. Brian Hyland at HBO Sports, Matt Boland at HBO, and Howie Deneroff at Westwood One radio share similar traits: they're all excellent producers and great bosses and friends.

There are the usual comrades that need to be thanked, including David Harmon and Marv Albert and Steve Horn. There are also the people that, for one reason or another, haven't been thanked in either of my previous books.

How can I repay John McCarthy, whom I met when I was in high school when he was my teacher? There isn't a first book, much less three of them, without Hannah Storm, who listened to my ideas for a basketball book and put me in touch with her terrific agent, Carol Mann.

Douglas Stark—the curator of collections at the USGA Museum in Far Hills, New Jersey—and research assistant Patty Moran were a delight even as I pestered them constantly for a couple of weeks.

And then there is Michele Matrisciani, who is my editor, my teammate, friend, and the person who didn't laugh when I called her up and said, "You know, I really believe Barry Bonds is the best player ever, and I'll bet the timing is right to put out a book that states that!" Thanks also to McGraw-Hill's Julia Anderson Bauer, who put up with my misspellings, one-sentence paragraphs, and revisions.

My in-laws, Irving and Barbara Levinson, assure me that their entire golf communities in Florida and New Jersey will buy and enjoy this book.

There are the kids: Wyatt, Heath, Alissa, and Jordan. Their dad isn't around every weekend to coach their teams, let alone attend all their games. The trade-off is that they are all, in their own way, becoming savants in sports knowledge. "Kathy Whitworth has 11 holes in one," chipped in Wyatt while reading an early draft of the manuscript. "You should put that in," said the 10-year-old, who reads his father's books, almanacs, encyclopedias, and anything by Bert Sugar. Does Heath, at five, really appreciate basketball star Bill Russell's winning 11 NBA championships? Actually, he does. Alissa even likes sports now that she understands the hard work involved in being part of a team like the color guard. Jordan, the 12-year-old, has passions that include reading, writing, and playing sports. The great thing about these kids is the bond they have with each other. I learn from them at least as much as they learn from me. Why I think it's important for them to appreciate Wile E. Coyote ("Super Genius"), Bruce Springsteen, Woody Allen, Shaquille O'Neal, and Phil Mickelson may be hard to explain. Then again, you should hear some of the music and see some of the shows they like!

I must acknowledge my true heroes, my parents. My father is the hardest-working individual that I know, and the most kind-hearted. He not only reads my books, he stays up late to watch or listen to me when I promote them. He attends local book signings. Here's the catch: he's not a sports fan! My mother, who has run a brilliant book-discussion group for the South Orange, New Jersey, library for 20 years, is the reason I love books, newspapers, and lively discussion. Phyllis Kalb is nothing if not fiercely loyal to her loved ones. I hope to provide the same security blanket to my children that my parents provided me.

I am most indebted to my wife, Amy. As a tribute to all she is to me and all she has given me, I offer this quote by the great European golfer J. H. Taylor from his 1943 auto-biography, *Golf: My Life's Work*, because Mr. Taylor was not only a superb golfer but a wonderful writer:

Whatever my merits or demerits as a husband my life has proved one thing I can and will say for all the world to know. Her courage in facing the rough and the smooth that life brings, her cheerfulness and devotion to home life and children—the constant and loving help given me in all my worries and anxieties, have been such as to cause me to wonder whether a better wife has ever existed. I take leave to doubt it. And in saying this I know that I am doing inadequate justice to what my wife has meant to me.

INTRODUCTION

"What do *you* know about golf?" chimes in Brent Musburger from his cell phone. "And what are you talking about, asking me who was better, Tiger or Jack? You're too young to remember Ben Hogan, but don't discount him." And I thought this was going to be easy.

I wrote *Who's Better, Who's Best in Basketball?* and a follow-up in the series, *Who's Better, Who's Best in Baseball?* The conclusions that I came to were that Shaquille O'Neal was better than all the other basketball players and that Barry Bonds was the best in baseball. Needless to say, these were controversial decisions.

I looked forward to the relative serenity of the golf research, comforted in the fact that I could not possibly make a controversial decision. Even more than the lack of serious candidates for number one (it had to be Tiger Woods and then Jack Nicklaus, or Jack Nicklaus followed by Tiger Woods), I was anticipating writing about a sport that featured sportsmanship.

In the baseball title I defended cheaters, in some degree because that's part of the sport's history. For more than 100 years, baseball players have used illegal pitches and illegal drugs, have stolen signs, and have done other things to gain a competitive advantage over their opponents.

How could I knock some known cheaters out of the top spots but not others? What if most modern-day players had "cheated"? Even more to the point, after my baseball book came out, many former players (including Mike Schmidt and Bob Gibson) said that they, being as competitive as they were, would have taken steroids if they'd been available when they played.

Golf doesn't have these problems. It's not that golfers are any less competitive than their baseball or football counterparts, but the sport has a character that the other sports do not. This is as fine a tribute to golf as there is.

One has to be honest in professional golf. Rule breaking is not tolerated by anyone. You don't even need referees in golf! This is the sport where accidental tap-ins cost players strokes in major tournaments. (The Masters, the U.S. Open, the British Open, and the PGA Championship are the four majors that are the yardstick for modern pro golfers.) This is the sport where a caddie can make an innocent mistake and cost his golfer a tournament. This is the sport that has technology to aid in yardage markers. But the PGA Tour has no plans to allow pro golfers to use binocular-like devices and GPS systems in competition. For instance, the USGA has 15 national tournaments, including the U.S.

Open (for men) and the U.S. Women's Open, and still determines yardages by pacing—you know, the old-fashioned way. Golfers can't even use carts, and Ben Hogan—after his severe automobile accident—wouldn't have even thought about asking to use one.

Of course, just because cheating isn't tolerated doesn't mean that it never happens. But golf takes care of its own problems. In 1985 Vijay Singh was embroiled in cheating allegations over an incident at an Asian Tour event. Singh was alleged to have altered his scorecard in an attempt to make the cut. Singh denied the allegations but was suspended by the Asian Tour.

Just the hint of a player altering his scorecard is scandalous in this sport. It's simply not worth risking one's reputation in golf.

Look at other professional sports. In late 2005 Argentinian soccer player Diego Maradona finally acknowledged that he had struck the ball with his hand in the famous "Hand of God" goal against England in the 1986 World Cup quarterfinals. After the goal Maradona said he quickly realized the referee had allowed the score but none of his teammates had rushed to celebrate with him—they were figuring the goal would be waved off. "I was waiting for my teammates to embrace me and no one came," said team captain Maradona. "I told them, 'Come hug me now or the referee isn't going to allow it.'"

Of course, Argentina won that match 2–1, on its way to the World Cup. Maradona, by the way, failed a drug test in 1991 and was banned for 15 months and was then selected with Pele as the best players in soccer history in 2002. Can you imagine that happening in golf?

In the fall of 2005, the number one college football team in the nation, USC, defeated Notre Dame on the game's final play when one player "pushed" a teammate into the end zone—a clear violation of the rules. After the game, losing Notre Dame coach Charlie Weis said it was a "worthwhile" risk for his opponent to take.

I can give chapter and verse of some of the most creative "cheating" in baseball history. The 1969 "Miracle" Mets defeated the heavily favored Baltimore Orioles in five games. In the sixth inning of Game 5 with the Orioles leading 3–0, umpires awarded first base to Cleon Jones of the Mets, saying he was hit on the foot by a pitch. Donn Clendenon then homered, bringing the Mets back within one run of the Orioles in a game they'd go on to win 5–3. More than 30 years later, Mets pitcher Jerry Koosman said, "That baseball *never* hit Jones. The pitch bounced in the dirt and rolled into our dugout. Immediately [Mets manager] Gil Hodges told me to pick up the ball and rub it on my shoe. I did and put a black shoe polish mark on it. Hodges in a split second grabbed the ball and ran out to the umpires, arguing that the ball hit Jones and here was the mark to prove it. He sold the umpires on it, they gave Jones first base, and that was a big play!

Some people call that cheating, but that kind of stuff went on all the time in baseball." Can you imagine that happening in golf?

NBA players have said that, at the end of a game, with 10 seconds left, they're not leaving the paint, regardless of the three-second rule. They know the refs won't blow the whistle in that situation.

In the NHL one of the most important issues is defining and enforcing the rules against obstruction. The real issue isn't obstruction. The real issue is cheating, having the proper respect for the rules, the officials, and the game.

The NFL had such a drug problem in the 1980s that 13 players were convicted of drug trafficking from 1976 to 1989. Players have gotten bigger and bigger despite the outlawing of steroids. No one is taking away the Steelers' four championships in the '70s despite the knowledge that several of the linemen used steroids.

No one is taking away any of Rafael Palmeiro's hits or home runs. He served his 10-day suspension, which was shortly after Major League Baseball took out a full-page ad in a national newspaper, congratulating him for his 3,000 hits. The message is clear: if a player can get away with cheating in team sports, the player, team, and league all benefit. For example, when a baseball player sets home run records, Major League Baseball benefits with higher attendance and television ratings, even if the records become knowingly tainted.

The blood-doping problem is—or was—pervasive in track and field, weight lifting, and cycling. It depends on who you believe.

Why is this sport of golf different from all other sports? Without players getting performance-enhancing drugs or trying to avoid getting caught or stay ahead of the testing, the emphasis is on the field of play.

We can judge golfers and compare them with others in their era or earlier. We still have those topics that will raise discussions among people of different generations—improved technology and training, chief among them.

Gary Player, one of the game's all-time greats, would like to change both the ball and the club for professionals. Without the power that often brings 400-yard drives, he believes today's superstars could come up short compared to his generation. "I just hate to see what's happening today with golf clubs that I consider to be illegal," Player remarks. "I'd stop the grooves being so deep [on the ball], and I'd stop the trampoline effect in the wood." Player has an easy but unrealistic solution. "The way to solve all the problems is to quit making metal clubs and go back to wood, but I say that with tongue in cheek," he explains. "If you gave Jack Nicklaus the conditions these guys play in now, none of them [modern-day players] could live with him. Also, there's nobody on the Tour today who could hit the ball as well as Lee Trevino or Ben Hogan." Player was one of the first players to utilize personal training and conditioning. He looked for competitive advantages, legally, to get higher scores and last longer than previous greats. And now he is putting down modern technology for allowing current players to post lower scores than his and other players of his generation. Interesting, isn't it?

There is also the wonderful argument of "quality of competition." Not all eras are created equal. Was it harder to win in the 1920s or the 1980s or the 2000s? Is the quality of Young Tom Morris's opponents inferior to the quality of the opponents of Harry Vardon, who came on the scene after Morris? Does Annika Sorenstam have more difficult competition than Mickey Wright had? Does Tiger Woods have it easier than Jack Nicklaus had it?

The methodology for this book will be to mainly judge the golfers by their accomplishments relative to the accomplishments of their peers. Sam Snead can't be rated higher than other golfers merely because he won more tournaments. Bobby Jones can't be rated higher simply because he had more majors than someone else. Players prior to the mid-1930s didn't have the Masters to play at. South African players were at a real disadvantage in playing major tournaments in the United States. For some, like Bobby Locke, their performances at the British Open have to be weighed and given greater stature. We have to put each player's record into proper perspective.

How do you rank the best golfers? How do you compare golfers in the era of the featherie ball (a sewn leather sphere stuffed with feathers) with golfers in the modern era of aerodynamically tested Surlyn balls and titanium-shafted clubs?

I do it the only way I know how. I compare players with players of different eras. I compare players with athletes in other sports. I compare players with pop-culture figures. I provide colorful, detailed biographies with little-known facts about each golfer. The book also branches out into other discussions, such as the following:

- How does Jack Nicklaus compare with and rank against Tiger Woods through a similar point in their careers?
- Where does 1920s great Bobby Jones rank against 1910 legend Harry Vardon?
- Was Mickey Wright the best woman golfer of all time, and did she dominate her competition like Palmer and Nicklaus did in their era?
- Who were the top golfers by decade?
- Who were the best amateurs? The best after the age of 40?
- Who are the best putters of all time?

The top 50 golfers of all time will be ranked. That's not a lot. There have been 41 male golfers who have each won at least three major championships. That's not including a ton of golfers who played prior to the 1960s, when it became common to play four majors a year. That's not including any women. That's not including golfers like Phil Mickelson, who won his second major at the PGA Championship in August of 2005. It was very hard selecting from a field so deep, cutting to just 50 top players.

There will be little suspense over the choice of number one: Tiger Woods. There are many people who disagree with me. Many experts that I spoke to at the 2005 PGA Championship and the 2005 Presidents Cup said I cannot make anyone but the great Jack Nicklaus number one of all time.

In a political op-ed piece that ran in the *Denver Post*, Paul Campos, a professor of law at the University of Colorado, came up with a great analogy. He used it in terms of cranky conservatives and naive liberals. I'm using it to justify the selection of Woods over Nicklaus.

In his article, entitled, "Any Time's Better Than Now," Campos writes the following:

One of my favorite examples is from Ernest Hemingway's *Death in the Afternoon*, in which he reviews bullfighting magazines covering roughly a century's worth of fights. He discovers that, in no matter what year the magazine was published, it's observed that the bulls of 20 years earlier were gigantic, fearless creatures who met their match in the peerless bullfighting artists of that era, so unlike today's small, cowardly bulls fought by fraudulent performers who are paid vast sums to bamboozle the gullible public.

Nicklaus was a gigantic, fearless creature. No one can seriously argue that point. But Tiger doesn't need any more time. He's better. He's the best.

And Brent, I know all about the great Ben Hogan. He's third.

TIGER WOODS
The Greatest of All Time

There has never been an athlete as well chronicled as Eldrick "Tiger" Woods. There aren't play-by-play accounts of Dan Marino's junior high games. Lance Armstrong went for plenty of bike rides that are unaccounted for. But Tiger was never anonymous. When he was two he putted against Bob Hope on the "Mike Douglas Show." At age three he shot 48 for nine holes. In March of 1991, when Woods was in ninth grade, *Sports Illustrated*'s Tim Crothers wrote a profile of Woods, quoting him as saying, "I don't want to be the best black golfer on the Tour. I want to be the best *golfer* on the Tour." Did Ted Williams tell people in high school that he wanted to walk down the street and have people remark, "There goes the greatest hitter of all time"?

He is the son of Earl and Tida Woods. He is as racially neutral as one could be. His father, from Manhattan, Kansas, is half-black. He's also a quarter American Indian and a quarter Chinese. His mother, from Bangkok, is half-Thai, a quarter Chinese, and a quarter white. One parent is Protestant, the other a Buddhist. In America, however, that means you're still seen as black.

"I just am who I am, whatever you see in front of you. . . . The bottom line is that I am an American, and proud of it!" Tiger joked in the mid-1990s that he thought of himself as "Cablinasian." That's short for the fact that he is one-eighth *Cau*casian, one-quarter *bl*ack, one-eighth American *In*dian, and one-half East *Asian* (a quarter Thai and a quarter Chinese).

Charles Barkley, former NBA player ranked 21 in *Who's Better, Who's Best in Basketball?*: "We shouldn't be looking at race, but we do. Tiger didn't realize it at first, but society makes you choose. Look, Tiger is a great role model for all kids, but particularly in the black community."

Because of Woods's popularity he has been a role model for the black community, as well as for all other communities. The game has been on a surge in popularity, and it can be felt in television ratings and attendance at tournaments and the number of weekend players. Woods is responsible for a chunk of that surge.

Tiger Woods has been criticized for not speaking out more for the black community. But his friend Barkley, who got him to open up and talk about racism in Barkley's book *Who's Afraid of a Large Black Man?*, told me, "No matter what happens, Tiger is going to get criticized. When that happens, you have two choices. You can be really honest and straightforward, or you can be guarded."

Charles Barkley: "I've gotten on him over the years for not talking more about his experiences growing up and for not taking stronger stands on racial issues. I've told him many times that we know people see him as black."

Dr. Richard E. Lapchick, a professor, civil rights activist, and author on the issues of race and sports, wrote this:

> What is it about Tiger Woods that makes us embrace him and at the same time let his contemporaries in tennis, Venus and Serena Williams, seem to be far less loved and embraced? Is it Tiger's brilliance on the course? His charm? Or is it that he has remained on the sidelines regarding social and political issues?

Rick Reilly, *Sports Illustrated* columnist: "When Tiger was 7, his parents installed the psychological armor. If he had a full wedge shot, the father would stand 15 feet in front of him and say, 'I'm a tree.' And the kid would have to hit it over him. . . . By 3 years old, Tiger was beating 10-year-olds, and then by 6 he'd already had two holes in one."

First Impressions

Charles Barkley: "Tiger is a 'Once in a Lifetime' guy. As an athlete, you know. I was great in my sport, so was Karl [Malone], Patrick [Ewing], but we weren't Michael. When I saw Michael Jordan play for the first time—at the 1984 Olympic trials—I knew. When I first met Tiger—at my golf tournament in 1994—I played a round of golf with him. I walked away from that saying that I just played golf with the greatest golfer who ever lived. How did I know? I just had seen some shit I had never seen before. When he hit the ball, it made a different sound. What is the common denominator that Tiger and Michael share? They have great skills, and they work harder than everyone else."

Dan Hicks, golf announcer for NBC Sports: "The first time I saw Tiger in person was at the 1995 U.S. Amateur in Newport, in the second of his three Amateurs. He defeated Buddy Marucci in the finals. He had this unbelievable 8-iron that came inches from the cup on the 36th hole of his final match. There was no doubt about it. He just got the job done. I mean, there was no doubt about this guy's game."

Tiger delayed turning pro and enrolled at Stanford University.

Rick Reilly: "I hit balls with him when he was a freshman at Stanford. I never saw anything like it. You could roll a ball to him, and he would hit it 250 yards. He was simply amazing."

The 20-year-old Woods won his third U.S. Amateur in 1996. It was the sixth straight year that he had won either the U.S. Junior title or the U.S. Amateur. He also joined Jack Nicklaus and Phil Mickelson as the only players to win the U.S. Amateur and the NCAA Championship in the same year.

After turning professional he entered eight PGA Tour events at the end of 1996 and won two of them. At the 1996 Disney World/Oldsmobile event, he shot a 21-under par 267 and defeated Payne Stewart by a stroke. At the Las Vegas Invitational, he trailed by four strokes entering the final round and won in a play-off over Davis Love III.

By 1997 he was the leading money winner on the PGA Tour and had won four tournaments, including the Masters. And he not only won the Masters, but he set a 72-hole record and won by 12 strokes! The greatest golfers in the world have been playing the Masters since 1934. No one ever did better than the 22-year-old Woods did. And the 12-stroke margin of victory? Well, I put it like this. In the last 15 years, a golfer has won a tournament by 10 or more strokes only three times. Tiger Woods has done it all three times.

Or put it in perspective this way. Nicklaus is considered by many to be the greatest golfer in history. He won six Masters Tournaments. One of those times he won in a play-off, finishing in a three-way tie. He won three other green jackets by exactly one stroke. In 1972 he won by three strokes. And he shot his then-record 270 in 1965, winning by nine strokes over Arnold Palmer and Gary Player. Palmer at the time called Nicklaus's performance "the greatest 72 holes of golf ever played." Sixty-three-year-old Bobby Jones said similarly, "It was the greatest playing in golfing history."

And Woods—almost out of the chute—topped it. Tiger's performance at the 1997 Masters was the top sports story of 1997 and one of the top sports stories of the decade. At the time, Nicklaus said Woods reminded him of himself 30 years earlier. "He has the same advantages when I first came out only he is longer than I was. He's hitting those short irons to the par-5s and just makes the course melt away," Nicklaus said at Augusta in 1997.

Woods was selected by the Associated Press as the Male Athlete of the Year (the first golfer so honored since Lee Trevino in 1971). And then, when it appeared that Woods would steamroll through the field at other majors, it didn't happen. Woods did not come close to any of the other three remaining majors in 1997. He revamped his swing, as a matter of fact. Tiger would not win any of the next 10 majors, until the 1999 PGA. Could he have won more had he not revamped his swing? It is a point of conjecture.

He won only one of the 26 tournaments he entered in 1998. In the majors he finished tied for 8th at the Masters, tied for 18th at the U.S. Open, 3rd at the British Open (one stroke back of Mark O'Meara and Brian Watts), and tied for 10th at the PGA. He shot a 66 on the final round at the British Open, but it was too little, too late after a 77 on the third round.

Tiger earned $6.6 million in 1999, nearly $3 million more than his nearest competitor, David Duval. The eight wins on the PGA Tour were an enormous number. No one else had won six times in one year on the Tour since Tom Watson did it in 1980. Tiger became the first player since Johnny Miller to win eight times in a year and the first since Ben Hogan in 1953 to win four consecutive starts.

In 1999 Woods won eight times on the PGA Tour, garnering more than $7 million. But he couldn't win any of that year's first three majors, the measuring stick for many people (including Tiger). He had one last major to shoot for in '99—the PGA Championship.

Jim Nantz, golf announcer for CBS Sports: "I'll never forget being in the tower for the 1999 PGA Championship. What I'll never forget about Tiger's tournament was the sheer exhaustion on his face, on his final shot on 18. He only needed about a two-footer, and after he knocked it in, his body went limp. He looked as if he didn't have an ounce of energy left in him. Remember, there were all kinds of doubts about him at this time. It is my contention that his second major was his hardest to ever win. He had made his mind up from a very early age on winning majors, and chasing Nicklaus's 18, and that wear and tear on him took a toll mentally. That tournament wasn't easy—Sergio Garcia gave him a great battle—and that win took Tiger out of the throes."

At the 1999 PGA Championship, Woods finished a stroke ahead of Garcia and got his groove back. Those doubts that Nantz referred to concerned Tiger's ability to win the majors. Was he just a shooting star that came back to Earth? No, Tiger was the real deal. Beginning with that 1999 PGA Championship, Woods won five of the next six majors, including four in a row (the Tiger Slam). Even Jones, in his 1930 season, never won four consecutive majors. Only Young Tom Morris (over the course of four consecutive British Opens) had ever won four straight majors.

Rick Reilly: "I've never seen a greater sporting achievement in my lifetime. Tiger's Slam—his four consecutive majors—was better than DiMaggio's 56-game hitting streak; it was better than the 1972 Dolphins winning every game they played. I mean, think about it. To win those four majors, he had to essentially go 551–0 against the top golfers in the world. With the fields of each tournament over 100, Tiger had to overcome the hot hand of any and all of them. It was remarkable."

The 2000 season was the greatest single year a golfer has ever had. Woods won the first three majors of the year. His nonadjusted scoring average of 68.17 was best in golf history, surpassing Byron Nelson's mark of 68.33 in 1945. He finished his year with 47 consecutive rounds of par or better. He won the British Open by eight strokes, giving him all four majors by the age of 24. Only four other players (Sarazen, Player, Hogan, and Nicklaus) had ever won all four majors—at any age! At the U.S. Open, Woods won by a record 15 strokes. The old record was 13, by Tom Morris Sr. at the 1864 British Open.

Dan Hicks: "I covered the 2000 U.S. Open at Pebble Beach and I think that is Woods's single best tournament of his career. On a course where the greens are not the truest, Woods put on a putting show. He put on a driving accuracy show. I mean, it wasn't a fair fight. To see the best players in the world admit to utter defeat is something that I haven't seen in any sport. I think that we'll never see a 2000 season like Tiger Woods had, and we'll never again see it from Tiger. We'll never see a single tournament dominated like Tiger dominated that U.S. Open."

Brandel Chamblee, Golf Channel analyst and PGA Tour member: "I played in that 2000 Open, and have the perspective of the field. He was unbeatable. He was Bobby Jones in 1930, or Ben Hogan in 1953, or Jack [Nicklaus] in 1972."

All the golfers marveled at how Woods lapped the field. The best quote was from Mark O'Meara. "Jack Nicklaus is by far the greatest golfer of all times in terms of records. But to me, Tiger Woods is the greatest player I've ever seen. He may not match Nicklaus's records, but it's hard for me to believe that there's ever been a player who could drive it, cut it, draw it, hit it high, low, has the short game putting, the mental toughness. If you were building the complete golfer, you would build Tiger Woods."

Woods won the 2001 Masters and in 2002 became the first since Nicklaus in 1972 to capture the U.S. Open and Masters in the same season. And then he hit another bump in the majors road.

He led the Tour in victories for a fifth time in 2003 with five more tournament wins. In 2004 he surpassed Greg Norman for most weeks at number one in the Official World Golf Ranking with his 332nd combined week at the top. But Vijay Singh ended Woods's consecutive weeks at number one (364 weeks) when Singh took over as the top player in the world in September of 2004. Tiger won only once in 2004 (defeating Davis Love III in the finals of the WGC-Accenture Match Play Championship) and finished 22nd, 17th, 9th, and 24th in the four majors.

Woods entered the 2005 season without a win in his last 10 majors. In fact, he had finished in the top five only twice in those 10 major tournaments. But as he did beginning with the 1999 PGA Championship, Tiger worked his way back on course to overtake Nicklaus. He won the Masters for a fourth time in nine years. He finished second in the U.S. Open. He won the British Open. And despite almost failing to make the cut at the PGA Championship at Baltusrol, he worked his way back into contention. He took two majors in 2005 and didn't miss the other two he entered that year by much. I wrote a column for foxsports.com that ranked Tiger's greatest seasons and decided that 2005 was his second greatest year, compared to his brilliant 2000 season. An accompanying poll found that 85 percent of online respondents agreed.

Woods almost won the PGA Championship in 2005 and in the process almost lost any chance he could have had at winning the championship. Here's what happened. Woods finished his final round and signed his scorecard at 2-under par. Bad weather moved in, causing a delay that didn't allow the rest of the field to finish their rounds before dark. The PGA needed an extra day to wrap up the tournament. Woods was the leader in the clubhouse, but a handful of golfers were leading Woods with a few holes left to finish. Tiger never showed up the next day, when the tournament concluded. He'd assumed that his score wouldn't hold up.

Jim Nantz: "We [CBS] had a camera awaiting his arrival on Monday. We figured he would be there with a cup of coffee, showing his face just to let his competitors know he was there. We never found him, obviously, as he never showed up. At one point on Monday morning, Phil [Mickelson] is −3 on the 17th hole. Steve Elkington is at −3. Tiger is in the books at −2. What if Elkington fell apart? Can you imagine the pressure that would fall upon Mickelson? Who knows what could have happened? The point is, Tiger prepared his whole life for these major championships. If he had been needed for a playoff—and instead the world found out that he fired up his plane the night before to get out of New Jersey—it would have been the biggest mistake of his life. He had no understanding of this. It wouldn't have been the equivalent of a double bogey. The analogy would be a 10-cup number. It would have been the biggest gaffe in sports history. It would be like [Scott] Norwood missing the field goal or Chris Webber calling a time-out at the end of the NCAA Championship game."

Of course, Woods took a chance, but the leaders held on. Mickelson won the PGA, and Tiger finished in a tie for fourth.

Who's Better, Who's Best
Tiger Woods or Jack Nicklaus?

There are only six golfers with more than 46 PGA wins at any age (Snead, Nicklaus, Hogan, Palmer, Nelson, and Casper). Woods should pass Nelson and Casper in 2006. Only Jack Nicklaus and Walter Hagen have won more majors than Woods. Nicklaus is the one that can be judged mano a mano with Woods on their major tournaments.

Most PGA Wins in Their 20s
1. 46 Tiger Woods
2. 30 Jack Nicklaus

Professional Majors Won by Tiger Woods
2005 British Open
2005 Masters
2002 U.S. Open
2002 Masters
2001 Masters
2000 PGA
2000 British Open
2000 U.S. Open
1999 PGA
1997 Masters

Most golfers play their best in their thirties, so Tiger's fans can expect many more years of production from him. Tiger turned 30 years old on December 30, 2005. To that point, he had won 10 majors (and 3 U.S. Amateur titles). Jack turned 30 years old on January 1, 1970. To that point, he had won 7 majors (and 2 U.S. Amateur titles). That puts Tiger in the clear lead over Jack by the time each had reached his 30th birthday.

Now Tiger's wins in those majors were more convincing, as I'll show. And Jack has many more top-five finishes. It's a razor-thin decision.

Jack, by his 30th birthday, had entered the four major tournaments 40 times.

At the 30th Birthdays, Record in Majors
1. Woods: 10 for 42 (winning 23.8 percent of the time)
2. Nicklaus: 7 for 40 (winning 14.5 percent of the time)

Woods was an amateur the first six times he entered the majors and yet made the cut in four of the six. In fact, his score was the lowest among amateurs at the 1995 Masters and the 1996 British Open.

How many majors will Tiger win? That has been a topic of discussion since Woods was a young cub. Author Tim Rosaforte was there when Tiger's father, Earl, made a toast to his son in the fall of 1995, when the teenaged Woods was winning the U.S. Amateur, announcing, "Before he's through, my son will win 14 major championships." Now that looks conservative. Bobby Casper, golf analyst and son of Hall of Famer Billy Casper, thinks that Woods can win majors well into the twenty-first century. I tend to agree.

Most Consecutive Events Without Missing the Cut

1. 142 Tiger Woods (from February 5, 1998, at the Buick International to the 2005 Byron Nelson Championship)
2. 113 Byron Nelson (1941–48)
3. 105 Jack Nicklaus (1970–76)

The 142 consecutive tournaments where Woods made the cut might be as impressive as his number of majors. At the Byron Nelson Championship, Woods needed a par on the final hole but pulled his second shot into a bunker and his bunker shot ran too far past the hole. Woods missed the putt and fell a shot below the cut line. Over the seven years of Tiger's streak, he won 37 tournaments, including eight majors.

Rick Reilly: "This streak is amazing. He accomplished this week in and week out, despite everything else that could have been going on in his life. He had the flu—he made the cut. He was fighting with his girlfriend—he made the cut."

Tiger's streak was 30 percent better than anyone else ever did. Although Tiger faced tougher competition, Byron never finished less than 17th. Nicklaus was the other great champion who was a grinder. And his best streak at making the cut was 105. That tells you something about Tiger's record.

Tiger Woods has the greatest set of skills any golfer was ever blessed with. He also has the competitive fire to compete each and every week. And then on top of that, he has the ability to turn his game up a notch for the four majors each year. Who's to say that if he didn't exist, Phil Mickelson or Ernie Els wouldn't have a string of majors? Who's to know if Tiger's competition appears not as notable as Nicklaus's because they're dwarfed by Woods's shadow?

From 1997 to 2005 there were four men chosen as the Associated Press Male Athlete of the Year. The athletes honored in that nine-year period were Tiger Woods, Mark

McGwire, Barry Bonds, and Lance Armstrong. The latter three have been accused of taking performance-enhancing drugs. Tiger has never been accused of taking any illegal substance. Nicklaus was never chosen as the Associated Press Male Athlete of the Year but Tiger was named it three times. It could have been bad luck that Nicklaus's greatest seasons were overshadowed by Sandy Koufax, Mark Spitz, Muhammad Ali, or Larry Bird. Or, maybe Jack didn't dominate the sports landscape the way that Woods does.

So Woods's athletic talent not only is superior but is also natural. He operates in a sport of honor. His worst offense has been to not alienate the majority of fans by speaking out on controversial issues. The other offense was a rare sportsmanship error, leaving the PGA Championship while he was still technically in contention.

I'm just saying that Woods is the greatest of all time, based on the numbers. I'm not even talking about the Jackie Robinson–type impact he's had on the game and how many fans he has brought to the table.

Brandel Chamblee: "Like Nicklaus, Tiger's genius is palpable. Woods has every tool available to him, and more important, he has the inextinguishable thirst to use those tools to their fullest extent."

In 2000, to commemorate the end of the century, *Golf Magazine* ranked the top golfers in history, placing Woods at 12th of all time. It is the contention here that in the last five years, he has won enough and gained enough ground to pass the 11 golfers ahead of him, including Jack Nicklaus.

It is time to realize that Tiger Woods is the greatest golfer of all time. Yes, in the coming years he may injure his back, totally redo his swing the wrong way, decide he would rather raise kids than play golf, or take a million other paths than the one track he has been on. But through the end of 2005, if he never played another round, it would be enough to consider Woods the greatest of all time.

JACK NICKLAUS
The Golden Bear

Jack Nicklaus has been considered the greatest golfer of all time since the mid-1970s. That's 30 years of setting the standard in his sport. Is he the greatest? As Jack himself said after he won his 14th major (surpassing Bobby Jones's mark), "The only measuring stick today is major titles. You can't compare stroke averages. The courses are so different." There is no question in my mind that the number of majors represents excellence at different types of courses, longevity, and pressure situations.

The question now becomes, has Jack been surpassed by Tiger Woods? Nobody has a résumé like Jack's. His references give out such positive feedback, you have to stop and wonder if it could all be true.

Jim Nantz, golf announcer for CBS Sports: "At this point, Jack Nicklaus is the greatest golfer of all time. Golf is a sport that we have to wait and look at the entire career. I can't put stock in what Jack did by the age of 30. I will say that Tiger is tracking to one day be the greatest."

Jay Randolph, Golf Channel commentator: "I began playing golf in 1950. [Note: The "Jay-Bird" is best known as a broadcaster, but he actually competed in four U.S. Amateur Championships in the early 1950s.] So I've seen the top players over 55 years. I would say that Nicklaus is the greatest—although Tiger could change that. Nicklaus had that uncanny ability to play his best at the majors—to focus on winning those events. He went through a stretch where it appeared he never missed a six-foot putt."

Gary Koch, NBC golf analyst and PGA Tour member: "Jack is the best of all time. He's the best primarily because of his longevity. He's played the game at the highest level for about 25 years. He won majors in 1962 and 1986. That's impressive. He had that ability to raise his game. Nowhere did his ability stand out more than at Augusta each year."

Dan Hicks, golf announcer for NBC Sports: "Because of Jack's longevity, because of the level of competition he faced, I'd have to say Jack over Tiger."

Brandel Chamblee, Golf Channel analyst and PGA Tour member: "Nicklaus's numbers are mind-boggling: 18 wins in the majors and another 19 runner-up finishes and 13 third-place finishes. Tiger, when he doesn't win the majors, doesn't seem to have as many close calls. That pushes Nicklaus ahead."

Nicklaus was named Golfer of the Century in 2000 by virtually every national and international media outlet and was named *Sports Illustrated*'s Male Athlete of the Century and number 9 on ESPN's list of 100 Greatest Athletes of the Century. He trailed only Michael Jordan, Babe Ruth, Muhammad Ali, Jim Brown, Wayne Gretzky, Jesse Owens, Willie Mays, and Jim Thorpe. No athlete can match his longevity. From 1962 to 1980, Nicklaus finished first, second, or third in 41 of the 76 major championships he entered.

Jack Nicklaus was born in January of 1940, which makes him less than four years older than football legend Jim Brown and only two years older than Muhammad Ali. Brown retired from the NFL in 1968. Ali, who fought well beyond what he should have, won his last big fight in 1978. Nicklaus finished in the top 10 of a major championship in the 1990s.

Every great athlete needs a break to get him started. It was his father's broken bone in his ankle that proved to be Jack Nicklaus's lucky "break." Charley Nicklaus, a pharmacist from Ohio, was a tennis player, 7-handicap golfer, and one-time college football player. After he broke a bone in his ankle, the doctors told him to walk on soft ground at first. He missed playing sports and decided to do his walking on the golf course. He took his son, Jack, along. This was Jack's introduction to golf. The pro at the country club, Jack Grout, took a look at Jack's swing and said to Charley, "I'd like to teach that boy before anybody gets ahold of him."

On the first nine holes he played, Jack shot a 51. The following year, he was shooting in the low 80s. Nobody practiced more than Jack, who took up the game at the age of 10. At 13 he was a 3-handicapper and had broken 70. By age 16 he had won the Ohio Amateur.

In 1955 Jack was the youngest player in the U.S. Amateur. His boyhood hero, Bobby Jones, was so impressed by Jack's drives that he decided to follow him for a round. So at 15 years of age, Nicklaus had impressed the man many considered to be the greatest of all time.

Nicklaus, like Jones before him and Woods after him, was one of the greatest amateurs in history. After the teenage Nicklaus won his first U.S. Amateur in 1959, he said he'd like "to do something like Bobby Jones." Jones played in his first U.S. Amateur Championship in 1916, when he was only 14 years old. He was eliminated in the third round by Bob Gardner, the defending champion. Nicklaus qualified for his first U.S. Amateur in 1955—a much more difficult feat than in Jones's day because there were 1,493 entries instead of 217. He was defeated that year by (a different) Bob Gardner. Jack was 19 years old when he won the U.S. Amateur title in Colorado Springs in September of 1959. In early October, Nicklaus had his first major tucked away—the U.S. Amateur—and headline writers gushed, "Amateur Champ Nicklaus Paralleling Bobby Jones."

It wasn't until November of 1961 that Nicklaus (who had won his second U.S. Amateur, at Pebble Beach, that year) announced he was going to turn pro. It put to an end an unbelievable six-year amateur career. When Arnold Palmer made his memorable come-from-behind victory at the 1960 U.S. Open, the second-place finisher was Nicklaus, who didn't pocket a dime due to his amateur status. Nicklaus was two shots behind Palmer, with his 282 the lowest score ever made in the U.S. Open by an amateur.

Why didn't Nicklaus turn pro sooner? Perhaps he was playing it safe. It could not be assumed that he could earn a decent living. Nicklaus was 21 and told the press that he planned to return to Ohio State for the fall quarter each year until he got his degree in business administration. Jack may have really thought that he couldn't earn enough money in professional golf to support his family. As it turned out, he made enough money to support a small country.

It's time to revisit the major markers in Nicklaus's career.

1962 U.S. Open

Jack's first professional victory—major or otherwise—came in 1962 at Oakmont, Pennsylvania, the site of the U.S. Open. It was memorable because the best and most popular golfer of the world at the time—Arnold Palmer—was heavily favored and yet lost to the young Nicklaus (whom Palmer called "that big dude") by three strokes in an 18-hole play-off.

In the play-off, Palmer (who had won the Masters in April) birdied the 9th, 11th, and 12th holes to close within a stroke of Nicklaus. But Palmer's putter failed him down the stretch. Nicklaus never three-putted in the play-off round.

Jack became the youngest golfer to win the U.S. Open since (guess who?) Bobby Jones in 1923. Jack's victory wasn't very popular among Arnie's Army, the very large Palmer fan base.

1963 Masters

The first time Jack Nicklaus entered the Masters was as an amateur in 1959, when he failed to make the cut. He not only made the cut in 1960 but finished in a tie for 13th. The next year, he did even better, shooting a 287 and finishing in a tie for 7th.

His first Masters as a professional was not vintage Nicklaus. He tied for 15th, so he didn't exactly get out of the gate like Tiger did.

It didn't take that long, however, before he sizzled in the majors. Tough conditions in the 1963 Masters meant higher scores than usual, including an opening round 74 for Jack. The next day, he shot 6-under par 66. He was in first place after the second and third days of the tournament.

He needed to shoot par on the final round to hold off Tony Lema by one stroke. A 12-foot birdie putt on 16 gave him the necessary margin. The victory made Nicklaus, at age 23, the youngest Masters winner (until Tiger). He was defeating fields of Arnold Palmer, Gary Player, Sam Snead, and other greats. It was an impressive start to his career.

1963 PGA Championship

It's terrible, but I can't put Dallas and 1963 in the same sentence without thinking of President Kennedy's assassination. Four months before the assassination, the city was host to the PGA Championship, which was played in 110-degree temperatures.

Nicklaus's win in the scorching heat gave him victories in the U.S. Open, the Masters, and the PGA. He became only the fourth golfer ever to accomplish that—joining Gene Sarazen, Ben Hogan, and Byron Nelson. It took Jack just 18 months to win the three different majors.

Nicklaus had to overcome the lead of Bruce Crampton, who had a three-stroke lead going into the final round. Crampton faded. Nicklaus made a sensational 30-foot birdie putt on the 15th hole and shot a 68 to win by two strokes over Dave Ragan and three over Crampton.

1965 Masters

This was the tournament when Nicklaus pulled away from Palmer, putting Nicklaus in the conversation for greatest of all time. He shot 67–71–64–69 to win the most prestigious tournament in the world 17 strokes under par. Previous to this, the fans didn't warm to him. He had won too much, too early. He threatened their favorite, Palmer. But by 1965 he had begun to receive tremendous ovations at Augusta.

Palmer called Nicklaus's performance "the greatest 72 holes of golf ever played." Sixty-three-year-old Bobby Jones said similarly, "It was the greatest playing in golfing history." In shooting a 64 over the 6,980-yard course, Nicklaus reached 11 greens in regulation figures with a wedge. Palmer and Gary Player, two of the greatest golfers of all time, finished in a tie for second place—a full nine strokes back.

1966 Masters

Golf was secondary to Nicklaus the week of the 1966 Masters. He made up his mind before the tournament began that he was going to win, he said later, referring to a promise to himself after his friend Bob Barton was killed in a plane crash en route to the Masters.

Nicklaus beat Tommy Jacobs and Gay Brewer in an 18-hole play-off to become the first golfer to win two Masters Championships in a row. Jack finished 11 strokes back of his 1965 score but still won the tournament!

In the 18-hole play-off, Jack shot a 70, Jacobs a 72, and Brewer a 78. On the par-four 18th, Nicklaus's second shot went into the crowd. But Jack chipped within a couple of feet and sank the putt to win his third Masters in four years. Even more impressive, he had tied for second in 1964, six strokes back of Arnold Palmer. If not for Palmer, Jack might have run off four Masters in a row.

1966 British Open

Nicklaus's one-stroke victory made him just the fourth man to complete the career Grand Slam. In the final of the 1966 British Open at Muirfield, three players were in contention toward the end of the championship. Dave Thomas took a par on the long par-five 17th hole. Doug Sanders did the same. Nicklaus needed a birdie on 17 and holed it. He made par on 18 and won his first British Open by a stroke. Jack, at 26, was the youngest to complete the feat until Woods did it in his amazing 2000 season at the age of 24.

1967 U.S. Open

On the 72nd hole of the 1967 U.S. Open at Baltusrol, Nicklaus blasted perhaps his greatest single shot: a 1-iron from 238 yards. The birdie would give him a tournament record, but (with a four-stroke lead) he needed only to stay away from taking a 7 on the hole to lose. He knocked his 1-iron to 22 feet. Minutes later he sank the long putt to win his second U.S. Open.

Jack shot a record 275 (breaking Ben Hogan's 19-year U.S. Open tournament record by one) at Baltusrol in Springfield, New Jersey. Three months after failing to make the cut at the Masters, Jack revamped his game. His 5-under par 65 in the final round was more than enough to beat Palmer, who finished four strokes back. Nicklaus would say after the round, if it wasn't his best round at any U.S. Open, it didn't miss by much. He had eight birdies on the final round. Playing the final 18 holes with Palmer, he still heard cheers on the holes where Palmer gained ground on him. Jack may not have had an army, like Palmer, but he had seven majors, just like Palmer.

1969 Ryder Cup

Nicklaus's first time playing on the Ryder Cup team was in 1969. In the closest contest in Ryder Cup history, 17 of the 32 matches went down to the last hole. The Ryder Cup came down to the final afternoon singles match between England's Tony Jacklin and Nicklaus. When Jacklin made a pressure 30-foot putt on the 17th hole, it drew the final match of the Ryder Cup even with one hole to go. In one of golf's most memorable moments of sportsmanship, Nicklaus conceded a two-footer to Jacklin after making a four-footer for par on the last green, resulting in the first tie in the match's history.

1970 British Open

"If a golfer is to be remembered, he must win the Open at St. Andrews," Nicklaus once said. Since Nicklaus turned pro, the British Open has been held at St. Andrews only eight times. Nicklaus won it twice; Tiger has won it twice.

In 1970 Doug Sanders was involved in an 18-hole play-off at the Home of Golf. Sanders had choked the day before, when he missed a three-foot putt on 18. Some say Sanders was never the same after that. Perhaps there was even divine intervention involved, after Nicklaus had conceded Jacklin's putt in the 1969 Ryder Cup.

Taking advantage of a reprieve, Nicklaus had gained a four-stroke lead through 13 holes of the play-off. But then the momentum changed. Sanders holed a birdie putt to pick up a stroke at the 14th hole. Sanders made another birdie on the 15th, while Nicklaus made par. The lead was cut to two strokes. Nicklaus bogeyed 16. The lead was down to a single stroke, heading for the last hole.

Sanders played first. He drove the ball and was 30 yards short of the final green. Nicklaus knew he could drive the ball onto the green 358 yards away. But if he made a slight mistake, it would cost him the championship. A cautious 4-wood, a wedge, and two putts would probably be enough for Nicklaus to win—or at least tie with Sanders.

Nicklaus drove the ball straight at the green, with no drift to the right. He overdrove it, and it skipped past the pin and up toward the gallery. It snagged in the heavy rough. After both men wedged to within five feet of the hole, Nicklaus, playing first, sank his putt and captured his second British Open—and first at St. Andrews.

1971 PGA Championship

By the time Jack was 31 years old, his slump in major tournaments was over. Remember, he had gone from the 1967 U.S. Open to the 1970 British Open without winning a major. Not bad, except for an immortal. But by the '71 PGA, he was back. Jack captured his second PGA Championship, giving him at least two victories in all four majors. It was also his 31st Tour victory. This one came fairly easy. Jack led after the second and third rounds and shot only 73 on the final round, but it was enough to win by two strokes over Billy Casper. Jack made his birdie putt on 17 and won the PGA Championship in Palm Beach Gardens, Florida. This was his 11th major counting his two U.S. Amateurs. His goal was Jones's mark of 13, which included six Amateur titles. The Golden Bear was well within reach.

1972 Masters

Nicklaus was the only player under par in 1972 at the Masters. He led all four rounds. He tied Palmer by winning his fourth green jacket. He was 32 and clearly in the prime of his career.

1972 U.S. Open

Bobby Jones died in 1971, so he wouldn't see when Nicklaus tied his record of 13 majors. Nicklaus won his 13th major in June of 1972 at Pebble Beach.

The course was playing as close to impossible as it could, with sudden gusts of wind. Jack's score of 290 was the highest score to win the Open since 1935 (when Sam Parks Jr. won with a 299). Even after Nicklaus shot 2-over 74 on the final round, he won the tournament by three strokes over Crampton and four over Palmer.

The debate over the best of all time was sounded by pro Hale Irwin after this Nicklaus victory:

> Jack probably is the best player ever to play the game. He is so much stronger than the average professional. He's so much longer. He can hit the ball so much farther than we can. When you're playing with him, you have to approach the whole thing realistically. You step on the first tee and know you're going to be outdriven on every hole. I wouldn't be correct if I said you don't feel his presence. He's there. One thing you can be absolutely sure of is he didn't get there by luck.

When Jack won the U.S. Open, it also put him halfway to Jones's Grand Slam. Furthermore it gave him possession of three of the four major trophies at once (he had won the 1971 PGA Championship). Nicklaus made a strong bid to win the British Open that year, but he finished a stroke behind Lee Trevino at Muirfield. That one-stroke loss to

Trevino goes a long way in my ranking Tiger (who completed his "Tiger Slam") ahead of Jack.

1973 PGA Championship

"I don't know if Bobby Jones is better, or I am. I do know that he achieved his in shorter time," said Nicklaus after his 14th (12th professional) major. Nicklaus wasn't the favorite going into this tournament in Cleveland, but his 72 holes included only 5 bogeys and 11 birdies. A closing 69 gave Nicklaus a 277 and a four-shot victory over runner-up Crampton.

Nicklaus's victory in August of 1973 was a bad moment for sports heroes from the 1920s. Hank Aaron would surpass Babe Ruth's home run total a few months later. Nicklaus didn't get as much fanfare (or hate mail) as Aaron, but Jones's record for majors had stood for 43 years.

1975 Masters

Jack won the 1975 Masters by the narrowest of margins. He defeated Tom Weiskopf and Johnny Miller by a stroke. Nicklaus finished the thrilling tournament with a 276. Hale Irwin tied a course record with an 8-under par 64 on the final day. Miller was 11 strokes off the lead after two rounds but then shot a 65 and 66. He just missed a birdie putt at the final hole that would have put him in a share of the lead. Weiskopf came from six shots back to overtake the front-running Nicklaus after 54 holes. When Weiskopf made a 12-foot birdie at 16, it put him one shot ahead of Jack with three holes to play. But Nicklaus didn't win all those majors for nothing, and on the par-three 16, he made a 40-foot sidehill putt that ultimately would win him his 15th major, his 13th as a professional.

1975 PGA Championship

This was Jack's 4th PGA Championship and his 16th major. It took place at Akron, Ohio. Crampton, playing before Nicklaus, shot a closing-round 69 and finished with a 278. Despite taking a double-bogey-6 on the final hole, Jack finished two strokes better than Crampton, with a 276. Sometimes a pitcher will give up runs when he has a big lead. In 1975, in the prime of his career, I can't see Nicklaus taking the double bogey on 18 if he needed better.

Jack was so good, he could shoot less than his best and still win majors. If Jack was ever going to win the Grand Slam, it would have been in 1975. He won the Masters in April. He blew the U.S. Open at Medinah by bogeying the last three holes, finishing two shots back. He missed the British Open Championship that year by a single shot. So he didn't miss the Grand Slam by much.

1978 British Open

Every great champion needs a competitor that pushes him or her to succeed. Nicklaus had three golfers that proved to be challenging adversaries to him at various stages in his career. His biggest competitive threat during his early career was Arnold Palmer (who was born in 1929); during the middle of his career it was Lee Trevino (who was born in 1939); and during his late career it was Tom Watson (born in 1949). By 1978 Tom Watson was looking like the next Nicklaus.

The greatest major that Nicklaus played in and didn't win was probably the 1977 British Open. That was called "The Duel in the Sun" and featured the final two rounds of Watson and Nicklaus going shot for shot. Jack shot 65–66, but Watson countered with 65–65 for a one-stroke victory.

The following year, Nicklaus would add his third and final British Open. That would break a string of 10 consecutive majors for Nicklaus, who had gone without winning a major since the 1975 PGA Championship. He came from behind on the final three holes and finished 7-under par for the tournament. It was his second win at St. Andrews and his third British Open. In 1978 he showed the world that he was far from finished.

1980 U.S. Open

Nicklaus didn't win a thing in 1979, and at 40 years old, he wasn't expected to be winning any more majors. Back at Baltusrol for the 1980 U.S. Open, he shot a 63 on the first day. He shot a 2-under par 68 on the final day and survived to win his fourth U.S. Open. His four-day total of 272 beat his own Open record, which he had set at the same club 13 years earlier.

1980 PGA Championship

Nicklaus continued to rewrite history books in 1980 by tying Walter Hagen for the most PGA crowns (five) and winning by the biggest margin since the Championship switched to stroke play in 1958. Nicklaus posted a 6-under par score of 274 for a seven-shot victory over Andy Bean.

Nicklaus would nearly add a sixth PGA Championship to his résumé in 1983 at Riviera Country Club in Pacific Palisades, California. Hal Sutton's opening round 6-under par 65 gave him eight strokes on Nicklaus. But 43-year-old Jack shot 65–71–66 on the final three days to finish in second place, just one stroke back of Sutton.

1986 Masters

On the final day of the 1986 tournament, the gallery was for Nicklaus, an obvious sentimental favorite at 46 years old. Seve Ballesteros—with a two-shot lead after 14 holes—took a bogey on 15, putting his drive in the fairway and trying to reach the green in two shots. The ball bounced in water, and eventually Seve would take a bogey on a hole that Nicklaus had eagled earlier. Nicklaus had trailed Ballesteros by six strokes with 10 holes to play. Seve wasn't the only one who blew this tournament. Greg Norman (who had made four consecutive birdies to get back into contention) got a little too aggressive. He was tied with Nicklaus on the final hole and was too hard with his second shot. The shot went into the gallery. Norman missed a putt on 18. Tom Kite missed a putt on 18. Again, was it divine intervention?

Nicklaus shot a back-nine 30 and won his sixth Masters, 23 years after winning his first. He finished the round 7-under par 65. He had turned back the clock, making himself and his fans feel younger.

Ernie Johnson Jr., golf announcer for TNT Sports: "I think the quick and easy answer on the Jack and Tiger debate is that Jack's greatest champion the game has ever known and that Tiger is the most talented guy to ever tee it up. Woods's willingness to attempt shots that other guys wouldn't think of, and then on top of that to deliver, is unmatched. I think the quality that Jack and Tiger share is all between the ears, and that is what separates those who excel from those who compete. There is that hard to define, yet impossible to ignore, and probably overused phrase—'the will to win.' They thrive on moments, situations, opportunities that have mere mortals shaking in their spikes.

"I can't speak from the experience of a tour player, like many of my colleagues can, so I can't and won't pick apart swing changes or compare the relative strengths and weaknesses of each player in their prime. I can only speak from what I've seen from the 18th tower in the course of our TNT coverage. I'll never forget one of those 'passing of the torch' moments at the PGA Championship at Valhalla, as Tiger and Jack were paired for the first two days. They came to the par-four 18th on Friday with Nicklaus needing birdie to make the cut. In trouble off the tee, he needed to hole his third shot from the fairway and danced a wedge inches from the cup. It would have been hard to imagine a louder roar from the gallery had it gone in. And as the two walked to the green there was a palpable feeling of respect and admiration for each other, and for the game itself. Sounds kinda flowery, but there was no denying it.

"At the 2005 British Open, Jack had the St. Andrews stage to himself . . . Tiger playing a few groups behind. It was on that Friday afternoon that those same qualities of respect and admiration were just overflowing. Our broadcast tower was located near the 1st green shooting back toward the 18th fairway and green. While Jack was making his way around the course in what would be his final round of competitive golf (though we didn't know that until late in the day), the crowd surrounding the 18th began building as Jack made the turn. Eventually wave upon wave of fans made their way to what would be the grandest stage for a sporting event that I'd ever seen. I remember turning my chair during a commercial break and seeing that there was no room to move on the street that runs alongside the 18th fairway separating the course from the hotels and shops at the Old Course. There were people on every balcony, heads sticking out of every window, and necks craning for a glimpse of Jack as he came to the 18th tee. We knew then that there was no chance he would play the weekend, but knew full well that we were in for something special. And it was just that every step of the way, as Jack nearly came out of his shoes with a missile off the tee . . . stood one last time on the Swilken Bridge for the photo op of all time . . . and then left himself a birdie chance. One of the most amazing facets of the whole thing was how the roars of those thousands who had staked out their spots to watch this theater fell absolutely silent as Nicklaus studied that putt. How could that many people make that much noise and then be that reverentially quiet? You know the rest of the story. The birdie putt fell . . . the place erupted . . . the ground shook . . . and the tears flowed. That's what happens when the greatest champion the game has ever known shows us all once again how he got there."

The Golden Bear had accomplished everything and more in the game of golf. While he probably wasn't the best in any one phase of the game, he was the greatest in history—until Tiger Woods surpassed him somewhere around 2005. Just as Jones surpassed Vardon and Nicklaus surpassed Jones, Woods has surpassed Nicklaus.

At their respective bests, Tiger has Jack beat. Tiger is just starting to add enough tournament wins and major wins to put the Tiger ahead of the Bear. Nicklaus played his entire career with an overlapping grip, and now that grip on history is overlapped as well.

3

BEN HOGAN
Practice Makes Perfect

Ben Hogan was born on August 13, 1912. His story is inspirational in so many ways. He was not the son of a hard-driving military perfectionist who bred his son to do a job. He was not the son of a rich pharmacist who took him to country clubs and gave him every advantage. No, he was the son of a mechanic and blacksmith who committed suicide when Ben was nine years old.

Success did not come early to Hogan, as it did to Tiger Woods, Jack Nicklaus, and Bobby Jones in their adolescence. Introduced to the game as a caddie in Fort Worth, Texas, at the age of 11, Hogan lost the caddie championship at 15 to a caddie named Byron Nelson. It was the beginning of a lifetime rivalry and friendship.

Ben was a natural left-hander who switched to the right side partly because of a scarcity of clubs. In those days, right-handers made natural left-handers *write* with their less dominant hand. There was no such thing as a left-handed golfer.

Hogan's career suffered at the same time the country did during the Depression years of the 1930s. After he turned pro in 1932, he entered the 1931 U.S. Open for the first time and failed to make the cut. Hogan spent seven years on the PGA Tour without winning a tournament. At various points, he ran out of money and nearly gave up his dream of having a professional golf career. Hogan was 27 years old—nearly the age Jones was when he retired—before he won a tournament.

Hogan had a natural hook that prevented him from breaking through sooner in his career. It was perseverance, patience, and practice that finally made him a championship-caliber golfer. When Ben nearly gave up his dream, it was his wife, Valerie (whom he married in 1935), who gave him the support he needed. In addition to being his wife, she operated as his entourage, swing coach, and psychologist.

It seemed like Hogan spent an eternity on the road without cashing a first-place check. He was not able to support himself, finishing in the top 10 only once a year from 1932 to 1934. He didn't finish as high as third until once in 1937. He had been financed at times by a wealthy Fort Worth businessman, but when Hogan ran out of money, he eventually had to go home and look for other employment. The turning point in Hogan's career came in 1938, when Ben was 26 years old, and the Hogans, existing for a few weeks on oranges, were down to their last $85. If he didn't win any money at the Oakland Open, he was through. The night before the tournament started, someone stole the two rear wheels off his car. He had to hitch a ride to play. But he shot well enough in the last round to earn a few hundred dollars, which enabled him to put wheels back on the car and keep them on the road. He started winning regularly soon after that.

By 1942, Bantam Ben (because he was only 135 pounds) was the leading money winner on the Tour. But he couldn't win the majors. Part of the reason was that he needed to play as much as he could to earn money, and the quantity of his play affected the quality, especially in regard to getting enough rest to compete in the majors. He spent as much time and energy traveling from one tournament to another as he did playing golf.

He was the leading money winner by the early '40s and was the Vardon Trophy winner in 1940 and 1941 for best scoring average. Hogan's career finally was successful, but World War II interfered. The Tour all but ceased to exist during the war years. The U.S. Open was canceled from 1942 through 1945. During the war, Hogan (in his early 30s) served as a lieutenant in the Army Air Corps. Of course, he wasn't alone in losing almost three years off his prime. Other great golfers to serve included Sam Snead, Jimmy Demaret, Lloyd Mangrum, and Horton Smith. Mangrum actually fought in the Battle of the Bulge and earned a Purple Heart.

By 1946 Hogan's childhood friend Byron Nelson had already accumulated five majors and was coming off an 18-win season in 1945. Hogan—who had lost an 18-hole playoff in a Masters to Nelson—had won 13 times in 1946 (no one has won more in a year since, and only Nelson ever won more, in '45) and had 30 tournament wins to date, but he had yet to win a single major.

At Augusta in 1946, Hogan had his chance for a major. He needed only a par at the 18th hole to tie Herman Keiser, who had three-putted the hole. Hogan hit his approach shot to about 20 feet from the hole, but he three-putted himself to give Keiser the crown. Two months later, at the U.S. Open at the Canterbury Golf Club in Cleveland, Ohio, Ben made an approach to the final green about 18 feet above the hole, but he struck his first putt two feet past the cup and then missed coming back. He lost by a stroke. After that there was the 1946 PGA Championship.

Remember, this was before stroke play for the PGA Championship. In the semifinals, Hogan defeated Demaret, 10 and 8, a huge victory over a great golfer. Hogan finished the front side 3-up before picking up three more holes on the back side to finish the morning round 6-up. Hogan shot a 31 in the afternoon round. He was 11-under par on the day. That set up a final between the 135-pound Hogan and the 220-pound Ed Oliver.

Hogan defeated Oliver 6 and 4. For the day, Hogan was 7-under par, playing the afternoon 14 holes in 8-under par. It was a magnificent display of golf. And it gave Hogan his first major triumph, at the age of 34.

How sweet was the first major? Consider the following. Prior to the 1946 PGA, Hogan had entered 15 majors (five Masters, four PGA Championships, and six U.S. Opens) without winning. After that he began a collection of majors. Just as he put an end to his seven-year winless streak on the Tour, he turned it all around and began winning majors. He won the 1946 PGA Championship. He won the 1948 U.S. Open. He won the 1948 PGA Championship.

The *2005 PGA Media Guide* sheds light on the 1948 PGA Championship that was played in St. Louis. In 1948 Hogan faced Gene Sarazen in the third round. After 27 holes Hogan was 4-up on the 46-year-old Sarazen. Gene got a stroke back with a birdie at the 28th and then picked up another stroke at the 34th. He birdied the 35th to get to within a stroke. Hogan held on and advanced. In the semifinals Hogan had to defeat Demaret, 2 and 1, in a match where both players were 10-under par. In the finals Hogan had to face Mike Turnesa. Turnesa's brother Joe lost to Walter Hagen in the 1927 finals, and his brother Jim was beaten by Sam Snead in 1942. This Turnesa faced the same result. Hogan won 7 and 6. For the week Hogan was 35-under for the 213 holes played. The grind of 10 rounds in five days was too much for Hogan after this year.

When Hogan finally began winning tournaments, World War II interrupted his career. Once Hogan finally began winning majors, a life-threatening automobile accident interrupted his career. In early 1949, when he was driving in the middle of the night with Valerie from Phoenix back home to Fort Worth, a bus skidded across the dividing line and hit the Hogans' car. Ben hurled himself in front of his wife, who was not seriously injured thanks to her husband. Ben, however, suffered a double fracture of the pelvis, a fractured collarbone, a broken leg, and other injuries. A short time later, blood clots formed in Hogan's legs and doctors operated.

His car accident of 1949 left him, with battered legs, unable to defend his PGA title. He didn't return to the PGA Championship until 1960, the third year after the switch to a stroke-play format. That Ben could come back and play one round of golf was a small miracle. There was no way he could play the ten rounds in five days that the PGA Championship required.

Hogan's comeback from the accident was one of the great comebacks in sports history. While many people predicted that he would never play golf again, he went from an extremely good golfer to an immortal, one of the best of all time. What happened to make Ben come back even stronger? Was it luck? It was hardly luck. Practice not only makes perfect, it made Ben Hogan a legendary golfer. As the 1949 season began, Ben had made adjustments in his swing that rid him of his chronic hook at last. He played around with his grip, and a weakened grip was the key.

"They used to laugh at me practicing," Hogan once said. "I'd practice, go out and play and then practice some more. Actually, I was a young fellow trying to improve my game. They laughed at me practicing so much, but soon they had to join me."

Lanny Wadkins, CBS golf analyst and PGA pro: "He was a workaholic. He didn't have a game that worked. He worked until he had a game. He set the standard for golfers who practiced and practiced and finally figured it out. And don't forget that it was harder to practice in Hogan's time. Nowadays, the ranges are perfectly manicured; you can hit hundreds of balls. Hogan had shag-bags and could hit maybe 100 to 150 balls at a time. The players today practice under perfect conditions."

Hogan was one of the most precise golfers on the PGA Tour. He would open a carton of new golf balls, take out a magnifying glass, and look at each ball, one by one. He would explain that some of the dimples have too much paint on them. Jones called him the hardest worker he'd ever seen. Gary Player called him the greatest striker of the ball ever.

It seemed like the entire nation rooted for Hogan when he made his return, at the first event in 1950, the Los Angeles Open. It's not like he was this cuddly, warm character like his contemporary Snead or a supreme gentleman like Nelson. He exemplified the working class, the man who had to put time and practice into succeeding. He was gone from the game for 11 months. His leg and shoulder injuries finally healed enough so that he could swing a club. He was still walking gingerly when he played his first tournaments, but he got by. Is it too much to say that he looked like many of the war veterans returning to the work force after sustaining physical wounds?

In that Los Angeles Open, he shot 73–69–69–69 in the final round. He had the tournament won, until Snead birdied the last two holes. It was a remarkable performance and had Snead saying, "The only things I fear in golf are lightning, a downhill putt, and Ben Hogan."

A short time later, Ben returned to Augusta for the 1950 Masters. He was 4-under par to tie Lawson Little for the lead through 27 holes. He had only begun playing again a few months earlier, and the fourth round was too grueling for him. Seven bogeys on the final round shot him out of the tournament. Despite getting a 76 on the final day, he finished with a 288 in a tie for fourth.

No golfer felt sorry for Bantam Ben in June of 1950, as he won the U.S. Open. He made it three U.S. Opens in a row the following year. (He won in 1948, didn't compete in 1949, and then won back-to-back in '50 and '51.) His 67 on the final round was one of the greatest rounds of golf he ever played. Afterward he commented, "I'm glad I brought this monster to its knees."

After winning the 1953 Masters (where Hogan played some of the best golf of his career, breaking the tournament record with a score of 274, which was surpassed later by both Nicklaus and Woods), he followed it up with a victory at the U.S. Open. He was urged to go to Scotland and attempt to win the British Open. It was the first and only time he played the British Open.

The Scots, taking an instant liking to Hogan, dubbed him the Wee Ice Mon. He was cheered big-time at the British Open and didn't disappoint. During the four rounds, at Carnoustie, Scotland, his drives on the 18th hole were almost identical. In fact, his divots from his second shots on that hole were all located in a space of about one square yard. He won by four shots and cemented his reputation.

But despite winning the first three legs of the Grand Slam, Ben chose not to enter the PGA Championship. With it coming so soon after the British Open, the ordeal of the 200-plus holes on his legs would be too much to attempt. Hogan attempted the British Open just once, and that was when he was 40 years old. He lost a lot of cracks at the PGA Championship, as well.

Hogan at the PGA Championship
1939: lost 3 and 2 in quarterfinals to Paul Runyan
1940: lost 3 and 2 in quarterfinals to Ralph Guldahl
1941: lost 2-up in quarterfinals to Byron Nelson
1942: lost 2 and 1 in quarterfinals to Jim Turnesa
1943: tournament canceled
1944: did not play (in the Army)
1945: did not play (in the Army)
1946: won tournament
1947: lost in first round
1948: won tournament

Here's the point one should remember about Ben Hogan. He lost time at the beginning of his career and at the prime of his career. He was 40 years old in 1953, when he won the first of three legs of the Grand Slam.

Everyone whom I talked to about *Who's Better, Who's Best in Golf?* asks or points out the number of majors that a player has won. They point to the nine that Hogan won. Well, hold it! That's not really fair to Ben. Players today compete in four majors a year for 20 years. Ben competed in two a year in his prime and had some of those prime years taken away. For comparison, Jack Nicklaus competed in 95 majors by his 43rd birthday; Ben Hogan competed in 39 majors by 1955, when he was 43 years old.

Ben Hogan's Record in Major Tournaments Broken Down
Prior to 1946: 0–15
1946–accident: 3–11
1950–55: 6–13
1956–60: 0–10

Hogan was an old 43-year-old by the end of the 1955 season. His putting had begun to erode. After not winning any of his first 15 major tournaments to begin his career, he won 9 of his next 24 majors.

If he played the PGA every year under stroke play, would he have won additional majors? If he played the British Open every year, would he have won a few more? If he didn't need the money from playing every nickel-and-dime tournament early in his career, would he have been able to concentrate on and rest for the majors that eluded him early? Yes, yes, and yes!

He won 68 tournaments, including four U.S. Opens, two PGA Championships, two Masters, and one British Open. The Wee Ice Mon finished in the top 10 in 16 consecutive U.S. Opens. He's considered the best ball striker in history, and no less than Nicklaus called him the greatest shot maker across the board.

Isn't it possible—heck, probable—that Hogan (at the clip he had established) would have won another six or seven majors? I figure World War II cost him two majors. And the accident cost him a few more.

Jay Randolph, Golf Channel commentator: "I saw him play many times in the '50s. He was simply remarkable. He was a machine, really. He got rid of his hook. He was an exceptional driver. Not the greatest putter in the world. He was hero to so many."

Hogan had a few last hurrahs on the golf course. His last victory was the 1959 Colonial. He competed in 1960 at the U.S. Open, where he played two rounds with a young Nicklaus. He was in contention until Arnold Palmer passed him. Nicklaus and Palmer passed him, literally. He didn't win in as many decades as Snead. He didn't win in the 1930s or the '60s. He had the 1940s and '50s—and entirely too much of that was taken away from him.

Hogan's last great moment on the golf course came at the 1967 Masters. He shot a 30 on the back nine at Augusta. The score equaled the nine-hole record at the time. Hogan was 54 years old. Hogan was the greatest golfer not named Woods or Nicklaus. Hogan died in 1997 at the age of 84.

4

SAM SNEAD
Longevity Counts

Samuel Jackson Snead was born on May 27, 1912, in Hot Springs, Virginia. The Sneads lived in the backwoods of Virginia for several generations. Sam's father, Harry, trapped wildcats, foxes, and hawks. Sam would later tell his manager, Fred Corcoran, how kids from his neighborhood went barefoot from May until late autumn's frost.

Young Sam cut a limb from a maple tree and whittled down a makeshift golf club. He shagged balls for his older brother, Homer, and would eventually get a job as an assistant in the pro shop at the Homestead resort hotel where his father worked as an engineer. Sam was a high school football player and competed in tennis, swimming, and track. Growing up in the Depression years, Sam was always motivated by money, which may account for his desire to play long after other contemporaries had retired. He was known for his fabulous swing. People claimed that he was double-jointed (which he denied), and people claimed that was the reason he could swing better than everyone else. Toward the end of his career, when his putting faltered, he went to a croquet style and kept rolling along. Although he was known as the longest straight driver of his time, he was actually better with his pitching clubs.

Sam Snead was a rookie on the Tour in 1936. By 1938, his swing had put him on top. According to Al Barkow's *The History of the PGA Tour*, Snead

> would outhit the reigning long-ball champion, Jimmy Thomson, going into the wind and mesmerize everybody with a wonderfully fluid swinging motion. Snead won eight tournaments, including the Canadian Open, and got seconds in the PGA and the Western Open. The entire Tour that year was worth $185,500, and out of that all-time high Snead took home $19,399.49. It was more prize money than had ever been won before by a professional golfer.

Like Hogan, with whom Snead is forever linked in history because they were contemporaries, Sam had trouble getting started. Snead won 27 times on tour before getting his first major championship title at the 1942 PGA Championship. He was the "almost" king, almost winning six majors before he won his first. He came close to winning two U.S. Opens, two PGA Championships, and two Masters.

One of Snead's near misses came in the 1938 PGA Championships at Shawnee Country Club in Shawnee on Delaware, Pennsylvania. In the semifinals, Snead defeated Jimmy Hines, 1-up. It took a finish of four consecutive 3s on Snead's part to win. In the finals, however, Paul Runyan beat Sam 8 and 7 to win the PGA Championship.

According to the *2005 PGA Media Guide*, at the 1940 PGA Championships in Hershey, Pennsylvania, Snead was matched in the quarterfinals with Gene Sarazen. Snead won the match 1-up. Snead was 3-down after the 28th hole but won the 29th with a birdie, won the 31st and 33rd holes with pars, and made birdie at 34 to take his first lead. In the finals Snead slugged it out with Byron Nelson, with Nelson edging Snead 1-up. The match went down to the final three holes, as Snead had a 1-up lead on the 34th hole with Nelson two feet away for birdie. Snead almost ran in a 20-footer that would have tied the hole. At the 35th hole, Nelson hit a wedge to within two feet, while Snead was six feet away. Snead missed his putt, and Nelson made his to go 1-up. At the final hole, a par-3, Snead hit his shot just off the green and missed his next shot. Nelson got within inches and tapped in the tournament-winning putt.

Sam never did win the U.S. Open. He had seven top-five finishes. His failure to win a single U.S. Open is a blot, not unlike tennis star Ivan Lendl never winning Wimbledon (despite winning eight majors in the other three major tennis tournaments). He was second (or tied for second) in 1937, 1947, 1949, and 1953. It was the 1939 U.S. Open that haunted Snead for decades. The Open that year took place at the Philadelphia Country Club. He thought he needed a birdie to win. But because there was no leaderboard in sight, he didn't know that even a bogey-6 would have been enough to put him in a play-off with Nelson, Craig Wood, and Denny Shute. Instead, he took several unnecessary chances at the 18th hole and wound up taking an 8 on the final hole to finish fourth.

World War II began, and Snead (like many others) enlisted in the Navy, but he delayed his induction by a week to play in the 1942 PGA Championship. He won his first major, defeating Jim Turnesa, who was an Army sergeant. Snead was not the popular man in the gallery that tournament. The fans were openly rooting for the enlisted man. So when Snead finally won an Open, he wasn't cheered, and his reward was a stint in the military.

Snead became a regular Tour player again after being discharged from the Navy with a slipped vertebra that did not hamper his golf game. He won six times in 1945. At the Pensacola Open, he was 21-under par. I can't make the point that he lost a few opportunities for majors because of World War II. While the war years cost him some victories, no one had the career longevity that Snead did, regardless.

He won the British Open in 1946. In those days the trip overseas was so cost prohibitive that even a victory at the Open didn't guarantee that a player would make his money back. Taking advantage of being overseas, Snead took a trip to South Africa, where he played a series of matches with Bobby Locke. Snead won only 2 of the 16 matches against Locke.

At the 1947 Open, in St. Louis, Snead had to hole a tough putt to tie Lew Worsham. In the play-off Sam said he was distracted by Worsham's heavy breathing. On the 18th both found themselves around three feet from the cup. Snead prepared to putt, and Worsham stopped and suggested a measurement. The tape showed that Snead's ball was a little farther away from the cup than Worsham's was. Snead missed his putt; Worsham made his.

Despite the annual near misses at the U.S. Open, Snead was entering the fertile period of his great career. He won the Masters three times in six years, beginning in 1949. That was the first year the green jacket was awarded to the Masters champion, by the way. Snead won the PGA Championship in 1949 and 1951 as well.

Earning about $35,000 per year, Snead was the leading money winner in 1949 and 1950. Just as Nelson's 1945 accomplishments are asterisked by Hogan and Snead serving in the armed forces, Snead's 1949 and 1950 accomplishments have to be viewed in the context that Hogan was laid up with his automobile accident.

Snead's final major, the 1954 Masters, was memorable because he defeated his archrival Hogan in an 18-hole play-off. Entering the final day, Hogan had a score of 214. Snead was three shots back, and an amateur named Billy Joe Patton had 219. Patton, trying to become the first amateur to ever win the Masters, aced the sixth hole. Though Patton failed to win, he made his presence felt by forcing Hogan into enough errors to leave him in a tie with Snead. In the 18-hole play-off, Snead won by a stroke.

While Snead had trouble at the Open, he was superb at the other majors. He won the PGA Championship three times (1942, 1949, and 1951). He played 17 years in match play at the PGA and won 78 percent of his matches (50–14). In 16 of the 17 years he played, Snead got by the first round. He was 3–2 in his five PGA finals. Only Sarazen played in more matches (82) than Snead, and only Sarazen won more (57) than Snead. Snead's best major was the Masters. He had 3 wins, 9 finishes in the top 5, and 15 finishes in the top 10.

Snead was also a great Ryder Cup player and captain. He played in seven Ryder Cups (on the 1937, 1947, 1949, 1951, 1953, 1955, and 1959 teams), including the first U.S. Ryder Cup team (1937) to get a victory on British soil. (There was no Ryder Cup played from 1938 to 1946 due to the war.) His record in Ryder Cup matches was 10–2–1 (6–1 in singles and 4–1–1 in foursomes). He was a three-time Ryder Cup captain as well.

Who's Better, Who's Best
Sam Snead or Ben Hogan?

Of Hogan's 1950 U.S. Open win, Snead once said, "He won one tournament in 1950, and I won 11. He got golfer of the year! That year I played 96 straight rounds and averaged 69.2!" That was Snead's greatest year, but the quote seems awfully harsh, considering the sentiment that went to Hogan.

In 1950 Snead parlayed his classic swing into his best year as a pro. In winning the Vardon Trophy, he averaged 69.23 strokes per round. That mark stood for 50 years (until Tiger Woods broke it).

Best Vardon Trophy Scoring Average (nonadjusted) (from 1950 to 1999)

1. 69.23 Sam Snead, 1950 (6,646 strokes, 96 rounds)
2. 69.30 Ben Hogan, 1948 (5,267 strokes, 76 rounds)
3. 69.33 Greg Norman, 1994 (4,368 strokes, 63 rounds)
4. 69.37 Sam Snead, 1949 (5,064 strokes, 73 rounds)

Best Vardon Trophy Scoring Average (nonadjusted) (from 2000 to 2005)

1. 68.17 Tiger Woods, 2000 (5,181 strokes, 76 rounds)
2. 68.87 Tiger Woods, 2001 (5,234 strokes, 76 rounds)
3. 69.00 Tiger Woods, 2002 (4,692 strokes, 68 rounds)

Will Woods's records hold up over five decades as Snead's record did?

Lanny Wadkins, CBS Sports golf analyst and PGA Tour member: "Snead did it day in and day out, year in and year out. He won tournaments from the '30s to the '60s. He was a tough cookie. I'd put him ahead of Ben Hogan. I'd put him ahead of Tiger Woods. He went head-to-head with Hogan only a couple of times—and beat him. Snead had the longevity. Yes, he missed winning the U.S. Open, but he won enough to make up for that. He was great at reading people—like a fox."

"Slammin' Sammy" Snead won 82 tournaments and 7 majors. Bantam Ben won fewer tournaments but one more major. The question is, do you value the career numbers or the peak value of Hogan? I take Hogan over Snead, but it's real, real close.

All-Time PGA Tour Winners
1. 82 Sam Snead
2. 73 Jack Nicklaus
3. 64 Ben Hogan

Most Years Finishing in the Money List Top 10
1. 18 Jack Nicklaus
2. 15 Sam Snead

Most Career Top-10 Finishes
1. 358 Sam Snead
2. 286 Jack Nicklaus

Youngest Professional to Shoot His Age or Below
1. 66 Sam Snead (4-under, fourth round), age 67, 1979 Quad Cities Open
2. 67 Sam Snead (3-under, second round), age 67, 1979 Quad Cities Open

Most Wins by Player After Age 40
1. 17 Sam Snead
2. 12 Vijay Singh
3. 10 Julius Boros

Snead won the 1965 Greater Greensboro Open at the age of 52 years, 10 months, and 8 days. That's the oldest anyone ever won a PGA tournament.

Snead was the oldest to make a cut at a PGA tournament, making the cut at the 1979 Manufacturers Hanover Westchester Classic at the age of 67. Snead won his first tournament in January of 1937 and his last in April of 1965. He won tournaments 28 years, 2 months, and 17 days apart. Only Raymond Floyd had victories as far apart as 28 years. Snead also won the Greater Greensboro Open a record eight times. He helped launch the Senior PGA Tour by winning the inaugural Legends of Golf in 1978 with Gardner Dickinson.

On November 17, 1974, an article in *Family Circle* magazine stated that Snead may be the best golfer who ever lived—at least according to panelists from the World Golf Hall of Fame. Snead emerged as the leader in the interviews with panelists Byron Nelson, Gene Sarazen, Arnold Palmer, Jack Nicklaus, and Fred Corcoran. During his 60 years in golf, Corcoran knew all the greats of the game and was a former tournament director of the PGA. Corcoran was also a former business manager of Snead's for years, so his comments were telling. Corcoran died in 1975, by the way, only months after the article was published. He stated, "I would have to say that Ben Hogan was the best golfer who ever played. He won his first tournament in 1940, when he was already 28 years old, but then he won the next two straight tournaments after that. To cure a natural hook, he probably hit more practice shots than anyone who has ever lived."

"The Hall of Fame Super-Panel's Report on Golf's Greatest" picked the best of all time. Nelson picked Snead for Best Long Irons and Best Mid-Irons. Sarazen picked Snead as Best Driver, Best Long Irons, and Best Mid-Irons. He also put Snead and Walter Hagen as Best Putter.

I value what those golfers said about Snead and what men like Wadkins and Jay Randolph told me, about how Snead should be ahead of Hogan. And, yes, I realize that Snead beat Hogan three times in head-to-head play-offs. If you have a historical ranking that weighs too much on longevity (top 10s, top 25s, etc.), the pick has to be Snead. Slammin' Sam had those 358 top-10 finishes. He had 473 top-25 finishes. Those numbers are outrageous. I just feel that Hogan was a better player when both were in their prime, similar to placing a premium on Tiger's peak over Nicklaus's longevity. So by my account, it's Hogan by a whisker.

Sam Snead died four days shy of his 90th birthday, in late May of 2002. Ironically, the man who mastered every stroke in the book died of complications from one.

HARRY VARDON
Get a Grip

In the summer of 2005, *New York Times* columnist Dave Anderson wrote, "In any evaluation of the best golfers ever, those are the four names, each from a different era, that will endure: Jones, Hogan, Nicklaus, and Woods."

Time has a way, like the ocean current, of washing away memories and names. Just as there rages a great debate in 2005 about the historical ranking of Jack Nicklaus and Tiger Woods, there was equally as strong a passion 75 years earlier about British great Harry Vardon ranked against Atlanta's Bobby Jones.

It is my contention that Vardon was thought of as superior to Jones up to 10 years after Vardon's 1937 death. What happened in the last 75 years to elevate Jones (and a host of others) over Vardon? Jones was visible for 35 years after Vardon passed away and held enormous influence among the growing (and increasingly American) fan base and media circles.

In 1928, headlines from the International News Service (similar to today's Associated Press) screamed, "Vardon called premiere golfer among all men." The article said, "Out of the whole world of divot-diggers there are only two that can be considered in the superlative class—Bobby Jones and Harry Vardon. The never-ending argument concerning the comparative greatness of this pair will continue unabated so long as nineteen holes exist; and until speech is denied them, the veterans will line up with Vardon and the youth of today will swear by the Georgia Peach."

Hmmm. It sounds curiously like the present-day argument with old-timers supporting Jack Nicklaus and the youth swearing by Tiger Woods.

Vardon was known as the Greyhound, for the way he made his move and overcame deficits against his opponents. But he was also known as the Master, for his skill level. His career overlapped the gutta-percha ball, which was replaced by the rubber-core ball, and he adjusted so well that three of his six British Opens came with the gutta-percha ball and three with the rubber-core. During Vardon's playing days more than 5 million people were introduced to the game, in large part due to the evolution of machinery, which allowed people to have a little extra free time to take up golf. More likely than not, he was the dominating personality that took his sport to the next level.

When the 51-year-old Vardon announced in 1921 that he was retiring from tournament play, it made worldwide headlines. This guy was as big as an athlete could get in the early '20s. Evidence of this was that his 1905 golf book *The Complete Golfer* became a bestseller on both sides of the Atlantic.

Jones took over where Vardon left off, dominating golf in the 1920s and culminating in his Grand Slam of 1930. It appears to me in combing the newsprint and stats that Jones had caught Vardon—but not passed him. Lawrence Perry's *Consolidated Press* article from July of 1930, headlined "Bobby Jones Rated on Par with Veteran H. Vardon," has this to say:

> Controversy is raging in England just now as to who is the greatest golfer that ever lived. The nominations are two—Bobby Jones and Harry Vardon. So far as this writer can learn, Jones is favored by the younger generation of Britishers, while those whose memory goes back beyond 30 years are either strong for Vardon or else inclined to place the great American youngster and England's historic golfing figure upon a par. Now, it was this writer's privilege some time ago to see Jones and Vardon opposed in a two-ball foursome and certainly that day the Atlantan showed to advantage. But of course, that was only one day and after all, this controversy is an English argument and should be left to the English.

Flash forward to February of 1938. Vardon had passed away the year before, and Jones had been retired for nearly eight years. The Associated Press named the Ten Greatest Stars of Golf. The headline: "Teacher Vardon and Pupil Bobby Jones Head Links 'Hall of Fame.'"

> Notwithstanding the glamour and impact of the achievements of the renowned Robert Tyre Jones, Jr., probably the greatest golfing competitor of all time, there hardly can be any dispute to the award of Number One position in golf's "Hall of Fame" to the great stylist, champion, and teacher Harry Vardon.
>
> Vardon was king of golf before Jones was born and 50 years old when their competitive paths first crossed at the 1920 U.S. Open at Inverness. Yet the old master even then was good enough to finish ahead of the youthful Jones and all others, except for Vardon's countryman Ted Ray.

Those are just some examples taken from syndicated newspaper columns that carried great weight in my justifying Vardon over Jones. Jones had the home-nation advantage with the media I found. And Jones had the more recent period of dominance. But the general consensus was, into the 1940s, that Vardon was *at least* as good.

When people think of Harry Vardon now, they think of the interlocking grip (which he popularized but did not invent). They also may think of the Vardon Trophy (given to the U.S. PGA Tour player with the best stroke average).

Golf historian Bernard Darwin from England (and nephew of the natural selection guru Charles Darwin) wrote the following in 1937 after Vardon died:

> When he was in his most glorious prime, people used to wonder whether he played better than had young Tommy Morris, who died when Vardon was five years old. When Vardon was older, people wondered whether he had played as well as Jones. The comparisons are futile. There were, of course, far fewer players than there are now, and far less writing about them in the newspapers; yet I doubt if any golfer has ever created the furor that Vardon did. Everything about his swing, his clubs, even his clothes (he was the first professional to wear knickerbockers) was eagerly discussed. "Have you tried the Vardon grip?" was almost as common a salutation amongst golfers as "Good Morning."

The quality of Vardon's play and the scope of his accomplishments might very well have been too overwhelming for us to properly appreciate a century later. Historians discount his feats—as is also the case with baseball's Cy Young, who performed in the same 1890s—because there is simply nothing similar to compare with. By naming awards for Vardon and Young, we keep their names alive, if not their historical place in their respective game's history.

So much of what we do know about Vardon is myth. The story goes that he couldn't play two rounds of golf in the same day on the same course: his tee shots in the afternoon kept falling into the divot holes he had made in the morning.

And, of course, there is the story that when the right-handed Harry was asked to name the greatest left-handed golfers of all time, he replied, "I never met one worth a damn." That, supposedly, is the origin of the phrase "left-handed compliment."

Harry Vardon was born May 9, 1870, in Jersey, one of the Channel Islands, just off the western coast of France. His father was a poor gardener. Harry learned golf as a caddie and didn't own his own set of clubs until he was 17.

He was a natural golfer. He never asked anyone for a lesson, and no one ever gave him one. Before Harry came along, golfers had been holding the shaft of the club in the palms of both hands, as they would hold a baseball bat. Harry used an overlapping grip, which locked his huge, powerful hands into one unit. He was only 5'9" and weighed about 150 pounds. But as Charles Price wrote in *Golf Magazine* in March of 1960, "His hands were large enough to belong to a man twice his size."

Did he develop the Vardon grip? Actually, he did not and never took or expected credit for it. Almost up until the time he won his first British Open (1896), he used the palm grip. He abandoned this grip because it had a tendency to make him overpower his shots with the right hand. The great amateur Johnny Laidlay is thought to have been the first to use the interlocking grip. But Vardon definitely popularized it and influenced many other golfers, due to his success on the links. Harry played with lighter clubs than most golfers and basically used just two woods, six irons, and a putter. He adopted an open stance, when a more closed stance was the style in his day.

Harry entered the Open Championship for the first time in 1893, at the age of 23. At St. Andrews in 1895, Vardon led the first round but finished ninth. Of course, the British Open was by far the most influential tournament in the world. In 1896, at the age of 26, he won his first British Open, defeating J. H. Taylor by four strokes in a 36-hole play-off at Muirfield. Taylor wrote the following in his 1943 book *Golf: My Life's Work*:

> Vardon's victory at Muirfield set him off on a trail of consistent successes which have never been equaled in the annals of the game. Vardon became a national hero, and in my judgment, proved himself to be the greatest player of all time. . . . Vardon won the Championship at Prestwick in 1898 by one stroke from Willie Park [Jr.] and won it the following year at Sandwich, and during this period he was unbeatable, as the fact of his winning the Cup three times in four years surely testifies. The confidence that his play engendered in the mind of the public can be shown by stating that whenever Vardon entered a competition he was freely tipped as the only possible winner and it became a question of who was to be the poor unfortunate who had the honor of chasing him home.

At the turn of the century, Vardon went on his first tour of America, which lasted for six months from autumn of 1899 to spring of 1900. He played up and down the country, traveling to Florida when the weather got too cold anywhere else. It was an exhausting business trip. His visit created a sensation. The game was booming in America, as courses were springing up everywhere, and people were reading newspapers and advertisements that featured Vardon.

While engaged in his tour of America in 1900, Vardon was hired to display his form into a net at Jordan-Marsh, a Boston department store. To relieve the monotony, he amused himself by aiming at the valve handle on a fire extinguisher that was projecting through the netting. The handle was no larger than a silver dollar. Vardon hit it so often that the floor manager begged him to stop for fear of flooding the store.

In his 1900 tour, he lost only one match in America, to Bernard Nicholls in Florida. Often he would play two amateurs at a time, playing their better ball. Vardon's services were sponsored and his matches organized by sporting goods manufacturers. Most people, in hindsight, look to this extended tour as groundwork for his getting sick soon after that.

Still at the top of his game, Vardon returned across the Atlantic to defend his Open Championship. He lost to Taylor but defeated him back in America to become the first man to win both the U.S. Open and the British Open.

The 1900 U.S. Open was the first time the world's best players played in the event. The greens in Wheaton, Illinois, were brushed in several different directions. It made putting an adventure. Vardon led Taylor by one stroke after 36 holes. He built his lead to four going into the final round by shooting a 76 to Taylor's 79. Taylor played the back nine on the final round in 36, which forced Vardon to post a 38, to win by two shots.

After Vardon holed out, the crowd surged past the ropes and onto the 18th green to greet the new champion. The crowd retired to the clubhouse and toasted the champion with "Auld Lang Syne."

The fourth British Open Championship did not come easily for Vardon. His doctor had advised him against playing at Prestwick because he was showing signs of weakness and fatigue. He came close to withdrawing. His fourth-round 78 was his worst, but it still left him six shots ahead of second-place finisher Tom Vardon (Harry's brother). It was his first British Open with the new ball. Afterward, Vardon was diagnosed with tuberculosis and was admitted to a sanitarium.

At this point in his career, Harry was 33 years old and had been either first or second at the British Open for seven of the previous eight years. He would write his bestseller and eventually recover enough to play again.

Even with tuberculosis Vardon never stopped smoking. He would play as part of the "400-pound foursome" in 1905, in which he and Taylor defeated James Braid and Alex Herd in 144 holes over four courses. Vardon even won a fifth and sixth British Open after getting sick.

For five months before the 1911 British Open Championship at Sandwich, he was under strict guidance by his doctor, being put on a special diet that consisted of a meatless breakfast and lunch, a balanced dinner, and only one glass of whiskey per day. He was also restricted to four pipes of tobacco—this rule bothered him the most. But the lifestyle changes worked, as he won his fifth Open Championship.

Then, of course, there was the memorable "Greatest Game Ever Played" at Brookline, Massachusetts. In 1913 Harry made his second tour of the United States in an effort to win back the U.S. Open. Now 43 years old, Vardon and countryman Ted Ray were shocked by Francis Ouimet in a play-off. In 1920, at the age of 50, with no stamina due to smoking and tuberculosis, Harry dropped seven shots in the last seven holes and Ray beat him by a stroke. By this time, it was over for Vardon. Being reduced to shaking, he couldn't putt anymore.

Aside from his three trips to the United States (where he won in his prime, finished second in a play-off at age 43, and finished second at age 50), the only major available to him was the British Open. In that event, he won a record six times and finished second another four times. He finished in the top three 12 different years. He didn't play every year either. Two bouts of tuberculosis kept him out of a half dozen British Opens, and World War I kept him from two others.

He was obviously a talent, even long past his prime. Walter Hagen saw him for the first time at the 1913 U.S. Open when Hagen was 20. Hagen recalled:

> I first saw Vardon at Brookline during practice rounds for the 1913 Open. He was practicing mashie shots off a downhill lie, and he was fading every one of them. The groove in his swing was so obvious you could almost see it. I was so impressed with his swing that during the last round, when my swing started to leave me, I started imitating his. And it worked, too. Fact is, I almost caught him with his own swing.

If one judges golfers on their mastery at the majors, then Vardon's seven majors are every bit the equal of Jones's seven professional championships (thirteen total championships, including the amateurs).

In Vardon's lifetime, it was assumed that he would always have a grip on the title as the greatest golfer of all time. Ironically, all the public remembered or cared about was his grip—not his hold on a mythical title.

When Vardon is called "the best golfer of his time" or "one of the best golfers from overseas," to me it is the ultimate left-handed compliment. He belongs in the same sentence with Woods and Nicklaus and Hogan and Snead. He deserves a spot in the top five of all time, ahead of Jones.

6

BOBBY JONES
The Distinguished Master Amateur

The name Bobby Jones is magical in golf. Since 1955 the United States Golf Association has presented the Bobby Jones award, its highest honor, given annually in recognition of distinguished sportsmanship in golf. The award seeks to recognize a person who emulates Jones's spirit, personal qualities, and attitude toward the game of golf and its players.

After retiring from golf in 1930, Bobby Jones built Augusta National and established the Masters as an invitational tournament. The Masters Tournament has been played at Augusta National since 1934. Whenever the discussion for greatest ever comes up, Jones's name is still mentioned. Only in two sports—golf and baseball—is there such a reverence for the past. No one considers Jack Dempsey anymore as the greatest boxer of all time. No one would put Bill Tilden ahead of later tennis players like Rod Laver, Pete Sampras, or Roger Federer. Only Jones and Babe Ruth still have names that carry a cachet from that golden era of the 1920s.

Ruth and Jones both performed for a nation that was between World War I and the Great Depression. Ruth was a larger-than-life slugger, the first of his kind. And Jones, too, was a worldwide hero and national treasure. No other golfer of his era had larger galleries and more fans than Jones had.

I'm convinced that the United States doesn't do the same hero worship that it once did, when the country was starving for heroes. Ticker-tape parades along the lower stretch of Broadway known as the "Canyon of Heroes" are a New York tradition that dates back to the late 1800s. Bobby Jones, an amateur golfer, was given two of them, once upon returning from Great Britain with the British Amateur and British Open Championships. The second came after he completed his Grand Slam. There hasn't been a ticker-tape parade in New York since October of 2000, when the Yankees won the World Series. While other cities may hold such parades, the Canyon of Heroes is reserved for presidents, astronauts, and other such luminaries.

Jones's putter, called "Calamity Jane," was made famous by Jones's rolling in putts like a 40-footer at the fifth hole at St. Andrews. Calamity Jane was a piece of hickory with a steel head. It was almost insane that both Jones (a modest kid from Atlanta who won everything in golf during his time) and his putter were national heroes.

It wasn't until the early 1900s that golf exploded in the United States. Prior to that the world's best golfers were, of course, from England and Scotland. Following Harry Vardon's emotional 1914 victory at the British Open (when he was 44), Europe changed for the definite worse. World War I began and most golf courses were taken over by the military, their clubhouses turned into convalescent hospitals. Many were used as gunnery ranges.

While Vardon was a little too old to fight in World War I, across the pond young Bobby Jones (born in 1902) was a little too young. He also wasn't very healthy, suffering from a stomach disorder and not even able to eat solid foods until he was five. His wealthy parents started him on golf at age six. What were the odds that this kid would become a legendary athlete?

Jones first appeared in a national magazine at the age of nine after he won the junior golf championship of the Atlanta Athletic Club, defeating a 16-year-old. Bobby won the Georgia Amateur at age 14, defeating his friend Perry Adair in the 36-hole final. Adair's father had already made plans to take his son to the 1916 U.S. Amateur to be held at the Merion Cricket Club in Ardmore, Pennsylvania. The Adairs took Jones along, making Bobby the youngest player ever to qualify for and play in a U.S. Amateur Championship. Even though he didn't win, he scored a huge upset over 1906 U.S. Amateur champ Eben Byers, and he didn't lose until the third round, when defending champion Bob Gardner beat him. He burst onto the scene and raised the level of expectations for himself.

Bobby couldn't win the National Amateur Championship in the next two years, as they were canceled due to the war. Jones reached the finals of the 1919 National Amateur but lost to Davey Herron at the Oakmont Country Club in Pittsburgh. Still, golf wasn't the only thing he was content on learning. Bobby began his freshman year at Georgia Tech; his major was mechanical engineering.

In 1920 he played in his first U.S. Open. The 18-year-old was paired with 50-year-old Vardon, who was making his third and last trip to the U.S. Open. Vardon had been a hero to Jones. Jones finished eighth—his first of 10 top-10 finishes at the Open in 11 tries.

The following summer, after college let out, Jones traveled to England to play in the British Amateur and the British Open. He was defeated in the fourth round by Alan Graham, 6 and 5. Jones stayed in Europe for the British Open, which was played that year at St. Andrews. After back-to-back holes where he took a 6, Jones withdrew—as in, he quit out of frustration. This would be the low point in his career. It was around this period when he realized that he had to overcome his temper, which more than once got the better of him, and his disappointment with not always winning. A few weeks later, back in the United States, he finished 15th at the U.S. Open. At the U.S. Amateur, he had Willie Hunter, the British Amateur champion, 2-down. Jones failed to play a shot safe, and his ball hit the tallest tree and dropped straight down. Hunter beat him 2 and 1.

Before any of the parades and the hero worship, Jones had to first start winning. Of course, his mind was on more than golf. In 1922 he graduated with a mechanical engineering degree from Georgia Tech and entered Harvard to study literature in the fall. He entered the U.S. Open and had a share of the third-round lead. But he fell one stroke short in the last round when Gene Sarazen had a final-round 68.

As he entered the 1923 U.S. Open, Jones was 0–11 in the 11 tournaments that mattered most to him (the British Amateur and Open and the U.S. Amateur and Open). In 1923 he barely played until summer, when he entered the U.S. Open at Inwood, on Long Island, New York. He had a big lead during the final round of the tournament and lost the lead on the final four holes. He pulled an approach shot out of bounds on 16 and was lucky to save bogey. He missed the green of the 17th and again made bogey. He took a 6 on the 18th hole, finishing with a 76.

Bobby Cruickshank came to the 18th hole needing a birdie to tie Jones. After driving the ball right down the middle, Cruickshank hit an iron shot straight at the flagstick. It landed about six feet shy of the cup. Cruickshank holed the birdie putt and forced a play-off.

The 18-hole play-off came down to the final hole. After Cruickshank laid up short of the water, Jones hit a mid-iron that would become a signature shot in his legendary career. The shot cleared the pond and nestled within six feet of the hole. Long before the 2004 Masters, when Phil Mickelson became the latest to shed the title "greatest ever to never win a major tournament," Jones finally overcame seven years of frustration by winning the 1923 U.S. Open.

In 1926 Jones was chosen for the Walker Cup team, so he stayed overseas to play in the British Amateur. He was defeated at Muirfield by Andrew Jamieson, 4 and 3, in the sixth round (the quarterfinals). Bobby decided to stay and enter the 1926 British Open, his first appearance in that tournament since withdrawing in 1921.

After the third round of the 1926 British Open, held at Royal Lytham and St. Annes, Bobby trailed Al Watrous by two strokes. He still trailed by those two strokes with five holes to play. Then Jones made par on the 445-yard 14th hole and had a birdie-3 on the 468-yard 15th. Jones and Watrous were still even on the 17th, when Jones made a pressure shot with a 4-iron, which would win him his first British Open. The amateur Jones, who played only a few tournaments a year to accommodate his studies, was becoming unstoppable.

After winning the British Open, Jones turned his sights on becoming the first ever to win the British and U.S. Opens in the same year. The U.S. Open was played in Columbus, Ohio. Jones was four strokes back of Joe Turnesa with nine holes to play. No problem for Jones, who played his last 12 holes needing only 46 strokes.

Later that year Jones went for his third major of 1926, the U.S. Amateur. He had won the tournament in both 1924 and 1925. But in 1926 George Von Elm defeated Bobby, 2 and 1, in the finals.

With the British Amateur quarterfinals, the U.S. Amateur finals, and victories in the British and U.S. Opens, 1926 was an amazing year for Jones. He didn't attempt to win all four in the next three years. He didn't play the British Amateur in any of the following three years. He won the U.S. Amateur for a third time in 1927 (in Minneapolis) and a fourth time in 1928 (in West Newton, Massachusetts). Jones added the 1927 British Open Championship as well. And in the U.S. Open, Jones finished 11th in 1927, breaking a nine-year string of first- or second-place finishes at the U.S. Open.

Jones would finish second in 1928 and win his third U.S. Open in 1929. In that Open, at Winged Foot in Mamaroneck, New York, Jones needed to make two long par-4s to tie Al Espinosa. It came down to a 12-foot putt up a sidehill that would break a foot or so from left to right on a slippery green. He made his putt and worked his way into the 18-hole play-off. Defeating Espinosa by a whopping 23 shots in the play-off, Jones had his third Open.

By the end of 1929, with nine majors, Jones had other interests aside from golf. He wanted to attend law school in Atlanta and to start a family with his wife. There was, however, one last goal in the game that neither Jones nor anyone else up to that point had ever accomplished. No one had won the four majors in a single year. The first would be the British Amateur, which Jones had not won in his two previous attempts. The British Open had eluded him twice before—once, you might say, on a called third strike. Jones wanted a victory at St. Andrews and the 1930 British Open.

There were many ways that Jones could have lost the British Amateur, the first leg of the Grand Slam. Three of the matches were won by just one hole. The first scare came in the fourth round, when Jones defeated Cyril Tolley on the 19th hole. In a dramatic sixth-round victory over Jimmy Johnston, Jones was 4-up with five holes to play and yet nearly blew the match. Jones needed to make an eight-foot putt on 18 to save the match. Jones described his opponent's threatening comeback as "the most brilliant golf under pressure I ever saw."

Then in the semifinals Jones faced George Voigt in another close call. Voigt took the lead for the first time on the 11th hole and increased it on the 13th hole when Jones sliced his tee shot. But after that Jones was flawless, and Voigt blew the two-stroke lead in the final five holes. The finals pitted Jones against Roger Wethered. The crowd, estimated at over 15,000, nearly trampled both Jones and Wethered after Jones won the match, 7 and 6, after the 30th hole.

Two weeks later it was on to the British Open at Hoylake. Jones won by two strokes over Macdonald Smith and gave quotes to reporters that he might retire and not return after that season. Then he came home to a ticker-tape parade in New York and took a train to Minneapolis, site of the U.S. Open.

At Interlachen Club in Minneapolis, Jones won the tournament with a blistering third round, when he shot a 68, despite bogeys on the final two holes. Before 10,000 fans the next day, he birdied the 18th hole. About an hour later, Macdonald Smith reached the 18th tee still two strokes behind, needing an eagle to tie. He made par, however, and Jones wrapped up his 3rd major championship in seven weeks and his 12th overall. And yes, they were counting majors even then. I found an Associated Press newspaper account that wrote that the 12th win of Jones's career beat the record of Walter Hagen, who had won 11 national titles, which included the British Open, American Open, and PGA Championship.

Then the only thing left for Jones to conquer was the U.S. Amateur at Merion, the site of his third-round defeat at age 14 and the site of his first U.S. Amateur Championship in 1924. Jones won his semifinal match easily (9 and 8) with Jess Sweetser, and in the finals it was another rout for Jones, who defeated Gene Homans 8 and 7. That made Jones the holder of all four major championships in one glorious year. It upped his record to 58–11 in match play at either the U.S. or British Amateurs.

Jones officially retired two months later, in November of 1930. He left the game on top, assuring him of immortality. He became a lawyer who played weekend golf. It helped, too, that he was able to make far more money by not playing golf than he could by turning professional. On November 13, 1930, Jones signed a contract with Warner Brothers. The deal called for him to create and star in a series of 12 short films, each 10 minutes in length. In June of 1931, Jones (and a man named Clifford Roberts) helped design and create the Augusta National Golf Club. Within three years, they launched the Masters Tournament.

Since Jones had quite the vested interest in the success of the Masters—and since he had to be somewhat like most great athletes who retire too young—he played in the first Masters Tournament in 1934. It only took a round or two for him to realize that he wasn't going to waltz through the field (although he did shoot a 72 in the third round). The other golfers treated him with the utmost respect. Writing a newspaper column, leading golfer Paul Runyan commented, "All he needs is a little competition to again be better than the best." Jones quickly realized that he did not want to pursue the comeback with any real zest. He finished 13th in the first Masters Tournament. Following the event he made a statement that he had not returned to general play and that he would restrict his competition to the Masters.

Beginning in 1947, at the age of 45, Jones developed syringomyelia, a crippling spinal disease that in Jones's day struck one out of a million people. The spinal pressure was terribly painful. An operation appeared to relieve the pressure, but in 1950, two years after the first operation, Jones suffered a relapse. The rest of his life was spent in pain, and he eventually wound up in a wheelchair. He began life as a sickly child, spent years at the end of his life with a painful, crippling condition, and died at 69 years of age. In between, he became an immortal.

I admit it. I don't get the reverence for Mr. Jones. A ranking of sixth best is generous for someone whom I believe to be the most overrated golfer of all time. He entered only 52 golf tournaments in his life. Many top golfers today enter 30 a year. Not only did he retire at age 28, but in three of his peak years (1923, 1924, and 1929), he played in only two tournaments: the U.S. Open and the U.S. Amateur.

The physical and mental anguish Jones experienced from playing in those tournaments were such a hardship that it was reported he lost a lot of weight during them. Was this nervous stomach related to the childhood sickness?

You have to give credit to the five men I have ranked ahead of Jones. They all played far more competitive, pressure-filled golf than Jones. Vardon played despite bouts of tuberculosis. Hogan played top-level golf after his near-fatal accident. Nicklaus, despite fame and fortune, put himself under the pressure cooker for decades after the age that Jones put his clubs down.

Jim Nantz, golf announcer for CBS Sports: "I do think you are underrating Jones. In his day the best golfers were the amateurs—not the pros. Forget the mere 52 tournaments—check out his record *in just the majors*. He was totally dominant. You have to take a look at those numbers."

I did and took Nantz's advice and tracked down Tommy Barnes, a 90-year-old Atlanta resident who was a close friend of Bobby Jones's and played the last round of competitive golf with him before Jones became afflicted with his disease.

Tommy Barnes: "I played him for the first time when I was 15 years old in 1936. Yes, the best players in the world competed in the national Amateurs back then—sometimes 15 times. I won the Georgia Amateur and competed in a bunch of national Amateurs against the best players in the game, like Gene Littler. I had a good business here, and I never gave thought to turning professional. I think Jones was the same way. He always could play. I played him many times in the 1930s and '40s—after he retired. He was a great driver and didn't have any weaknesses in his game."

Jones had a heavily crafted image of sportsmanship and excellence. In short, he owned the press. One sportswriter, O. B. Keeler, covered Jones the way "Access Hollywood" covers Jennifer Aniston. The legendary sportswriter Grantland Rice once said, "Bobby Jones is not one in a million persons. . . . I should say he is one in ten million—or perhaps one in fifty million." Yet he was mortal. He smoked. He drank. He picked up his ball in frustration at the 1921 British Open and withdrew. He took four strokes to get down on the final hole of the 1923 U.S. Open, allowing Cruickshank to tie him for first place. If he had lost that play-off, it might have been the biggest choke in golf history. He almost gave away sure titles at the 1929 and 1930 U.S. Opens, as well.

I'm not saying Jones wasn't worthy of admiration. He certainly had character. He twice called penalties on himself at the U.S. Open. One incident probably cost him the 1925 U.S. Open, where he finished 72 holes in a tie and lost in a second 18-hole play-off.

In the first round of the tournament, Jones hit an approach shot to the 11th green that fell short. The ball settled in deep grass on an embankment. Jones's clubhead brushed the grass and moved the ball. Or did it? No one but Jones saw it happen. He immediately informed an official that he had violated a rule. It cost him a stroke, and he nearly didn't make the cut. He shot 70 the next day, but his final score would merely tie Willie Macfarlane. Jones would hear no accolades for doing what he saw as right. His famous quote was "You might as well praise me for not breaking into banks."

On the other hand, he was also a competitive sportsman. In the 1930 British Amateur, Jones (in his fourth-round match against Cyril Tolley) hit a shot that landed on the green, bounced once, hit a spectator on the chest, and then rebounded about 10 feet from the hole. There are those who felt that Jones had deliberately hit that approach into the crowd, knowing his ball would not go through (because of the crush of fans). And in the 1930 U.S. Open, on the 17th hole of the final round, Jones stepped to the tee as the leader. He hit a poor tee shot, and the ball hit a tree and was never seen again. Jones asked the referee what to do. The referee answered that the ball had gone into the water hazard and that Jones was permitted to drop a ball. If only that referee, Prescott Bush (who went on to become a U.S. senator), had the same diligence in finding Jones's ball as his grandson George W. would one day have in seeking out weapons of mass destruction, then Jones might never have won the Grand Slam. Bobby took a penalty shot, dropped another ball, pitched onto the green, and made 5. But that was a controversial decision.

Who's Better, Who's Best
Bobby Jones or Harry Vardon?

Just look at the one overlap in their careers: in 1920 when Vardon was 50 years old, sick with TB, and suffering the shakes with his putter, he still was three strokes better than an 18-year-old Bobby Jones. Jones ended his competitive golf career at age 28 and he was never a contender in his infrequent tournaments after that. Jones had no lengthy track record.

A Better Analogy

Bobby Jones and Jimmy Carter If Michael Jordan had stuck to his first retirement in 1993 at the age of 31, there would have been comparable situations. Jordan had been an amateur champion (winning an NCAA title as a freshman), a two-time Olympic champion, and a three-time NBA champion and had no worlds left to conquer. But, of course, Jordan came back twice more—once successfully and once not so successfully.

A baseball analogy might be drawn with Sandy Koufax, who, like Jones, had a seven-year period of total domination in his sport and retired young (at the age of 30)—but in Koufax's case, he retired because of injury. Also, Koufax became a near recluse in his retirement, whereas Jones was a constant presence at Augusta for decades.

A football analogy might be found with NFL-great Jim Brown, who retired after leading the league in rushing in eight of his nine seasons. Brown retired for a movie career that didn't quite take off. While both Brown and Jones retired for the big screen after reaching their athletic goals, Brown was never regarded with the same level of esteem in his sport that Jones was in his.

Looking for a comparison in track and field, one might consider Bob Mathias, who, like Jones, was sickly as a child. Mathias suffered from anemia and at age 12 had to take hundreds of iron shots. By the time he was 17, Mathias grew to be 6'2" and 190 pounds. Mathias made the 1948 U.S. track team and won the Olympic decathlon, the champion of which is universally acknowledged as the greatest all-around athlete in the world. And then Mathias repeated in 1952. But his name recognition and legendary status seem to have waned over time, which wasn't the case with Jones.

I have to go outside of sports to find an analogy to Jones. I suppose I have Georgia on my mind, because former president Jimmy Carter reminds me most of Bobby. Carter was from Plains, Georgia, about 150 miles from Jones's Atlanta. In the decades since he left office, Carter has gained much respect for his role as an international mediator and peacemaker and has used his position as a former president to further many charitable causes. In short, his reputation and legend grew after he left office. In 2002 Carter won the Nobel Peace Prize. Carter spent only four years of his life as president. Jones played only 52 golf tournaments in his lifetime, and, like Carter, some of his biggest contributions to the game, as a writer and ambassador of golf, came long after he left the limelight.

WALTER HAGEN
The Mirthful Professional

There are hundreds of golfers over more than a century to consider when ranking the greatest of all time. If one chooses to place a premium on major championships, then Walter Hagen ranks very high. If one ranks golfers by their popularity, their influence, their number of tour victories, or what their contemporaries thought of them, the Haig still ranks among the very best.

He was a fabulous player in a fabulous sports era, the golden age of the 1920s. He gets left behind in the greatest-ever arguments for two reasons: the legend of Bobby Jones and the fact that his name (Hagen) sounds similar to that of another golfing great (Hogan).

Walter Hagen was born in Rochester, New York, on December 21, 1892. He was the son of a blacksmith. He wasn't as wealthy as Jones was growing up, but he wasn't as poor as Vardon. He learned to play golf as a caddie at the country club at the age of seven and got paid 10 cents an hour.

Young Walter also spent his time stuffing birds and reptiles—and it is even said that on one occasion there was a strange disappearance of a neighbor's cat. Walter was given a license to practice taxidermy in the state of New York. It was his fallback career if he couldn't make a living in sports. After working his way up the ranks at the country club, he became an assistant manager in the pro shop. Walter was a good athlete in every sport he attempted, and he became proficient enough at golf to finish 11th in the 1912 Canadian Open. By all accounts, he was a natural athlete, whose confidence aided him in every sport.

He entered the 1913 U.S. Open at Brookline and tied for fourth place in the most memorable of leaderboards. That was the tournament where the unknown caddie Francis Ouimet defeated Vardon and Ted Ray. Hagen was in contention until the final nine holes.

At this time, Hagen (who was also an excellent billiards player, hockey player, and polo player) still harbored hopes of making the major leagues as a baseball player. He was a good semipro baseball player and was offered a contract for the 1915 season with the Philadelphia Phillies by manager Pat Moran.

He would have given baseball his full attention if, at the age of 22, he hadn't won the 1914 U.S. Open at Midlothian. I tend to believe that Hagen's aptitude for so many other sports is what made his golf game so good. The grip he used on his putter was taken from the odd winding used on a polo mallet. He learned from billiards the hazards of one bad shot. He knew from baseball that every great player has slumps and how to ride them out.

"I'm in the big league in golf now, so why bother with baseball?" said Hagen at the time. But golf wasn't exactly big league—until Hagen made it big league. He dressed like a rich man, elevating the status of the professional golfer. He refused to be treated like a second-class citizen, lower than the country club members or the amateur golfers. He became such an attraction that the clubs had no choice but to open their doors and changing rooms to the professionals.

He was a modern golfer almost out of place in his era. He would have understood private planes. He had an entourage that traveled with him. He claimed that he never wanted to be a millionaire, he just wanted to live like one. He was larger than life with a vivacious personality and expanded his fortune and name by taking his popularity beyond golf.

To do that, he needed the help of two men. Until the 1929 crash, Jesse Livermore (known as the Wolf of Wall Street) always picked up Hagen's first-class travel tabs. This would include Rolls-Royces in England. And Bob Harlow's association with Hagen, as his manager and publicist, began in 1922. They were inseparable for more than 20 years, and Harlow was responsible for much of what Hagen is remembered for—his showmanship.

Hagen developed quite the reputation as a showman, and Harlow encouraged it. Unlike the well-known golfers who were slaves to the practice range, Hagen played it differently. In a 1963 interview, Sir Walter revealed that many times when competitors thought he had left the golf course to go to his hotel, he went instead to a different golf course in another part of town and practiced for three or four hours. He liked the psychology of sports, psyching out the other players. It helped his image if people thought he was a playboy who cared little about golf matches. Hagen wrote in his 1956 book, *The Walter Hagen Story*, "I set up shots the way a movie director sets up scenes, to pull all the suspense possible from every move."

Harlow found ways to make Hagen (already the wealthiest pro golfer to that point in history) richer. When Babe Ruth was bragging that in 1927 he was making $80,000—more than the president of the United States ("After all, I had a better year," cracked the Babe)—Hagen made more than that every year.

Hagen, during the Florida real-estate craze of the 1920s, was paid $30,000 a year to act as a part-time pro to the Jungle Club in Fort Lauderdale. Walter was nothing more than an ornament for the club. He had to merely play in some foursomes with potential investors. He probably just attached his name to it.

After winning the 1921 PGA Championship, Hagen passed up a chance to defend his title. Harlow hooked him up on a series of matches with Australian Joe Kirkwood, a well-known trick-shot artist. Hagen was already considered a colorful player, so Harlow proposed that Hagen go on tour with Kirkwood. They developed a successful act and played all over the world.

Hagen was the antithesis of Bobby Jones. He was the furthest thing from an amateur that one could be. Jones never won a single dollar in prize money. Hagen was the player who psyched out opponents. He had a little trick of starting with a shorter drive than his opponent, who soon became all confident with the idea that he was outdriving Hagen. Then Hagen would begin to pound his next drives, dropping them 40 yards beyond his opponent's ball. It is of little wonder that he was the best match-play golfer of all time. He played with opponents' heads.

In 1919 Hagen didn't enter the PGA Championship, although earlier that summer he did win his second U.S. Open, this time in an 18-hole play-off with Mike Brady. The night before the play-off, Hagen hooked up with his showbiz friend Al Jolson, who was playing in a theater in town. As Hagen described it years later:

> On the night before my play-off with Mike, Al and I and all the chorus girls piled into a couple of open cars and drove out to a seashore club where we danced and romanced. Al and I were dressed in tails, and the girls were dressed to the nines. Sometime during the night, a well-meaning friend said, "For Gods-sake, Walter, get some sleep so you'll be in shape for the play-off tomorrow. You can be sure that Brady has been in bed and sleeping hours ago." I just laughed. "He may be in bed right now, but he ain't *sleeping* any more than I am."

It's legend that Hagen rushed out to the course in the morning—still in his tuxedo—and the officials gave him time to change his clothes. Hagen won the play-off by a stroke, incidentally, to win the Open. He supposedly told Brady on the second tee, "Mike, you really ought to roll those sleeves back down. You're letting everyone see how your muscles are quivering."

The PGA Championship was the second major tournament in the United States; it was established in 1916. Hagen reached the semifinals in the first year of the match-play tournament, and then the tournament was canceled the next two years because of World War I. Hagen's dominance of the PGA Championship in the 1920s is one of the most incredible feats in golf history. If not for Jones's Grand Slam, Hagen's run of PGA Championships was probably golf's most outstanding feat in any of the majors.

In 1921 Hagen reached the finals and defeated two-time PGA champion Jim Barnes, 3 and 2. Walter didn't defend his title the following year; instead, he opted to play in exhibitions.

He again reached the finals in 1923 and faced Gene Sarazen. They needed to go to the first extra-hole finals in the short history of the tournament, and Sarazen won 1-up on the 38th hole. Hagen needed a birdie on the 38th hole to halve the hole and came within inches of holing his bunker shot and within inches of getting his birdie.

He won all six matches to win the PGA in 1924. He also won all six matches to win the PGA in 1925, although he needed to survive a first-round match with Al Watrous. Hagen won on the 39th hole. He had to come back against Leo Diegel, who was 4-up after the front nine. Hagen won a third consecutive PGA Championship in 1926 and a fourth straight in 1927.

Diegel finally extracted revenge on Hagen, defeating him in a 1928 match at the PGA Championship. It ended Hagen's string of 28 consecutive victories over the top professionals. Going into that match, Hagen was 32–1 in his previous 33 matches—the loss being to Sarazen in the 1923 finals. By then Hagen was 36 years old and on the downside of his great career.

How do we put these 28 consecutive wins in the PGA—and 4 consecutive championships—in proper perspective? To me, it's comparable to Björn Borg winning 5 Wimbledon titles in a row and Pete Sampras winning 6 in seven years.

Although his greatest success came in the PGA Championship, Hagen had the aforementioned pair of U.S. Opens, as well as four British Opens. Before Hagen no American-born golfer had ever won the British Open. His first overseas trip to play in the British Open came in 1920. The high winds at Deal were unexpected for Hagen, who finished 55th. The next year, he returned and finished sixth.

Hagen, who usually gave good quotes to reporters, claimed that the British golfers played it too "safe." Hagen boldly stated that he would take chances and become the first American-born golfer to win the British Open. He did exactly that in 1922. He won in 1924 as well. In 1928 he left early for Britain to play English golfing great Archie Compston. Compston crushed Hagen, 18 and 17, in a scheduled 72-hole match.

One week later it was Hagen who won the British Open. Walter had previously lost to Compston so badly (and was compensated so well) that you almost wonder if it had been another setup. In that 1928 British Open, Hagen shot 292 to better runner-up Gene Sarazen by two and Compston by three.

No one gave much chance for Hagen to win the 1929 British Open. His career was on the downside, and he was an old 37. He was captain of the Ryder Cup team that played at Leeds, England, in the spring of 1929. Hagen, in a display of sportsmanship, let everyone on the team play at least one match, instead of using just his stars. Great Britain stunned the United States by a 7–5 count, and in the big singles match, George Duncan routed Hagen, 10 and 8.

But Hagen rebounded from his stunning loss to Duncan by defeating him (and everyone else) in capturing the 1929 British Open title. In fact, he shot a 66 on the final round to win his 11th major, this time by six strokes.

Hagen won 11 majors, which is a huge number when you consider that in Hagen's era there were only two or three to shoot at every year (depending on whether players made the expensive trip to the British Open), as compared with the modern era with four every year. Jones—if you don't count the British Amateur or U.S. Amateur titles—won 9 majors. By the end of 2005, only one player—Nicklaus, with 18—had won more than Hagen's 11 majors.

Who's Better, Who's Best
Walter Hagen or Bobby Jones?

Was Walter Hagen better than Bobby Jones? At the height of their careers, they played against each other just once. Hagen recounted the match in a May 1963 *Golf Magazine* article by Robert J. Allen:

> As Bobby continued to win one amateur match after another, often beating the pros in the open tournaments, his reputation kept growing. In the opinion of most golf experts, I was considered practically unbeatable when I wanted to bear down, so there grew a lively debate as to which one of us would win in a special match contest. By 1925, the clamor fanned by all the golf writers for such a match was irresistible. Golf impresario Bob Harlow finally got both Jones and myself to agree on the match, a 72-hole contest with the first 36 holes being played on Bobby's home course at Sarasota, Florida, and the final 36 on the course I favored at Pasadena, Florida.
>
> I was determined to give him the beating of his life. I did—I won the match 12 up and 11 to play!

For the match, Hagen received a huge fee for the mid-1920s. He received $7,600. He used $800 of it to buy Bobby a set of diamond and platinum cuff links. Was this a genuine gesture to a man who couldn't accept prize money? Was it another setup in Hagen's career?

Hagen didn't have Jones as a competitor in 8 of the 11 majors he won. He still faced everyone else. He probably had tougher competition than Jones did, although that's debatable. They were an interesting pair. Jones, the true amateur, never accepted a dime for his golf, and Hagen never turned one down.

Hagen won 40 PGA tournaments from 1916 (long before Jones began to win) to 1936 (long after Jones retired). I'm not sure that Hagen was better, but I wouldn't have bet against him. He died in October of 1969.

MICKEY WRIGHT
The Greatest Female Golfer

Baseball fans know that the greatest Yankee of all time—and perhaps the greatest player of all time—was Babe Ruth. But the most talented Yankee was known as "the Mick," the beloved Mickey Mantle. In women's golf it was another great Mickey who picked up where Babe left off. In the LPGA that's Mickey Wright, who picked up where Babe—Didrikson, that is—left off.

Mickey Wright was born in 1935 (a few years after Arnold Palmer and a few years before Jack Nicklaus) and won more tournaments than either of them in the same era. She dominated the LPGA at a critical juncture in its history. She won 79 tournaments in the years from 1959 through 1968, which worked out to be almost eight victories per year. Although one lady (Kathy Whitworth) would end her career with a few more wins, Wright is the one generally considered as the greatest woman golfer of all time.

Wright, from San Diego, took up golf for the first time at the age of 10, when her lawyer father got her interested in the sport. She grew to 5'8" and weighed between 140 and 150 pounds. "I was bigger than anyone in my class and had a slight inferiority complex. I wanted to be noticed for something besides my size. So I got into golf," she told sportswriter Harold Ratliff in 1965.

She won her first tournament at age 13 and turned professional at 19. She (and other women) were able to turn pro because of the efforts of female sports pioneer Babe Didrikson Zaharias, the woman who first caused a surge in the women's golf game and broke new ground in the 1930s and '40s.

Babe was one of a handful of women pros who began the LPGA in 1950. In the 1954 U.S. Women's Open, at Brookline, Massachusetts, Babe was paired for the final two rounds with Wright, the U.S. Girls' Junior Champion. Didrikson, battling cancer at the time, won her third U.S. Women's Open by a whopping 12 strokes.

That tournament would be a last hurrah for Didrikson, who died less than two years later. Wright's arrival on the scene coincided with Babe's departure. Wright finished fourth, 17 shots back of Babe. Later in 1954, after finishing second in the Women's Amateur,

Wright turned pro. She was one of 17 LPGA members. By 1963, just nine years later, there were 120 LPGA members.

From the get-go Wright's tireless drive was apparent through the competitive goals she set. Her priority was to become the best female golfer in the world. When she started she was a weak putter. She was always a long hitter, that being the best part of her game. Practicing Ben Hogan–like to reach her goals, she turned herself into a decent putter and wedge player. Her first professional victory came at the age of 21 at the Jacksonville Open in 1956.

In her era the four majors in women's golf were the U.S. Women's Open, the LPGA Championship, the Western Open, and the Titleholders Championship. She won 13 majors—all by the age of 31. She won the LPGA Championship in 1958, 1960, 1961, and 1963; the Western Open in 1962, 1963, and 1966; the Titleholders in 1961 and 1962; and the U.S. Women's Open in 1958, 1959, 1961, and 1964. That's a career Grand Slam, and she racked up three majors in 1961 alone!

She earned the trophies, but she didn't earn the money that Arnold and Jack did. When asked her thoughts on the difference in prize money between men and women, she had this to say in a 1964 Associated Press interview:

> It's not the difference in earnings that bother me. It's just that it seems like a phony value system to me. Purses like the men get are completely out of line. It's self evident that something is wrong when a golfer makes $20,000 for a weekend of work, while a professor or scientist can't make that in a couple of years. Thank heavens we don't have that on the women's tour. I certainly would mind it because value systems are important to me.

This quote was published at the peak of her career. And her peak, like the year she had in 1963, was one that not even Nicklaus ever enjoyed or that Tiger Woods has accomplished to this point. Wright entered 28 tournaments in 1963 and finished in the top 10 in 27 of them. She finished first a record 13 times. She was either first or second in more than 70 percent of the tournaments she entered that year. For the entire 28 tournaments she played in 1963, Wright earned a total of $31,269. Also in 1963, Nicklaus won the Masters—he received $20,000 for that one tournament alone.

Here is how good Wright was in 1963. Writers and broadcasters were asked to vote for first, second, and third in the annual Associated Press Female Athlete of the Year poll. Many of the voters just stopped after writing down Mickey Wright's name. It was the third straight year Wright had topped the LPGA money list and the first time any lady golfer had won as much as $30,000 in a year. Wright had almost as good a year in 1964

(24 top-10 finishes in 27 events, including a win in the U.S. Women's Open, and $29,910 in earnings) and repeated as the Associated Press Female Athlete of the Year.

Like female athletes before her, Wright wanted to forge new territory and advance women's sports in prestige and popularity by pumping up interest in the women's game. To accomplish this, she agreed that more players would be paid out of the total purse, with the winner getting less of a percentage. The move would hurt multiwinner Wright but would help the other, struggling tour members. I believe her biggest feat was bridging the gap between the founding women of the LPGA and the next generation of stars who would reap the benefit of Mickey's accomplishments.

At the premiere event in women's golf, the U.S. Women's Open, she won four times. In 1958, at Forest Lake Country Club in Detroit, she won by five strokes over her nearest competitor, Louise Suggs, and earned $1,800. She repeated the following year, when the event was held at Churchill Valley Country Club in Pittsburgh. She won by two strokes. A bad final round cost her the 1960 U.S. Women's Open. But in 1961 she won by a commanding six strokes at Baltusrol in Springfield, New Jersey. The story goes that she was putting horribly before that Open, but she solved her problems on a Howard Johnson hallway carpet. And really, what problem can't be solved on a HoJo's hallway carpet?

In 1964 she won 11 events, including the U.S. Women's Open (in her hometown of San Diego) for a fourth time, sharing the record for winning the most Open titles with Betsy Rawls. She also won the LPGA Championship to become the only player in LPGA history to win that title four times. She shot a career-low 62 (setting an LPGA record for the lowest final round by a winner) and came from 10 shots down in the final round to win the Tall City Open, marking the largest come-from-behind win in LPGA history (Annika Sorenstam tied her record in 2001).

By 1965 Wright, nearing 30 years of age, had accomplished all her goals. She had always taken three months off each winter, but in '65 she took a semiretirement to go back to college. She entered only 11 tournaments.

In 1966 the lady golfers finally got a little bit of money thrown to them. The previous year the total purse money for the women's Tour was $356,316. The growth of televised sports and the interest in golf raised the annual LPGA prize money to $509,500 in 1966. In the first week of that September, the top six women golfers came together in Springfield, Ohio, for the first annual Ladies' World Series of Golf, a made-for-TV show. A group of 13 Springfield businessmen put up a record $32,000 purse for the 36-hole tournament. That was nearly three times as much as any previous women's tournament had offered.

The six golfers who competed were Wright (recently returned from her brief sabbatical), Kathy Whitworth, Carol Mann, Sandra Haynie, Clifford Ann Creed, and Sandra Spuzich. On the first day, Mann shot a 68. The second and final round saw Wright birdie 10, 11, and 12 with putts of 12 feet, 15 feet, and 8 feet. She added four other one-putt greens and sank a 25-foot chip shot. Mickey finished with a 67, and 136 for the tournament. She won easily by four strokes. The sponsors handed her a $10,000 check. Sandra Haynie finished second. Mann had slipped to third place but received a check for $5,000, responding by kissing all 13 of the sponsors.

Women's golf was on its way. They increased their visibility and marketability for television purposes. The LPGA developed new stars. Wright was the conduit between Didrikson and the Kathy Whitworths, Nancy Lopezes, and Annika Sorenstams that followed. Sorenstam earned more than $2.2 million in 2005 alone. Thanks, Mickey!

Wright won 82 tournaments and entered only 230. That is a terrific percentage. In 1969, the same year that the other Mickey (Mantle) retired, Wright stopped playing on the Tour for a variety of reasons, including an adverse reaction to sunlight, aversion to flying, and foot problems.

Not only did Mickey Wright have an adverse reaction to sunlight, she never was comfortable in the limelight either. She didn't seek out attention when she played. And she certainly didn't seek it out when she retired. She was merely the greatest golfer in women's history, dominating the 1960s, winning a tournament in each of 14 straight years, from 1956 to 1969.

9

BABE DIDRIKSON ZAHARIAS
The Other Babe

John Lennon wrote a song called "Woman Is the Nigger of the World." I thought about this song a lot while researching the life story of Babe Didrikson Zaharias. "We make her paint her face and dance," Lennon sang. But Mildred Didrikson would not paint her face and dance.

When she was born, in Texas in 1911, women were not expected to star in sports. She didn't want to paint her face and dance. She did, however, want to become the greatest athlete of all time. She grew up in Beaumont, Texas, and played all sports, on any team that would have her. She played on the boys' basketball team in high school and took on males in every sport. She got her nickname after hitting five homers in a baseball game. In 1932 an insurance company from Texas (the Employees Casualty Company of Dallas) won the U.S. Track and Field Championships. Mildred Didrikson made up the entire team. In a span of three hours, the 21-year-old Didrikson competed in 8 of 10 events, winning 5 outright and tying for first in a 6th. She set world records in the javelin (139 feet 3 inches), 80-meter hurdles (11.9 seconds), high jump (5 feet 3.19 inches, tying for first), and baseball throw (272 feet 2 inches). Didrikson also took first in the shot put (39 feet 6.25 inches) and long jump (17 feet 6.625 inches) and finished fourth in the discus. In doing so, she qualified for the 1932 Olympics.

In the 1932 Olympics she won two gold medals in track and field. She might have won more in a later era. Women were limited then to just three events. It was at those games that she was asked if there was anything she didn't play. She answered, "Dolls."

After the Olympics there wasn't much that she could do to earn money. She barnstormed around the country. She played baseball for the House of David team. She was an excellent basketball player and bowler. She took up golf in 1933 and shot a 77 in her first round. She took lessons from the great champion Tommy Armour, and her practice sessions on the range were legendary. It was said that she would hit 1,500 balls a day to practice. Babe also was an excellent irons player and had a terrific touch on the greens.

She became a leading amateur but again needed to find a way to make money. She turned professional when a company offered her $300,000 to make movie "shorts" (20-minute pictures that were shown in theaters). Bobby Jones had accepted a lot of money to also make movie shorts, and their success opened a door for Babe. Later she fought to regain her amateur status in golf.

In 1932 sportswriter Grantland Rice called her "the greatest woman athlete of all time." Six years later Alan Gould, an Associated Press sportswriter, listed 10 women whose athletic feats merited a spot in a mythical hall of fame. The women, listed alphabetically, were Mary K. Browne, Didrikson, Gertrude Ederle, Sonja Henie, Suzanne Lenglen, Helen Wills Moody, Elenora Sears, Glenna Collett Vare, Joyce Wethered, and Hazel Hotchkiss Wightman. Gould wrote in 1938, "It's safe only to say that competitive interest and scope of women's sports have increased greatly in the post-war period, which gave impetus to all athletic activity." Before the 1930s women tennis players had to wear long skirts. The women Gould listed changed society's image of what female athletes could do.

Didrikson didn't start playing golf until 1933, but her golfing, combined with her Olympic and other achievements, led the Associated Press in 1959 to vote Babe the "Greatest Female Athlete of the first half of the twentieth century." She received the bulk of the votes cast in the AP poll: 319 first-place votes out of 361.

In 1938 Babe married a professional wrestler named George Zaharias, who was known at the time as the Crying Greek from Cripple Creek. George loved Babe and made his wife his full-time job. He managed her career. They never had children, and they weren't allowed to adopt kids, because they traveled too much and wouldn't be considered "good" parents. For insight into how the media of that time portrayed her, I turned to a 1947 *Time* magazine article:

> There are few men in the land who can out drive husky Babe Didrikson. . . . When she spotted a photographer trying to take her picture, she yelled, "I'm not so bad that you have to have your thumb over the lens, am I?" . . . She is still the world's top woman athlete, but she is no longer the rough and tumble tomboy. She wears silly hats, nylons and red fingernail polish when she dresses up. The retreat from tomboyishness began when she married cauliflower-eared George Zaharias.

She had her amateur status restored in August 1947, and she won her first U.S. Women's Open in 1948, the third year of the event. At this point she was the number one female athlete in the world.

The Start of the LPGA

In September of 1950 Didrikson was in Wichita, Kansas, for the U.S. Women's Open at the Rolling Hills Country Club. Twelve competitors, including Babe, went over their plans to create a professional women's golf tour.

"We all wanted this thing to fly, and for that to happen, we had to stick together," said founder Louise Suggs to Bob Stratton for Knight/Ridder newspapers in 2000.

In the early days of the LPGA, there were enough talented ladies to play a competitive tour, but there were so many other things it took to make it work. Babe "was the Tiger Woods of our tour," said cofounder Marilynn Smith. "She was a big hitter with a flair for the dramatic. She loved interacting with the galleries and they loved her for it." In the first year of the LPGA, Babe won two-thirds of the tournaments and earned $14,800, making her the leading money winner on the Tour. The next year, she won 7 of 12 starts and took home $15,087. She was abrasive, and sometimes her competitors didn't appreciate her cockiness. She would walk into the clubhouse and ask which one of the ladies was going to finish second that week. Babe knew that she was the most popular figure on the Tour and demanded more money than anyone else.

By the early 1950s she was finally making some real money, thanks to the new LPGA Tour and endorsements, movies, and the like. She also began to drift from Zaharias. Her constant companion became Betty Dodd, a player on the Tour. In April of 1953 Babe learned she had cancer and underwent the first of two surgeries. Doctors removed the tumor but found that the cancer had spread into her lymph nodes. By the next year she had completed an incredible golf comeback, winning her third U.S. Women's Open— by an incredible 12 strokes—just 14 weeks after her second surgery. That year, 1954, saw Babe win five titles and her sixth Associated Press Female Athlete of the Year award. Eventually, pain in her spine from the cancer had reduced her to about 80 pounds. Dodd as well as the grieving husband kept a constant vigil at Babe's bedside. Didrikson passed away at the age of 45.

In 2000 ESPN voted Didrikson number 10 among North American athletes of the twentieth century. CNN/*Sports Illustrated* named her as the second greatest female athlete of all time (trailing only Jackie Joyner Kersee), also in 2000.

The story of her amazing life was the subject of a fascinating exhibit at the PGA Museum in Far Hills, New Jersey, in the spring of 2005. The highlight of the exhibit, of course, was Babe's golf career. The museum also had a uniform from the House of David, the baseball team Babe pitched for in 1934. The House of David played against the top Negro League teams of the day, including the Homestead Grays and Kansas City Monarchs. Babe (who, unlike her male teammates, wasn't required to have a beard) pitched the first two innings of many of those games. Think about it. Babe most likely faced the great slugger Josh Gibson or was a mound opponent of Satchel Paige, one of the few athletes in history whose legend can match hers.

Babe has a legacy that is comparable to many of the greatest athletes of all time. Certainly, she has to be considered among the greatest female athletes ever. She can be compared with Satchel and the great Negro Leaguers of the 1930s for she faced many of the same barriers that they did. She can be compared heroically with NHL star Mario Lemieux or cyclist Lance Armstrong, two other champions who battled cancer and then returned to the field of play.

She might have been the first athlete to go public with cancer in the prime of a career. There is little doubt that if she had been born in a later time, she would have been considered a great athlete (probably golfer), especially by today's standards. If she had been given longer to live, she would have accumulated many more golf titles. There aren't many golfers named something other than Tiger who have won a major by 12 strokes. As it is Didrikson may have been the greatest athlete in the first 50 years of the 1900s.

Who's Better, Who's Best
Babe Didrikson or Mickey Wright?

During the 1988 Centennial of Golf in America celebration, *Golf Magazine* named Babe Golfer of the Decade for 1948 to 1957. Wright was named Golfer of the Decade by the same magazine for the years 1958 to 1967. Mickey was 24 years younger than Didrikson, but they crossed paths competitively once in a U.S. Open. Wright faced tougher fields, her records were more tangible, and it's Wright who gets the nod.

A Better Analogy

Babe Didrikson and Satchel Paige   Satchel Paige was as talented a baseball player as there ever was, but he was such a legendary figure that half the stuff was made up. He lied about his age. He didn't get a chance to compete with the Major Leaguers until 1948. He had to make money in the '30s and '40s by barnstorming, playing in vaudeville, and the like.

Didrikson—who was known at various times as the Amazing Amazon, the Texas Tornado, and Whatta-Gal Didrikson—had to barnstorm around the country herself. In 1935 Babe went on a one-month tour with Gene Sarazen, that year's Masters champion and the winner of seven majors. She would occasionally outdrive him. This was comparable to the winter tours that Paige took with Bob Feller and other Major Leaguers.

Didrikson and other sources claimed she won 17 consecutive golf tournaments in 1946 and 1947. She didn't. After winning 13 straight, she lost in the first round at the National Open in Spokane, Washington, in August of 1946. Babe conveniently erased this tournament when she spoke of her streak. After losing in Spokane, Babe won four more tournaments.

This is no different than the tall tales that Paige used to tell. Maybe Satchel did pitch in 2,500 games and win around 2,000 of them. Maybe he did throw 100 no-hitters, as he claimed. You get the point.

To me it's not terribly important if it was 13 tournaments in a row or 17. You have to be really, really dominant to win that many golf tournaments in a row.

Susan E. Cayleff, Ph.D., author of *Babe: The Life and Legend of Babe Didrikson Zaharias* **(1996) and** *Babe Didrikson: The Greatest All-Sport Athlete of All Time* **(2000):** "The analogy you make to Paige is a good one. But Babe could compete in legitimate venues once she turned her attention to golf. I think a better analogy would be more along the lines of Jackie Joyner Kersee because of her versatility. Also, both of these women had larger-than-life personas. If Babe had been born 60 years later, she would have played golf. Track and field doesn't yield the same income. Softball/baseball barnstorming was somewhat of a moneymaker; but then as now really there is only tennis and golf that provide viable livings for women. A current-day athlete would most likely aim for one of those two sports."

10

BYRON NELSON
Lord Byron

Byron Nelson caddied from the time he could lift a bag and discovered early in life that his future would be in golf. Born in Texas on February 4, 1912, Byron to this day still answers to Lord Byron and resides in Roanoke, Texas.

Shortly after losing his job with a magazine in 1932, Byron boarded a bus to Fort Worth to play in an open tournament in Texarkana, Texas, hopeful of winning the $500 in prize money. When he arrived at the club, he asked tournament officials what he had to do to become a professional and enter the tournament. They told him to pay $5 and announce that he was playing for money. It was a good move, as Nelson won $75 in that tournament.

That announcement is what signaled the start of a new era in golf. Bobby Jones and Walter Hagen were no longer competing. Now the stage was left for Nelson, Sam Snead, and Ben Hogan.

There is no mystery to Nelson's nickname. After his Masters victory in 1937, which made him the then-youngest winner at the Masters, O. B. Keeler of the *Atlanta Journal* gave him the nickname Lord Byron, and it stuck. It would be Byron's first great moment in the game. Byron set records that stuck as well. He was the most accurate and consistent shot maker of his day.

Byron continued to live up to his nickname at the Spring Mill Course of the Philadelphia Country Club in the 1939 Open. He hit the pin six times during the regulation 72 holes, each time with a different club. His score of 284 placed him in a three-way tie with Craig Wood and Denny Shute. In the first play-off round, both Wood and Nelson shot 68. An eagle-2 on the third hole of the second overtime gave Nelson his second major.

Some of Nelson's most sensational golf came at the match-play PGA Championships. In 1939 he steamrolled into the finals, easily winning his first five matches. In the quarters he shot 99 in 27 holes to whip Emerick Kocsis, 10 and 9. He then defeated Dutch Harrison, 9 and 8. In Nelson's 156 holes of golf, he was 28-under par. Nelson then met

Henry Picard in the finals, and the match went into overtime before Picard won 1-up on the 37th hole.

Byron came back in 1940 to win his first PGA Championship. According to the *2005 PGA Media Guide*, he defeated Snead in the finals, 1-up. Snead had a 1-up lead on the 34th hole, with Nelson two feet away for birdie. Snead almost ran in a 20-footer that would have tied the hole. On the 35th hole, Nelson hit a terrific wedge shot to within two feet. Nelson went 1-up on that hole. On the 36th and last hole, Byron hit a 3-iron to just 10 feet away. He got close enough to tap in for the major championship. Nelson almost had his second Masters Championship in 1941. He finished second, however, three strokes back of Wood.

If there's a criticism of Nelson's record, it is that during his peak years, he did not face the top competition because many of the greats served in World War II. But Nelson beat everyone in his time. Just look at the 1941 PGA Championship.

Byron eliminated Ralph Guldahl, 4 and 3, in the third round. He knocked out Hogan, 2-up, in the quarterfinals. He knocked out Gene Sarazen, 2 and 1, in the semifinals. Nelson eliminated two of the top 20 players of all time—and three of the top 50 in succession. Nelson lost the finals of that PGA Championship, by the way, when Vic Ghezzi squared the match with Nelson by making up three strokes on the back nine. On the final hole, tied, Ghezzi missed his four-foot putt for the championship. At the 37th hole Ghezzi had another chance to win with a 10-foot putt for birdie. He missed again. On the 38th hole both Nelson and Ghezzi chipped to within three feet. Even the referee couldn't determine who should putt first, so they tossed a coin. Nelson won the toss and missed his putt. Ghezzi barely made his, and Nelson lost in the finals.

The play-off at Augusta in the 1942 Masters Tournament was one of the great events in sports history. Two of the 10 greatest players in history went 18 holes in a play-off for the most prestigious tournament in the world. Nelson defeated Hogan in a magnificent display. Byron was down three strokes to Hogan after five holes. Hogan was continuing his hot play; he had come back eight strokes on Nelson in the final two rounds. Nelson got hot and was 6-under from the 6th hole through the 13th. It was like a great heavyweight fight, with Hogan coming back with birdies on 14 and 15 to cut Nelson's lead to one stroke. Nelson played conservatively with the late lead and won 69–70.

In 1942 Nelson reached the semifinals of the PGA but lost in overtime on the 37th hole, this time to Jim Turnesa. The PGA Championship was canceled in 1943. But in 1944 Byron lost in the finals for the third time, this time to 28-year-old Bob Hamilton, a 10–1 long shot. Nelson was dejected afterward, telling reporters, "Four times in the Championship finals, and I've won only one; maybe I should give up the game." It was a good thing he didn't, for the best was yet to come.

Byron had an excellent year in 1944, finishing with the lowest stroke average, 69.67, which was the record at the time. Hogan broke the record in 1948, Snead bettered the record in 1949 and 1950, and Tiger Woods now holds the record. In 1944 Nelson also won eight tournaments, which was one short of Paul Runyan's record of nine wins in a calendar year. But this was nothing compared with what Nelson accomplished in 1945.

It seemed that he won everything in 1945. (The Associated Press recognized him as the Male Athlete of the Year.) It remains the greatest year a golfer has ever had. Here are the records that Nelson set in 1945:

1. 11 consecutive victories
2. 18 wins in a calendar year
3. 68.34 stroke average (7,657 strokes in 112 rounds)

Let me put the three records into perspective.

First, you have to consider his 11 consecutive victories. It was actually 10 in a row if you don't count the Miami Four-Ball Tournament that Nelson won with Jug McSpaden. I understand there's a big difference between winning an individual tournament and a team competition. But I don't care if it's 10 or 11 consecutive wins. No one before or since has won as many as seven golf tournaments in a row. And the only golfers with six consecutive victories are Woods and Hogan. Winning 11 (or 10) consecutive tournaments is more impressive than making the cut in 113 consecutive tournaments, as Nelson did. It is as impressive as Joe DiMaggio's 56-game hitting streak, set in 1941.

Detractors will point out that when Nelson won some of these tournaments, many of the top golf stars were overseas in uniform. (Nelson was classified 4-F because of hemophilia.) Nelson had a stock response to his detractors. He would say that all he could do was to let the record speak for itself. "The best that any man can do is to be the best in his time. There probably were some good players in the service, but there were some good ones that weren't there, too."

His closest call came in his first singles tournament following the Four-Ball Tournament. He beat Snead in an 18-hole play-off. After Nelson finished his last round, Snead three-putted; Nelson won his second straight tournament and wouldn't come close to losing for months.

He was "in the zone" for 11 wins in a row, finishing 280 in one tournament and under that in every other one. The pressure got to be a problem after he'd won four in a row. By winning four consecutive tournaments, Nelson had tied the record set by Johnny Farrell in 1927. A week later at Durham, Snead won his fifth straight.

And then there were no more tournaments for two months, until mid-June. Nelson was in fine form to resume his quest. He won in Montreal, Philadelphia, and Chicago before heading to Dayton and the 1945 PGA Championship.

The pressure from having won seven straight tournaments was increasing. Nelson defeated Sarazen (4 and 3), Mike Turnesa (1-up), Shute (3 and 2), and Claude Harmon (5 and 4) to get to the finals against a newcomer to the Tour named Sam Byrd (a former Yankees outfielder). Byrd had a 2-up lead after the first 18 holes. But Nelson went in front on the 29th hole and finally won, 4 and 3, a few holes later.

Nelson won in Chicago again, and then he won the All-American Open, defeating Sarazen and Hogan. The next week, in Toronto, Nelson won the Canadian Open. He finally lost in mid-August to amateur Fred Haas Jr. in the Memphis Invitational.

Nelson's 18 victories in a calendar year is also incredible. It has been written that he won 19, but that includes a 36-hole tournament in New Jersey. Only 72-hole tournaments are counted. The closest anyone has come since Nelson won 18 tournaments in a calendar year was when Hogan won 13 the very next year (1946).

The most impressive of Nelson's 1945 records was his 68.34 stroke average. That has been bested only once in 60 years—by Tiger Woods in 2000 (with a 68.17 stroke average). Lord Byron's detractors talk about the level of competition in 1945, even without the players lost to the service. Nelson would be the first to admit that the field is much deeper today and that maybe 10 to 15 players could get hot enough to win a tournament in 1945. But let me just say this: golf is a sport where one competes against the course, not the competitors.

In 1945, at the Seattle Open at the Broadmoor Golf Course (par 70), Byron breezed through the four rounds, shooting 62–68–63–66 for 259. The gallery went wild with this display. At the time, it was the lowest tournament score in history. Over the course of the next 44 years, Byron's score of 259 was beaten only once (by Mike Souchak, who shot 257 in the 1955 Texas Open). The 259 is still one of the top scoring records of all time.

In 1946 Nelson continued to play well. He nearly defended his PGA title, but with everyone back from the war, Nelson was defeated in the semifinals by Ed Oliver, as Nelson blew a 2-up with just five holes left. A bogey on the final hole cost him the chance to advance. Still, even after winning 6 tournaments in 1946 (and 25 over the previous three years), he retired for the most part.

His longtime sparring partner Hogan was now dominating golf. Hogan was in the service for Nelson's big wins. And Nelson was retired for Hogan's run of dominance. Hogan and Nelson were the same age, but Nelson retired after 1946, when he was 34 years old. Like Jones, Nelson had accomplished everything he had set out to do in golf.

Byron Nelson was a professional golfer in the days when they had to schlep their own bags and drive their own cars. They didn't own or charter private planes. At the end of a tournament on Sunday, it might take two days of travel to get to the next spot on the tour. Nelson, a hemophiliac, would be in jeopardy of massive bleeding from a simple cut. And he had a nervous stomach and used to lose his breakfast or lunch before he played crucial matches.

Though Nelson retired in his mid-30s, he won 52 sanctioned tournaments. Even at the end of 2005, that ranked ahead of everyone but Snead, Nicklaus, Hogan, and Palmer. Nelson made the cut 113 consecutive times, in an age when the cut line determined if a player received a check. In 60 years this mark has been passed only by Woods.

In 1958 the Masters Tournament dedicated a bridge on the famous course to Byron. The Nelson Bridge crosses Rae's Creek, taking golfers to the No. 13 tee. The Nelson Bridge commemorates Nelson's play on Nos. 12 and 13 at the 1937 Masters, when, on the final day, Lord Byron went 2–3 on the two holes and made up six strokes on Guldahl.

And for those who wonder why I rank Byron Nelson (and his five majors) ahead of players with more majors (Player, Watson, Sarazen, Palmer, Trevino, and Faldo), the reason is this: the other players all competed at the British Open many times, but Nelson didn't. He lost the chance to play—and potentially win—some majors when championships were canceled for World War II. If he had played as many majors as these other golfers, he wouldn't be Lord Nelson—he'd be Major Nelson.

Jim Nantz, golf announcer for CBS Sports: "You have to find a place somewhere in the top 10 for Byron Nelson. You can put the dapper, friendly Mr. Sarazen just outside the top 10. But Byron is a lot closer to Hogan than you would think."

11

GARY PLAYER
The Most Frequent Flyer

On November 1, 2005, Gary Player celebrated his 70th birthday. I have a particular theory about Player. He has spent so much of his life in airplanes that the "time travel" has slowed down the aging process. Perhaps he really is decades younger, the age that he looks and acts.

He's been called the Black Knight because one of his superstitions is to always wear black. He's known as Mr. Fitness as well. He responds to Laddie and is known worldwide as the International Ambassador of Golf. Maybe he really is something like "Austin Powers—the International Man of Mystery," who can travel back and forward through the years.

Gary was born in Johannesburg, South Africa. When he was 14 he started playing under the tutelage of Jock Verwey of Johannesburg. (Verwey was later to become his father-in-law.) Player turned pro at 17 and worked for Jock until he was 21. In April of 1958 he won the Kentucky Derby Open at Louisville; he was the youngest competitor to win a pro tournament in the United States in more than two decades. He was the runner-up in the 1958 U.S. Open.

He couldn't have accomplished much without his wife, Vivienne. Viv had a 2-handicap when she and Gary got married. Not only was she supportive but she also was able to point out flaws in his game.

He won the 1959 British Open at the age of 23, becoming the youngest player to win that event since 1868. His record lasted for 20 years, until Seve Ballesteros won the British Open at an even younger age (22).

Did the champion 23-year-old Player have staying power? Well, just two months shy of his 63rd birthday, he became the second-oldest winner in the history of the Champions Tour with his victory at the Northville Long Island Classic in 1998. Earlier in 1998, in gusty winds at Augusta, he became the oldest golfer ever to make the Masters cut, breaking the record set by Sam Snead 25 years earlier. And at 69 years old in 2005, he was able to shoot better than his age with a score of 68.

And how did Player, a little man no more than 5′6″, have the strength and endurance to maintain his jet-setting schedule over 50 years? He was the first golfer to work out and train like a madman. He followed a strict diet and exercised to minimize the effects of jet lag and to perform so well for so long. In 1965 he hired a former Mr. America, Roy Hilligan, to train him. While other golfers were puffing cigarettes, Player was doing a zillion squats. The South African Player needed great strength: at one point in his career, he traveled with his six children and more than 30 pieces of luggage that sometimes took as many as three taxis to transport.

He's traveled more miles than any athlete in history—he's so proud of that fact that he trademarked it. With over 13 million air miles, he is The World's Most-Traveled Athlete. Joe DiMaggio wanted to be known as "the greatest living ballplayer." Gary wants to be known as most-traveled athlete. Of course, Gary insists that he has traveled more miles than anyone else in history—athlete or otherwise. He may be right.

Let's examine this. Athletes, politicians, and other human beings just didn't travel from one end of the world to the other prior to the 1950s. Airlines didn't offer jet service until the 1950s. Player started traveling when it became possible. In the 1960s his trips from Johannesburg to New York were 45-hour, propeller-driven ordeals on which Player and his wife, Vivienne, brought their six children. Adding all the flights he has taken as a course architect to the more than 200 projects he has around the world, Player says, "I've traveled more than any human being who's ever lived."

In his prime he flew at least twice each year to the United States, twice to Britain, once to Australia, and once to wherever the World Cup was being played. Plus he also made numerous side trips and took an occasional trip to the Far East. Look at his 163 tournament victories around the globe. He won the South African Open 13 times. He won the Australian Open seven times. Player didn't travel 13 million miles over five decades to lose.

Player won the Masters in 1961 when Arnold Palmer, needing only a par on 18 to win, hit his approach into a bunker and took a double bogey. Player started the fourth day six strokes in front of Palmer and started the final day birdie-birdie. Putting the pressure on Gary, Palmer played the front nine in 33. Player finished his tournament with an 8-under 280 and watched on television as Palmer blew up on the last hole, after a round of magnificent golf.

In 1962 Player added his third major. He became the second foreign-born golfer to win the PGA Championship, beating Bob Goalby by one stroke. Goalby birdied 14 and 16 on the final round, but Player parred the final two holes to maintain victory. Player was so mentally drained that he shifted in the final holes to a 3-wood instead of his driver for his tee shots, to gain the extra accuracy he felt the club would give him. Player's victory was decided on the final putt on 18, and he stayed bent over the cup as he reached in for his ball.

Player became the first foreign-born player in 40 years to win the U.S. Open since the Scot Willie Macfarlane had won in 1925. Player won in 1965, defeating Kel Nagle by three strokes in the 18-hole play-off. The victory meant the world to Player, who became just the third player following Gene Sarazen and Ben Hogan to win a career Grand Slam. Only Jack Nicklaus and Tiger Woods have since accomplished the feat.

After giving his caddie $2,000, Player (figuring that he had made most of his money and earned most of his fame in the United States) decided to turn the rest of his $25,000 check over to USGA charities. He requested that $5,000 go to the Cancer Fund, in honor of his mother (who died when he was eight), and that the rest be funneled into junior golf programs.

He fell into a "minor" major slump following his victory in the 1965 U.S. Open. He wouldn't win another major until the 1968 British Open. It was there that a spectacular eagle on the 14th hole on the final round at Carnoustie gave Player a two-shot lead. He hit a 3-wood four feet from the cup. He still had to make great recovery shots on 15 and 16.

At the 1969 PGA Championship in Dayton, he was heckled about South Africa's racial policy. He was shoved by demonstrators and picketed. The NAACP planned protests for future appearances by Player. "This is a heckuva way to have to play," he commented. Fans yelled in his backswing, and death threats were made. He had FBI protection for several months. Early in 1971 he played with an entourage of police officers in the gallery of every tournament. At the 1971 U.S. Open he received a direct threat against his life. He couldn't understand why he should be held responsible for something (apartheid) that wasn't his doing.

In 1972 it was a miracle 9-iron shot that gave Player his second PGA. Gary bogeyed the 14th and 15th holes and pushed his tee shot far to the right on the 16th. Unable to see the flag, Player lofted the ball over a tree and pond to within four feet of the hole. Player birdied the hole and went on to score a two-stroke victory.

Still in the prime of his career, he had injury problems. He had an operation to remove a cyst from his leg. Then he had bladder surgery. He spent 12 days in the hospital and didn't hit a golf ball in 40 days. But nothing could keep this most optimistic of men down. Not being protested. Not having serious and painful operations. Not being away from his home for long stretches.

Because he was still recovering from the two operations, he didn't play in the 1973 Masters. But in 1974, nearing his 39th birthday, he won another Masters. He charged into second place, one stroke behind leader Dave Stockton, after the third round. After nine holes he took the lead and never relinquished it.

This win tied him with Harry Vardon for the most majors by a foreign-born player. He didn't have much time to savor the victory. After he put on the green jacket for winning the Masters, he left immediately for Spain to play in the Spanish Open. Following that he had commitments to play in Japan and South Africa before returning to the United States four weeks after the Masters.

At the age of 43, at the 1978 Masters, Player teed off seven strokes behind Hubert Green. It was no problem for the man in black. Gary birdied the 9th, 10th, 12th, and 13th holes. On the 15th he faced a crucial second shot, a 520-yard par-5 with a pond in front of the green. He pulled out a 3-wood and told himself, "Laddie, you need another birdie. You've got to go for it."

The shot cleared the water and wound up on the front-right edge of the green, about 65 feet short of the cup. He got down in two putts for the birdie. He picked up another birdie on 16 and holed out from 18 feet for the final birdie on 18, giving him a 64 and a total of 277, which won him his third Masters.

Player is regarded as one of the best bunker players in the world. He proved that his reputation was well deserved in the 1990 British Open. Player was in nine bunkers in all. Eight times he got up and down in two strokes. The ninth time he holed out.

Player won nine majors in an era competing against Nicklaus, who most experts believe was the greatest player of all time. Nicklaus and Player finished first and second in eight PGA Tour events. Twice they finished first and second in a major championship. In the 1965 Masters, Player finished nine strokes back of Nicklaus's 17-under par 271. In the 1968 British Open, it was Player who won the major, with Nicklaus finishing two strokes back.

What makes the Black Knight so fascinating to me is his apparent contradictions. In 2005 he was quoted as saying, "Gary Player would change both the ball and the club for professionals." Without the power that often brings 400-yard drives, he believes today's superstars could struggle. "I just hate to see what's happening today with golf clubs that I consider to be illegal," Player remarks. "I'd stop the grooves being so deep [on the ball], and I'd stop the trampoline effect in the wood." Player defended the golfers of his generation, who didn't have the benefit of modern technology that allows players to drive the ball 400 yards. But in 1965, when Player won the U.S. Open in St. Louis, it was with fiberglass or graphite shafts in all the clubs; he became the first man ever to win on Tour using those types of shafts.

It's interesting that the man who was picketed by the NAACP would win the 1974 British Open with a black caddie, Rabbit Dyer. Player told Rabbit to wear his badge at all times. Rabbit responded, "Don't worry, Laddie. I stick out like a fly in buttermilk. I don't need no badge." It was the first time a golfer with a black caddie won the Open Championship.

And it's interesting that one of the world's foremost travelers would be content to spend so much time now at home on his huge farm in South Africa.

Gary Koch, NBC golf analyst and PGA Tour member: "You have to give Gary Player his due, because whether you think he is genuine or whether you think it's all schtick, nothing was handed to him. It was very trying, all the travel. And yet, he looks great. I was with him at the 2005 Presidents Cup, and he looks closer to 55 than 70. He really believes in his positive approach. Nicklaus and Palmer were very gracious to him when he went through his troubled times."

Who's Better, Who's Best
Gary Player or Arnold Palmer?

Player won more majors, lasted even longer than Palmer, and traveled a path that was logistically much harder. Arnold Palmer won seven majors, plus the U.S. Amateur Championship. He also finished runner-up in 10 majors, losing play-offs at the U.S. Open to Jack Nicklaus in 1962, to Julius Boros in 1963, and to Billy Casper in 1966. Player won nine majors and finished second in six others, including the 1962 Masters, where he lost to Palmer in an 18-hole play-off.

Gary Player won the career slam, which Palmer never did. Player won 163 professional worldwide tournaments. Player won the British Open in three different decades, whereas Palmer won all seven of his majors between 1958 and 1964.

The experts that I talked to were cautious in labeling Player over Palmer. They asked me, "Do you mean, who did more for golf?"

In golf ability, Player was the better golfer.

A Better Analogy

Gary Player and Secretariat At the 2005 Presidents Cup, Player coached the International Team against Nicklaus's United States Team. The night before the finals, the International Team, knowing how much Player loves racehorses, gave him a painting of Secretariat, who Gary considers one of the five greatest athletes in the last 50 years. President Clinton told Player that he had the same opinion of Secretariat, telling Player that when he was in the White House, he voted for Secretariat as one of the five best athletes when they asked him to vote.

There was no better competitor in his sport than Player, and none better in racing than Secretariat. We'll never again see what Secretariat accomplished, finishing 31 lengths in front of the field at the 1973 Belmont Stakes. We'll never again see a golfer with Player's travel stamina. Tiger Woods, at 30 years old, would have to play nonstop for the next 40 years to equal it. Player and the great racehorse shared a stamina that few creatures could hope to match.

12

ARNOLD PALMER
Mr. Modern Era

The sports that are popular today are in large part popular because of television. In the late 1950s two sports saw their popularity surge because of airtime. In 1957 the Baltimore Colts and New York Giants played an epic battle for the NFL Championship. The NFL's popularity skyrocketed. In golf Arnold Palmer was his sport's answer to football's Johnny Unitas. One of the greatest competitors who ever lived, Palmer was a magnetic personality who brought fans to the television set.

Palmer took chances. He went for birdies and eagles. He went for miracle shots. Sometimes his play gave him dramatic, come-from-behind victories. His dynamic style made him a superstar. Did Palmer popularize televised golf? Or did the advent of television make Palmer the first millionaire golfer?

Arnold Palmer, from Latrobe, Pennsylvania, was easy to root for. Growing up he wasn't one of the country club elite. In 1921 his father worked at the Latrobe Country Club as golf pro, construction worker, and greenskeeper. When the Depression came Milfred (Deacon) Palmer was allowed to work as the head golf pro as well. Although his dad was the club pro, the Palmer family didn't actually belong to the club, and Arnie (born in 1929) was permitted to play only on Mondays, when the club was closed.

His father gave him a set of sawed-off clubs to play with when he was three years old. At seven Arnie shot a 55 for nine holes. One of his biggest thrills was shooting a 71 in his first high school match at age 14.

Palmer enrolled at Wake Forest University in 1947 and was roommates with Bubby Worsham (whose brother Lew was the 1947 U.S. Open champ). One night, Worsham asked Palmer to ride with him to a dance. Palmer declined, and an hour later Worsham was killed in a car accident. The accident was too much for Palmer to take. He quit school and joined the Coast Guard for three years. Arnie eventually reenrolled at Wake and won the U.S. Amateur title in 1954. The following year, at the age of 25, he turned professional. Palmer's arrival on the Tour coincided with the decline of Ben Hogan and Sam Snead. In essence he had the field to himself since Jack Nicklaus was 11 years younger and didn't show up on the scene until 1960. Add to that that Arnie was fan friendly and handsome (as compared with the grumpy and sour Hogan and the hillbilly Snead)—fans easily embraced him. He really had the stage to himself. For example, when Palmer won the Masters in 1958, the leaderboard below Arnie included the likes of Doug Ford, Fred Hawkins, Stan Leonard, and Ken Venturi.

Palmer had his greatest success early in his career and in the right places. The Masters was first broadcast on television in 1956, but covering only the last three holes. The sport found an audience with the passing of each year. Palmer, of course, first played Augusta in the mid-1950s. He finished seventh in 1957 and won the Masters for the first time in 1958. A star was born. He loved playing before a large gallery, and the galleries became filled with his fans, dubbed Arnie's Army.

Beginning in 1958 Palmer won four Masters in the next seven years, finishing second, third, and ninth in the years he didn't win. No one had ever won the Masters four times (only Nicklaus and Woods have done it since). Palmer's year in 1960 was as good as he ever had, and only a handful of players ever approached his achievements before or since. He played in 27 tournaments and won 8 of them. He finished in the top 10 in 20 of 27 tournaments. Yes, he was lucky that Snead and Hogan were way past their prime and that Nicklaus wasn't even in the radar yet. But, man, he dominated.

Palmer's Record in the 1960 Majors
Masters: 1st
U.S. Open: 1st
British Open: 2nd
PGA Championship: 7th

At the Masters he won his second green jacket in three years. Needing a birdie on one of the last three holes to tie Venturi, Palmer found himself 50 feet short of the hole on the par-three 16th. He attempted a bold putt that hit the pin so hard the ball almost bent the flagstick. He saved par on that hole. On the 17th he canned a 30-foot putt for his tying birdie. And on the 18th hole he won the tournament outright with another birdie.

At the U.S. Open, at Cherry Hills Country Club in Englewood, Colorado, Arnie started the final round in 15th place, seven strokes back of the leader, Mike Souchak. Arnie vaulted over 14 rivals in the last 18 holes. He shot a 65 to win his second consecutive major. In second place was young 20-year-old Nicklaus, whose 282 score was the lowest ever by an amateur in the U.S. Open.

At Cherry Hills it seemed that everyone in Colorado was in Arnie's Army. He relished it and played to the crowd. They wanted to see miracles, and sometimes he delivered.

His gallery gave him a psychological and physical lift, like home crowds give basketball, baseball, and football teams.

Palmer was halfway to the Grand Slam. He arrived at St. Andrews and pumped up interest in the British Open. Of course, Palmer was a fan favorite at St. Andrews in Scotland. The Palmers were Scots. Arnie's great-grandfather had immigrated to Pennsylvania from Scotland.

A driving rainstorm postponed the last day of the tournament. Arnie was one hole back of Kel Nagle. Arnie went birdie-birdie the next day to finish his round, but Nagle made a birdie-3 at 17 and beat Palmer by a stroke.

That one-stroke difference deflated Palmer as he headed to Akron, the site of the 1960 PGA Championship. He opened with a 67 there, for a share of the lead. But he finished in a tie for seventh, his downfall coming on the 16th hole of the third round. Palmer took a 7 after a series of mishaps in the sand.

At this point in his career, he was one of the best drivers in the game. He stood 5'11" and weighed around 175 pounds. But he was solid muscle and could outdrive the bigger opponents. He had a go-for-it-all personality and was a charger. He had great final rounds. His confident, gambling style, while great for galleries and television viewers, led Palmer to some of the most disappointing losses in golf history.

Palmer won back-to-back British Open Championships in 1961 and 1962. He won the Masters for a third time in 1962 and a record fourth time in 1964. The 1964 Masters was his final major. He was 35 years old.

I suppose this is where the folks who tell me I'm crazy for putting Tiger Woods (at age 30) ahead of Nicklaus begin nodding. There was no one around in the summer of 1964 who didn't think Palmer was going to win more majors, especially coming off a Masters victory by six strokes.

The most distressing defeat came earlier, however, in the 1962 U.S. Open at Oakmont, a home game for Palmer. Twenty-two-year-old Ohio State student Nicklaus caught Palmer in the final round and went on to upset him in the 18-hole play-off by three strokes. Palmer, who had already won the '62 Masters, was hoping for another run at the Grand Slam.

Another tough defeat came in the 1961 Masters, when he took a double-bogey-6 to lose to Gary Player by a stroke. Palmer almost blew the '62 Masters when he shot an uncharacteristic 75 on the final round, which dropped him into a three-way tie. But he defeated Player and Dow Finsterwald in the 18-hole play-off the next day.

They say Snead had it tough at the U.S. Opens. He did, but even Snead never lost three 18-hole play-offs in three different U.S. Opens. Palmer did, losing in 1962 to Nicklaus at Oakmont; in 1963 to Julius Boros in Brookline; and in 1966, the king of chokes, to Billy Casper in San Francisco.

In the 1966 U.S. Open, Palmer was leading by seven strokes with nine holes to play. He still had a six-stroke lead with six holes to play. Casper, in second place, shot a 32 on the final nine. Palmer, meanwhile, bogeyed five of the last nine holes. Arnie had made the turn in 32 strokes. He shot 39 on the back nine. In the 18-hole play-off the next day, Palmer blew another lead, and Casper had the U.S. Open Championship.

Did that loss take the wind out of Palmer's sails? At the 1967 U.S. Open, Palmer finished in second place to Nicklaus. That loss is considered the baton-passing event. From that point no one put Palmer and Nicklaus in the same sentence.

Arnold Palmer never won the Masters Tournament after 1964. He didn't even have a top-10 finish at Augusta after 1967 (when he was 38 years old). Palmer never won a U.S. Open after 1960. He never won the British Open after 1962. And he never won the PGA Championship. At the PGA Championship he played 121 rounds of golf in his career. He had only 18 rounds under par. He shot only 13 rounds in the 60s.

In 1964 he put together four of his best PGA rounds: 68, 68, 69, and 69. His 274 was good enough to win most years but not this one. Palmer finished in second place, three strokes back of Bobby Nichols. In 1968 Palmer finished tied for second, one stroke back of Julius Boros. And in 1970 he finished tied for second, two strokes back of Dave Stockton.

Now I know Palmer ushered in the television era. I know what Arnie's Army meant, as he brought casual fans to golf. He also moved a lot of merchandise. Mark McCormack, who knew Palmer from college golf tournaments, started a sports-management company in 1960 called IMG. McCormack got the company off the ground with a handshake deal with Palmer. IMG worked for Palmer, creating a slew of outside business interests for him. IMG soon signed Nicklaus and Player as well. Palmer's reputation as a trusted pitch man soared even as his golf game declined.

But enough adulation is enough. In 1970 the Associated Press named him Athlete of the Decade for the 1960s. Were the voters on drugs or something? Forget the fact that Bill Russell led his Boston Celtics to nine NBA championships in the decade. Forget the fact that baseball's Willie Mays performed brilliantly, as did Hank Aaron. And Jim Brown was the best running back ever. If Russell, Mays, Aaron, and Brown were the wrong color or temperament for the voters, they could have at least selected the best golfer in the 1960s—Nicklaus.

Palmer was not as good as people remember him to be. He was a heckuva great guy and an exciting athlete to watch. His close losses in the biggest events—sometimes to Nicklaus—reminded me of Wilt Chamberlain's play-off losses to Russell.

But Chamberlain's teams were inferior to Russell's teams. And Chamberlain was destroyed in the press. Palmer became an even greater hero, win or lose. Go figure.

Palmer, for all that he meant to the game, gets the nod with his seven majors over Tom Watson, who had eight majors. I'll give Palmer the credit he tells everyone about, with his National Amateur title in 1954 and his longevity, winning at least one PGA Tournament for 17 consecutive years (a feat only Nicklaus has matched). Palmer was much more than Tom Watson, who you will read about shortly. Palmer was as big as President John F. Kennedy and Yankees slugger Mickey Mantle in the early '60s. The big difference was that Palmer lasted and lasted. People don't want to let go of their heroes. With Arnold Palmer, they never had to. He's overrated as a top-five player, but if the discussion is expanded to the top 12 players, or the most influential or most beloved players, there's always room for Arnold.

13

TOM WATSON
Mr. One-Putt

Tom Watson was born on September 4, 1949, in Kansas City, Missouri. His father, a successful investment counselor, was a scratch golfer. Tom took up the game at the age of six and competed against his older brother and father. In time not only would he defeat them, but he would pass everyone else in his era, usually with his putter. There may be players who putted as well as Watson (Billy Casper, Bobby Locke, Jack Nicklaus), but no one could have made as many pressure putts as Mr. One-Putt.

It wasn't just golf that interested Tom. In high school he was the quarterback on the football team, and he played basketball as well. But his best sport was golf. He won the Missouri State Amateur Championship four times. After he got a degree from Stanford University, he gave the pro tour a try. I mean, what else are you going to do with a degree in psychology?

In his early days on the Tour, he began to develop a reputation as someone who jumped out in front of tournaments but couldn't seal the deal. He joined the pro tour in 1971 and didn't win a tournament in his first three years.

At the U.S. Open in Mamaroneck, New York, Watson led the tournament after the third round. He not only was poised to win his first tournament but was ready to break through in a major. In the final 18 holes of that '74 Open, he shot a 79, his worst round of the year. He didn't make a putt longer than three feet after the first hole. He didn't record a birdie, and he fell to fifth place.

After his game fell apart that day, Byron Nelson took Watson aside and gave him some advice. He told him that he liked Watson's golf swing but that he didn't use his legs as well as he should. Nelson also advised Watson to move his hands ahead on his irons so he would have better control of them. And most important, Nelson mentored Watson.

Two weeks later Watson won his first professional tournament, the Western Open. He won his last tournament on the Tour in the 1998 MasterCard Colonial. The stretch between his first and last victories—23 years, 11 months, and 24 days—was the third longest in PGA Tour history, giving Watson the longevity that only a handful of others, including Sam Snead and Nicklaus, had. Only a handful of golfers had the peak performance that Watson had from 1977 to 1982.

The second tournament that Watson won was, appropriately enough, the 1975 Byron Nelson Classic in Dallas. Watson shot a final-round 65, getting birdies on four of the last nine holes. He turned over a portion of the winnings to the charity that sponsored the tournament, in honor of Mr. Nelson.

If there was a theme that screamed out to me in everything I read about Watson over his quarter-century career, it was that he was a mensch (a Yiddish word that means one who does good deeds). He had great reverence for the game and for those who came before him. When he defeated an aging Arnold Palmer early in his career, he would say that without Palmer, none of his success (or the success of anyone else on the Tour) would be possible. When he battled Nicklaus in the great duels, there was a spirit of class and sportsmanship. At the British Open in 1975, when he faced the pressure of winning his first major, Watson lost his temper at a cameraman who got in his way when he was driving. Four hours later, when he was presented with the trophy, Watson said, "I would like to apologize to the movie cameraman I encountered at the third tee. I was just momentarily upset."

Those are the small gestures. He made some larger ones as well. In 1990 he resigned his membership from the Kansas City Country Club because Henry Bloch (a Jewish businessman and cofounder of H&R Block) was not admitted as a member. Watson, whose resignation was front-page news, had a personal interest. His ex-wife and his kids were Jewish. "It's something that I personally can't live with because my family is Jewish. It's not something that's very appealing to me: the possibility that my family isn't welcome—because of their religion." Within a few years the country club began to admit minority members, and Watson was back in the club.

When Watson's game went into decline, he did the right thing for longtime caddie Bruce Edwards and encouraged him to work with someone else. And then in 2003 Watson had a bittersweet year, enjoying his finest year on the Champions Tour while at the same time teaming with Edwards in his battle against Lou Gehrig's disease. Watson donated his $1 million annuity for winning the Schwab Cup to ALS research and patient care. Throughout the course of the season, he helped raise nearly $3 million for ALS-related causes. It wasn't a gesture. The man genuinely cared about Edwards and fighting the ravaging disease.

None of these actions, taken individually or together, make Watson a hero. They do, however, make him a class act. You don't have to always agree with Watson's politics to admire his principles. In 1994 CBS announcer Gary McCord angered Watson by using terms such as "bikini wax" and "body bags" while on the air. Watson felt the choice of words was inappropriate for a golf tournament and wrote a letter to McCord's boss, which got him removed from future Masters assignments. This came from Watson, a one-time liberal from Stanford in the late '60s. But it was consistent with Watson's feelings toward the game of golf and how he always did what he believed to be proper.

What he accomplished on the golf courses made him an athletic hero, someone Johnny Miller described as "without question, one of the five greatest players who ever lived." Watson is most known for his winning eight majors. He had a great shot at more, especially early in his career. He led late in the 1974 and 1975 U.S. Opens and at the 1975 Masters. He didn't win a major until the 1975 British Open, when he won at Carnoustie. In that tournament he holed in a 30-foot chip shot for an eagle on the 14th hole. Tied in the 18-hole play-off with Jack Newton, Watson made par on 18. Newton just missed a 12-foot putt, and Watson had his long-awaited first major.

He didn't win another tournament until 1977, when he won five times including the Masters and the British Open. At the Masters, Watson was the coleader with Ben Crenshaw entering the final round, three strokes ahead of Nicklaus. Although Nicklaus put the pressure on with a final-round 65, Watson shot 67 to win his first green jacket. More important, he proved that he could withstand a charge by the greatest player in the greatest tournament. No longer would Watson have to answer questions about fading down the stretch of tournaments.

After Nicklaus and Watson had their duel at Augusta, they waged an even better battle at Turnberry at the British Open. In the third round they matched 65s to separate themselves from the field. Their epic battle in the fourth round was one of the greatest and most dramatic finishes in golf history.

Watson came from three strokes down to defeat Nicklaus by one shot. Watson shot 65 to Nicklaus's 66. Watson tied the match on the 15th hole with a 60-foot putt. Watson went ahead on 17, where he made birdie. Nicklaus rolled in a 32-foot putt for birdie on 18, but Watson only needed to make his 2-foot putt for the tournament-winning birdie.

If Watson never won anything else after that 1977 British Open, it would be enough to merit his inclusion in this book. But of course, he would go on to do so much more. He won the British Open again in 1980, 1982, and 1983. In that 1983 tournament Watson separated himself from a crowded leaderboard with a magnificent iron shot on 18, which got him close to the hole. Hale Irwin and Andy Bean finished one stroke back. After the tournament Watson received a telegram from Australian great Peter Thomson, welcoming Watson to the "five-times" club. But Thomson won his five British Opens at a time when the best American players didn't attend (at least not every year). It wasn't until Palmer went and conquered the British Open in 1960 that it became a very big deal.

Watson won four of his five British Opens in Scotland, where he became known as "Toom" Watson.

Watson added a second Masters victory in 1981, when he was acknowledged as the best player in the game. He dominated the era. He won 29 times in a six-year period, beginning in 1977. In that same span of time, Nicklaus won 10 times. No one else won more than eight. Watson won at least three titles a year from 1977 to 1982.

In 1982 Watson finally won the U.S. Open. In one of the most dramatic finishes in golf history, Watson beat Nicklaus once again in a major, this time at Pebble Beach. They were tied as they approached the 17th hole in the final round. Watson's 2-iron failed as he hooked the ball into thick grass on a severe downslope. He was doomed for a bogey. Then came the signature shot in Watson's career, a real miracle. Standing ankle-deep in the rough, with heavy winds to deal with, Watson hit a very high chip shot that was certain to roll 7 to 10 feet past the cup. Yet the ball broke right, straight into the cup. The crowd roared, and Watson went on to birdie the 18th and take his long-awaited U.S. Open crown. It was his eighth and final major. Only Nicklaus, Walter Hagen, Tiger Woods, Gary Player, and Ben Hogan have more professional majors.

Watson never did win the career slam, never getting a PGA Championship in 23 appearances. But he was voted the best golfer of the 1980s, and that is saying a lot. Harry Vardon dominated the 1910s. Bobby Jones was the master of the 1920s. Nelson, Hogan, and Snead dominated the 1940s and '50s. Palmer was the man in the 1960s, and Nicklaus the king of the 1970s. You better believe that Watson being the best player in the '80s means something.

And on top of all of that, he's a mensch, too.

Who's Better, Who's Best
Tom Watson or Arnold Palmer?

In a six-year stretch beginning in 1977, Watson won 29 tournaments and six majors. In a six-year stretch beginning in 1960, Palmer won 32 tournaments and six majors. Call that a draw.

Although Watson won eight professional major championships to Palmer's seven, Palmer won 62 times on the PGA Tour, compared to Watson's 39 wins. That's enough to push Palmer ahead of Watson in this book.

A Better Analogy

Tom Watson and George Brett There was no bigger or better-known Kansas City Royals fan than Kansas City native Tom Watson. The best player in Royals' history, George

Brett, played for the team for 21 seasons, from 1973 to 1993. Those were roughly the same years that Watson had his Hall of Fame golf career.

The Royals finished in first or second place each season from 1976 to 1985. Those were the only seasons that Kansas City made the postseason. Watson had a long career but won his eight majors from 1975 to 1983.

Brett had his best and most dramatic moments at Yankee Stadium, defeating the Yankees. Watson had his against Nicklaus, in the finals of the most prestigious tournaments in the world. In a long line of those who were going to be the "next Nicklaus," Watson accomplished Nicklaus-like feats for a decade, but it wasn't close to what Jack did for the length of his career.

14

BILLY CASPER
The Most Underrated Golfer Ever

Billy Casper was born on June 24, 1931, in San Diego, California. He played in an era with not only three of the greatest golfers of all time (Arnold Palmer, Jack Nicklaus, and Gary Player) but some of the most dynamic personalities of all time. He never could compete with their legendary status and marketing abilities, which makes him the most underrated golfer ever. He wasn't exactly a matinee idol. But he could handle the stick.

Recently, I asked Billy's son Bobby, a golf pro and analyst, how his dad was doing. When told he was doing great three years after hip-replacement surgery, I thought it was terrific. After all, Billy Casper wasn't hip even in his younger days. In his early days he was described as heavy or rotund or portly. He played at around 240 pounds. Then, after developing allergies, he saw a doctor who put him on a strange diet of buffalo meat. He joined the Mormon Church and spent the nights before rounds in fireside sessions of church members. While his faith gave him inner strength, he certainly lacked the charisma or connection with the galleries that opponents like Palmer and Player had.

It's not a put-down. He just wasn't hip. In 1971 he was a member of the U.S. Ryder Cup team but couldn't play in the singles competition. Why? Casper was nursing a broken toe incurred while groping in the dark to find his hotel bathroom.

He came out of the caddie shacks of San Diego and attended Notre Dame. He joined the pro tour in 1955. He nearly took the PGA Championship as early as 1958, finishing second by two strokes to Dow Finsterwald in Colorado Springs.

Casper won his first U.S. Open while eating a sandwich. Well, it's true. He went into the final round at Mamaroneck, New York, with a three-stroke lead, but Bob Rosburg and Mike Souchak were making a late charge. Casper holed a 12-foot birdie putt on 14, which would prove vital as he bogeyed 15 and 17. It was his short game that put him over the top. He one-putted 31 of the 72 holes with an experimental mallet-headed putter he'd never used before. When he finished his round, he went into the clubhouse for a sandwich, watching as Rosburg and Souchak had birdie chances on 18 to tie him. Neither one could catch Casper, and he became the 1959 U.S. Open champion.

Casper, for a big man, wasn't the long hitter one would expect.

Bobby Casper, radio golf analyst for Sirius and Westwood One (and Billy's son): "On a par-5, when he had opportunities to go for a green, he'd lay up to a yardage he could handle. He managed his game well—connected all the dots—and had a phenomenal short game. Once he got close in a tournament, he knew what had to be done."

Sometimes that strategy paid off—and sometimes it didn't. He was criticized for playing too conservatively, especially at the Masters, where he refused to go for the green on his second shot on the par-5s. He always played well at the Masters, but he rarely took the big chances that were necessary to win. He finished fourth at Augusta in 1960, seventh in 1961, fifth in 1964, and second in 1969.

At the 1969 Masters he was one stroke back of George Archer with one hole left to play. Casper's approach shot was about 35 feet from the pin. He didn't get his birdie and ended up finishing second.

He finally won the Masters in 1970, defeating his longtime friend from San Diego, Gene Littler.

Bobby Casper: "I don't remember the '66 Open, but I remember watching the '70 Masters on TV. I was 10 years old and expecting him home the next day—but then, he got into that play-off. I couldn't even watch it the next day because it wasn't on television."

What the young Casper missed was this: Billy one-putted six of the first seven holes to take a five-stroke lead. And he won by five strokes. Casper was Mr. Consistency. He will long be remembered as a great putter, one of the best ever. (Casper would say many times that Bobby Locke was the greatest putter, and the feeling was apparently mutual.) Casper won 60 professional tournament championships, 51 of them on the PGA Tour.

There aren't many who have topped those 51 Tour victories. You can count them on one hand (at least until Tiger Woods gets his 52nd). Only Sam Snead, Jack Nicklaus, Ben Hogan, Arnold Palmer, and Byron Nelson have more. And Nelson had but one more tournament victory than Casper.

This is how consistent Mr. Casper was. He won a tournament in 16 consecutive years, from 1956 to 1971. Only two players (Nicklaus and Palmer) have won a tournament in 17 consecutive years.

In the late 1960s, the era of the "Big 3" (Palmer, Nicklaus, and Player), Casper won almost as many tournaments as the Big 3 combined. That was when Palmer began his decline, Nicklaus was in a three-year slump, and Player didn't play all that much in the United States. But you get the point. This Casper was quite a player.

He was PGA Player of the Year in 1966 and 1970. He won the Vardon Trophy five times for having the lowest scoring average on the PGA Tour. And he did this despite the allergies.

In 1964 Casper visited Dr. Theron Randolph in Chicago about his weight. He was told that he was allergic to certain foods—well, it seemed he was allergic to everything. He was put on that diet of buffalo meat (which earned him a nickname of Buffalo Bill). By 1965 Casper had dropped a ton of weight. On January 1, 1966, he and his family formally joined the Mormon Church.

Bobby Casper: "He got to a point where he had a lot of allergies to the chemicals on the golf courses. He went to a doctor in Chicago. Dad always had a lot of protein in his diet. The doctor told him if he would rotate the protein—and have chicken only once a week—that it would get rid of a lot of the toxicity. He was told he could eat a lot of fish, buffalo meat, venison, elk. Sure, I had it, too. It helped his diet. He lost a lot of weight and got down to about 185. I'm sure it helped his golf game."

Apparently, Casper became more patient as a person, more mild mannered. He began spending his nights on tour at "fireside chat" gatherings of Mormon friends. He did so on the night before the finals of the 1966 U.S. Open in San Francisco, showing friends pictures of his recent trip to South Vietnam.

The next day, Casper shot a 32 on the back nine. Although he was seven strokes down with nine to play against Palmer, Casper putted his way into an 18-hole play-off the next day. Despite trailing him after nine holes, he defeated Palmer by four strokes in the play-off. Palmer never really recovered his mastery in the majors. Even Arnie's Army began pulling for Casper during the comeback. In this U.S. Open, Casper was a putting machine, needing just 117 putts on the 90 holes.

The next month, he was scheduled to play in the PGA Championship, which that year was held in Akron, Ohio. He gave the PGA Tournament director a list of things needed for him to play. The list included an air-conditioned house due south of town, an electric cooking range, and an arrangement of buffalo meat. You see, he was allergic to the industrial fumes of the city as well as to chemical reactions of gas cooking, and he couldn't eat food that had been exposed to fertilizer and noxious gases. He had boycotted tournaments in Akron since 1962, but not for political reasons. He boycotted for atmospheric conditions. But because he was the U.S. Open champ and the number one player in the world, PGA officials found everything to make life easier for him. Casper played and finished third.

Besides the majors and the many other tournament wins, Casper had a splendid record in Ryder Cup competition. Here are his stats for the Ryder Cup:

8 years (1961, 1963, 1965, 1967, 1969, 1971, 1973, 1975)
37 matches

20–10–7 record
6–2–2 in singles
23.5 points won

No U.S. player has represented his country in Ryder Cup competition more often than Casper has. (Lanny Wadkins and Raymond Floyd also have eight times on the team.) No one has played more than Casper's 37 matches. No one has won more than Casper's 23.5 points. Casper's 10 singles matches played are topped only by Palmer's 11 for a U.S. player. And no other U.S. player has topped Casper's foursome matches or four-ball matches.

Casper had more than 50 championships against the very best competition. His career spanned the same time as the careers of Palmer and Nicklaus. That was 25 majors that they divvied up between themselves and didn't leave to anyone else. Casper had his moments against them (Casper defeated Palmer in the 1966 Open), and they had their moments against him (Casper lost to Nicklaus in the 1971 PGA Championship). Casper's low number of majors can be explained this way: he didn't enter the British Open but for a couple of times. The trip must have been too hard for a payoff that was not that big. When Casper won the Masters in 1970, he entered the British Open in hopes of a possible Grand Slam.

He never got the publicity that others received. His personality had something to do with it. It was once written (it must have been the late Jim Murray) that "an empty car pulled up beside the clubhouse, and Billy Casper got out." Even Casper occasionally complained that despite his pair of U.S. Open victories, he had to eat buffalo meat to get his name in the papers.

Who's Better, Who's Best
Billy Casper or Nick Faldo?

Faldo had a record almost completely opposite of Casper's. Oh, he played on even more Ryder Cup teams than Casper, but he played on the European side. Faldo won twice as many majors (six) as Casper but won far fewer times on the PGA Tour. Faldo had only nine PGA Tour wins and only 27 on the European Tour. He didn't last as long and didn't face as tough a competition, so the edge here goes to Casper. I'm calling Casper the most underrated golfer of all time, and that's accurate. A golfer can't be anonymous if he wins three Masters, like Faldo did. Casper had the ability to win a great deal, almost always stayed in contention, and yet (because of his low-key personality) almost never gets mentioned in the "greatest of all time" arguments.

15

ANNIKA SORENSTAM
The Female Tiger

As I write this on a late November evening in 2005, Annika Sorenstam just completed her victory at the ADT Golf Championship, the LPGA's version of the Tour Championship. This marked her fourth time winning the event. It wrapped up a dream year for Sorenstam on the golf courses. She won 10 tournaments out of 20 that she entered in 2005. She won the LPGA Player of the Year for an eighth time. She was the money leader on the LPGA Tour for the eighth time. She won the Vare Trophy for the lowest scoring average for the sixth time. She completed the "triple crown" by winning the most tournaments for the most money with the best average for the fifth time in her 12-year career. And most of the United States hasn't realized her greatness.

Rick Reilly, *Sports Illustrated* **columnist:** "Annika has the most repeatable swing. She never hurries it. I love watching her play. She has the best tempo, next to Ernie Els. Combine that with the fact that she's super competitive. Every week she wins by 10 strokes and is still totally under the radar. Much of that is her doing, as she hid from public speaking."

She has staked her claim to being the best LPGA player in history. She has dominated her opponents the way Didrikson did in the 1940s and Wright did in the '60s. The next year or two should see Sorenstam approach the long-standing records for victories and major championships. She is the female version of Tiger Woods, playing as much against the history books as against the international field of opponents.

Annika was born on October 9, 1970, in Stockholm, the capital of Sweden. She and her younger sister, Charlotta, grew up loving sports, although Annika didn't play golf until she was 12. When she was younger than that, she wanted to be like Sweden's Björn Borg, the tennis champion who won five Wimbledon titles in a row beginning in 1977.

Sorenstam's parents—Tom, a 7-handicapper, and Gunilla, a 12-handicapper—were avid golfers, and Annika soon surpassed her parents at the game. By the time Annika was 16, she was working with Henri Reis, a regional coach in the highly successful Swedish youth golf program. Though she was ranked as high as 12th among Swedish junior tennis players, she quit that sport around her 16th birthday, when she got seriously into golf.

Sorenstam became a member of the Swedish National Team in 1987 (remaining with the team until 1992) and enjoyed a very successful amateur career. She would go to the United States and accept a scholarship to the University of Arizona in 1990.

"When Liselotte Neumann won the U.S. Women's Open in 1988, it opened the door for a lot of us [from Sweden]. Se Ri Pak did the same thing for the Koreans, and Karrie Webb did it for the Australians," Sorenstam told *USA Today*.

Dottie Pepper, winner of 17 LPGA Tour events and 1992 Rolex Player of the Year: "Annika's closest competition has been Karrie Webb and Se Ri Pak. Webb is in the Hall of Fame, and Se Ri Pak will be when she gets her 10 years in. In the beginning of Annika's career, in the mid- to late '90s, it went back and forth between Karrie and Annika. Annika would be the first to tell you that Karrie pushed her. If you add Webb's and Se Ri Pak's majors together, they equal 10. Annika has nine by herself."

In 1992 Sorenstam was the World Amateur champion, runner-up at the U.S. Women's Amateur Championship, and the second-lowest amateur at the U.S. Women's Open. She won seven collegiate titles during her career at the University of Arizona.

She turned professional in 1993 and only played a handful of events on the LPGA Tour, electing to play 10 tournaments on the European Tour. She finished in second place four times in Europe, placed third on the Order of Merit (the European ranking system), and was voted the European Tour's Rookie of the Year.

In 1994 she was the LPGA Rookie of the Year. The following year she won her first Player of the Year honors, on the basis of her three wins on the LPGA Tour, including the U.S. Women's Open at Broadmoor where she defeated Meg Mallon by one stroke. She was only the second international player to ever win the Player of the Year, following Japan's Ayako Okamoto in 1987.

The worldwide attention came quickly in 1995. Sorenstam became the first European to win both the LPGA's Rolex Player of the Year award and the Vare Trophy for the lowest scoring average. Sorenstam also led the European Tour (the WPGET) Order of Merit on the strength of her two wins, and she won the Australian Masters on the Australian Tour (ALPG Tour).

Sorenstam had another great year in 1996, as she went over $1 million in career earnings. More than $200,000 of that came from her whopping six-stroke victory at the U.S. Women's Open, as she defended her title and won her second major. She shot an eagle and four birdies in her final-round 66 at Pine Needles Lodge & Golf Club in North Carolina. She won her second Vare Trophy for lowest scoring average that year.

She married David Esch in January of 1997 and had her most victories in a season (six). That year she captured her second Player of the Year Award, finishing ahead of Webb, who was partnered with Sorenstam in a golfing pas de deux for LPGA supremacy during this time.

She won another Player of the Year (her third) in 1998 as well as the Vare Trophy (her third). After that, Sorenstam went through a slump. While she won a lot of money, she stopped winning majors after her two U.S. Women's Opens in 1995 and 1996. In fact, she didn't even have a top-10 finish at a major for three years.

Remember the Bobby Jones story? He played competitively from the age of 14 until his retirement at 28. He didn't win anything of consequence in his first seven years (described as his "seven lean years"). He won everything in his final seven years (his "seven fat years").

Sorenstam certainly didn't have many "lean" years. She went from a Hall of Fame career (her 18 LPGA wins were the most of anyone in the 1990s, and she didn't even win her first until 1995) to a historic jump in numbers that was truly Barry Bonds–like (let's call it "her seven muscular years").

Dottie Pepper: "Annika has taken golf to an athletic dimension that hadn't been seen before—at least, not in women's golf. Before Annika, players didn't hit the gym the way they do now—they didn't prepare in the same manner."

She began a grueling exercise program with a zillion sit-ups per day. She has been the hardest working woman on the Tour. She has become steely-eyed in her determination and passion to win. If this reminds anyone of Sorenstam's Orlando neighbor Tiger Woods, well, it should.

Sorenstam's game is marked by her iron play. Anytime she has a mid-iron in her hands, the ball has a chance to go into the hole. Putting was never her strength, and she dedicated herself to improving that part of her game with former men's pro Dave Stockton.

Averaging only 252 yards per drive, she was 26th in driving distance in the late 1990s on the LPGA Tour. In 2005, Sorenstam was 4th (out of 161) in driving distance, averaging 263 yards per drive. What has made her so great is her accuracy as a driver, finishing 12th in driving accuracy in 2005.

Dottie Pepper: "The best of Annika's game is that she has no weaknesses. She has not one glaring weakness. Put it like this: if Tiger Woods drove the ball with the accuracy and distance that Annika does, they would just hand him every trophy without playing it out. Annika's short game has gotten so much better over the years. Both Annika and Tiger are workaholics. Working with Tiger has given Annika more creativity. One of the wedges in her bag even belonged to Tiger. He has made her a better player."

Sorenstam took Hall of Fame ability and pushed it to even greater heights. Here are the numbers for her, as she skyrockets up the rankings.

Year	Victories	Tournaments	Awards
2005	10	20	Player of the Year, Vare Trophy
2004	8	18	Player of the Year
2003	6	17	Player of the Year
2002	11	23	Player of the Year, Vare Trophy
2001	8	26	Player of the Year, Vare Trophy
2000	5	22	

6 "lean" years (1994–99): 18 wins in 122 tournaments (14.8 percent)
6 "muscular" years (2000–05): 48 wins in 126 tournaments (38.1 percent)

In the last four years alone, Sorenstam has won 44.9 percent of her tournaments. She's raised the level of her game at the majors, dominating them as well.

After winning her two early U.S. Women's Opens, Sorenstam missed the cut at that tournament in 1997, by shooting 77 and 73. She then made the cut but finished 41st in 1998. And she missed the cut at the 1999 U.S. Women's Open. She went without a major in 1997, 1998, 1999, and 2000.

Sorenstam at the Major Championships
First 7 years (1994–2000): 2 majors in 25 tournaments (winning 8 percent of those entered)
Last 5 years (2001–2005): 7 majors in 20 tournaments (winning 35 percent of those entered)

She won the Kraft Nabisco Championship in 2001, 2002, and 2005. She won the Women's British Open in 2003. She won the LPGA Championship in 2003, 2004, and 2005. She won these despite going through the personal pain of separation and then divorce from her husband, Esch.

Gone is the talk of early retirement. It has been replaced by talk of catching Kathy Whitworth's LPGA record of 88 tour victories. When 24-year-old Sorenstam began playing on the LPGA Tour in 1994, Whitworth's record of 88 tournament victories would have been a very lofty goal indeed. Whitworth accomplished the victories over two decades. Sorenstam, with 35 in a four-year stretch (2002–05), had 66 at the end of the 2005 season.

Who's Better, Who's Best
Annika Sorenstam or Kathy Whitworth?

I don't think Whitworth deserves to be ranked ahead of Sorenstam. If you make the analogy that Whitworth's career resembled Snead's, then Sorenstam's resembles Tiger Woods's career. It is not premature to rank Woods ahead of Nicklaus or Snead, or to rank Sorenstam ahead of Whitworth.

Dottie Pepper: "Kathy Whitworth had 88 wins! That's one for every key on the piano! It's a huge number. It's a bigger number than anyone had in the history of the sport. Kathy had the longevity. I played on the Tour beginning in 1987, and I played with her a bunch. Even late in her career, she still rarely missed a putt. She played with her old putter that she still uses, with the smallest of sweet spots. She played with clubs that didn't have a lot of forgiveness. She just had so many shots, and was so creative. But Annika is still 22 wins away, and the career span of Whitworth would mean that I would still put her ahead of Sorenstam."

A Better Analogy

Annika Sorenstam and Tiger Woods Tiger has made no secret of his goals as he attempts to catch Nicklaus's record for the most wins in the majors. Sorenstam has nine majors. Among the women only Patty Berg (15), Mickey Wright (13), Louise Suggs (11), and Babe Didrikson Zaharias (10) have more wins than Sorenstam.

Wins at Majors Through 2005
Tiger Woods: 10 first-place finishes in 41 majors
Annika Sorenstam: 9 first-place finishes in 45 majors

Woods is credited with helping Sorenstam become a more creative player around the green. His competition is tougher and, despite that, he has more major championships, although far fewer tournament wins.

Sorenstam is best known, perhaps, for a tournament for which she failed to make the cut. She accepted an invitation in 2003 to compete at the Colonial Championship on the PGA Tour. This was big news. A lot of the PGA Tour members complained—publicly and privately—that she was taking a spot away from a deserving man. Vijay Singh said that he hoped she would miss the cut. He withdrew from the tournament to spend more time with his family.

Sorenstam shot a 71 in the first round. She shot a 74 in the second round and missed the cut by four strokes. She hasn't attempted to play on the PGA Tour since. My opinion is that her missing the cut doesn't constitute a failure. Most PGA golfers don't win in their first PGA event. If she played regularly, she would compete with the men and might win some. But I also think that it would hurt the LPGA.

Once the Major League Baseball owners integrated by signing Jackie Robinson, it was the end of the Negro Leagues. It didn't take very long, and it cost many people their jobs. If Sorenstam, Michele Wie, or any other woman competes regularly on the men's tour, then there would be a greatly reduced interest and viability in the women's tour. I applaud Sorenstam for playing the Colonial and applaud her also for not playing more on the men's tour, which if she had played more would likely have resulted in personal success for her and suicide for the LPGA.

Having dominated the action in the LPGA for more than a decade, Sorenstam is the female Tiger. Since 2002 through 2005 Webb has won just once on the Tour. There isn't anyone approaching Sorenstam in 2006 except the record books.

There are lessons to be learned from history, however, about leaving the stage as an all-time great. There are graceful exits and disgraceful exits. There was the great hero of Sorenstam's youth, fellow-Swede Björn Borg, who retired from tennis at the age of 26, burned out after 11 Grand Slam singles titles. There are athletes who hang on too long, going for statistical goals. (LPGA fans can remember Whitworth, struggling for years to catch Sam Snead's victory total.) There are athletes who leave the games they love on a stretcher. There are athletes who soil their reputations in their quest for athletic supremacy (we can safely put Barry Bonds in this category).

Here's hoping that both Annika and Tiger leave the game with their health and their names intact, with their accomplishments plastered all over the record books. They are part of the elite group of athletes that have made this the real golden age of sports. We can say that we lived in a time when we were able to see Tiger Woods and Annika Sorenstam and Lance Armstrong and Roger Federer and Roger Clemens and Barry Bonds, and Michael Jordan right before that. How lucky are we?

16

GENE SARAZEN
The Sand Wedge Inventor

When Gene Sarazen passed away in 1999 at the age of 97, he was remembered for so many things. He hit, arguably, the most memorable shot in history, his 1935 double eagle in the second Masters Tournament. He was the first to win the four major professional championships. He won seven majors. He was a member of six Ryder Cup teams. At only 5′4″, he was one of the shortest golfing legends. To a later generation of fans, he was the host of a long-running, popular television program, "Shell's Wonderful World of Golf." And he was a charter member of the World Golf Hall of Fame. But his main contribution to the game was inventing the sand wedge in the early 1930s.

Arnold Palmer said that "Gene set some standards for the game of golf—with the sand wedge, for instance. It probably should have been called the Sarazen wedge."

You know the Ralph Waldo Emerson quote "Build a better mousetrap, and the world will beat a path to your door." That was Sarazen, and the sand wedge was his better mousetrap.

One day, while taking flying lessons, he watched the tail of the plane drop as the plane rose and it occurred to him: a golf club might have the same effect on a ball. He called the Wilson Sporting Goods Company, which he endorsed, and had them send him 12 niblicks (an iron-headed golf club with the face slanted at a greater angle than any other iron except a wedge; a 9-iron). He figured that by putting a flange (a protruding rim, edge, or collar used to strengthen an object, hold it in place, or attach it to another object) on the back of a niblick and angling it, he could hit behind the ball and explode it out of the bunker. He then went to the store and bought supplies to spend hours a day, filing away until he got it just right. Soon he was showing off his club and demonstrating how he could get up and down in two strokes from traps. Of course, necessity has also been called the mother of invention. Sarazen had always had a terrible time playing out of sand bunkers.

Eugenio Sarceni was born in Rye, New York, in 1902. He was the son of Italian immigrants. His father was a well-educated man in Italy, but he had trouble with the English language and was a carpenter in the new country. Eugenio had different ideas and started as a caddie at the age of eight at the Larchmont Country Club. When he was 15 he quit school to join his father in construction so the poverty-stricken family could get by. A few years later, Eugenio Sarceni, upon seeing his name in print for the first time after success in a local golf tournament, changed his name to Gene Sarazen.

One case of pneumonia gave Sarazen the springboard to his long and happy life. While working with his father as a high school dropout, Sarazen spent weeks in the hospital after contracting pneumonia. The doctors, concerned that his work environment was contributing to his illness, prescribed an outdoor job. So long to the construction business and picking up nails. Sarazen had a doctor's note to play golf! More than 80 years later, another case of pneumonia finally ended the life of Sarazen.

Sarazen's father never did give his son his blessing to play golf. This was another case of an immigrant parent (similar to Francis Ouimet's father as portrayed in *The Greatest Game Ever Played* or Lou Gehrig's mother as portrayed in *Pride of the Yankees*) not able to grasp the concept of playing a sport for a vocation.

After his hospital release, Sarazen got a job as a club professional, entered tournaments (including the 1920 and 1921 U.S. Opens), and, in the spring of 1922 at the age of 20, won his first tournament (the Southern Open). He didn't face any moral dilemmas about turning pro and accepting the prize money. He needed the income from golf tournaments. His first major came soon after turning professional, in the 1922 U.S. Open. That was a very significant victory for Sarazen. He defeated a field that included an Atlanta kid the same age as him (Bobby Jones, who finished second). That year's British Open champion, Walter Hagen, finished fifth.

He shot a 2-under par, tying a course record at the Skokie Country Club in Illinois. His birdie on the 18th hole of the final round proved to be the difference, as he waited out Jones and Hagen to finish their rounds.

Sarazen entered the 1922 PGA Championship in August. This time Jones wasn't there (he was, of course, an amateur), and neither was defending champion Hagen (he was, of course, making more money playing exhibitions). Sarazen met Jock Hutchison in the quarterfinals. The match went to the 35th hole, with Sarazen winning, 3 and 1, after trailing Hutchison for most of the match. In the semifinals Sarazen met Bobby Cruickshank in what was called "The Battle of the Midgets" (since neither golfer was taller than 5′6″), and Sarazen won, 3 and 2. Sarazen defeated Emmett French in the finals, 4 and 3. In winning the PGA, Sarazen became the first person to win both the U.S. Open and the PGA Championship in the same year.

At 20 years of age, he was on top of the golfing world. He defeated Hagen in a 72-hole challenge match. Jones was still in his seven lean years. And in the 1923 PGA Championship, the 21-year-old Sarazen took home his third major, defeating the great Hagen in one of the most exciting matches in the 87-year history of the PGA Championship.

It was the first time the Championship needed to go to an extra hole to determine the winner. Sarazen had a 3-up lead, with nine holes to play. Hagen's birdie on the 35th hole squared the match. The final hole was halved. Sarazen's tee shot on the 38th hole hit into a heavy rough. He made a magnificent second shot, dropping short of the pin and coming to rest two feet away from the birdie. Hagen came close to holing his bunker shot and pulling off a near-miracle finish. Sarazen thus won his second straight PGA title.

After the '23 PGA, Sarazen suffered a slump. Hagen began to treat the PGA Championship as his personal playground. Jones won a batch of U.S. Opens and British Opens. Sarazen didn't win much of anything, although he was runner-up to Jones in the 1928 British Open and to Tommy Armour in the 1930 PGA Championship.

In 1928 old friend Hagen told Sarazen that he never would win the British Open without the right caddie—and loaned him his, a man named Skip Daniels. Sarazen didn't win until 1932 but, having taken every piece of advice the older caddie offered him, gave full credit to Daniels.

Sarazen's first victory at the British Open in Sandwich was record-setting. His 283 defeated Macdonald Smith by five strokes. When Sarazen walked up to the 18th green on the final round, he was within grasp of his first British Open. "I said to my caddie, 'Dan, maybe I'm a little dizzy from all of this, but do you know that I have this championship won?' He said, 'Yes, sir, you can take four putts and still be safe.' I said, 'Dan, I know that, but I am going to try and sink this one from 50 feet.' I missed doing it by ten inches, and then the roar went up. Lady Astor grabbed my arm, and I don't mind telling you I never felt a greater satisfaction in my life."

Years later, Sarazen would recount the story of his 1932 British Open Championship. He told people that he must have spent $20,000 traveling overseas to compete about 10 times before finally winning.

But in 1932 even a Jones exhibition match was more newsworthy than any championship final. No one had replaced Jones yet in the minds of the golfing world. So it was Sarazen who began gobbling up the tournaments. He won 14 tournaments between 1930 and 1932. After he returned from Sandwich in 1932, he won the U.S. Open, shooting a 32 on the back nine of the final round.

In the week of the 1933 PGA Championship at Blue Mound Country Club in Wisconsin, Tommy Armour said that Sarazen "was all washed up as a championship contender." There's nothing like proving the experts wrong. Sarazen won the PGA Championship for the third time in 1933 and after the final match told the audience that he was "pretty good for a washed-up golfer."

He *was* marketable and hot. He began playing exhibitions to make money. He didn't play in the inaugural 1934 Masters Tournament but instead played an exhibition match elsewhere.

In 1935 Sarazen made money by touring with Olympic star Babe Didrikson, as she made her golf exhibition debut. They were teamed together in a series of exhibitions, usually in New England.

And then there was the dramatic shot at Augusta. It was the most dramatic finish of the Masters, at least until 1986, when Nicklaus won at the age of 46. Sarazen started the last round in the 1935 Masters three strokes behind Craig Wood. When Sarazen and his playing partner, Hagen, walked up to hit their drives on the 15th hole, they heard a roar from the clubhouse. Wood had just birdied the 18th. Sarazen would have four holes to make up three shots.

On his second shot at 15, Sarazen chose a 4-wood for the 220-yard shot. He was going for the green in an attempt to get a birdie. The shot was perfect. It landed 10 feet in front of the green, bounced three times, and rolled in. In a single shot Sarazen had erased his three-shot deficit to Wood.

That was his seventh and final major title. Although he won the second Masters Tournament, Sarazen was past his prime when the tournament came into being. Given that he was the same age as Jones, who had retired at age 28, Sarazen must have seemed very old to still be playing competitive golf in his late 30s. He finished second at the 1940 U.S. Open, losing a play-off to Lawson Little.

Sarazen spent a decade playing golf around the world and hosting his television show. He competed in 35 Masters Tournaments and was an honorary starter in 19 others. It was a rich and full life, although if he had listened to his father and become a cabinet-maker or something else, he would have been spared life's ultimate screwing. He never made a dime off his invention. The Wilson Sporting Goods Company owned all the rights to Sarazen's sand wedge.

A Better Analogy

Gene Sarazen and Danny Biasone Sarazen was the inventor of golf's sand wedge and one of the first great golf professionals. Biasone was one of the NBA's pioneers, along with men like Walter Brown, Ned Irish, and Eddie Gottlieb. Sarazen was the son of Italian immigrants. Biasone was himself an Italian immigrant. He was born in 1909, so he was roughly the same age as Sarazen. As the owner and founder of the Syracuse Nats, Biasone conceived the 24-second clock for the NBA, figuring that a faster game would help. It sure did help, as the league averaged 93 points per game in the first year of the shot clock, compared to 79 in the last year before the shot clock. Biasone became known as "the father of the 24-second clock."

Some inventions are so perfect—like the sand wedge and the shot clock—that they don't need the least bit of tinkering and remain useful for decades. Gene Sarazen would often say that he changed his name from Sarceni to Sarazen not to hide the fact that he was Italian but because it "sounded like a violin maker." No matter the name, he hit just the right notes.

17

LEE TREVINO
The Merry Mex

Lee Trevino is one of the classic rags-to-riches stories. First, the rags part: He quit school in 1953 at the age of 13 to go to work to help bring money into his poor household. He had never met his father and instead was raised by his mother and grandfather, who worked as a grave digger. Their house in North Dallas did not even have electricity or indoor plumbing.

As poor as they were, Trevino lived next door to the Glen Lakes Country Club in Dallas, where he got started in the game caddying by the age of eight. He was self-taught and got good enough to hustle the local golfers. He dropped out of school in eighth grade and found work on a golfing range. He became so good at golf that he couldn't find any more games, as golfers stopped taking him on to avoid being one of the many he'd beat. Eventually, Trevino became the protégé of Hardy Greenwood, the owner of the driving range where he worked as a teen.

Trevino didn't have a classic swing. In fact, it was quite unorthodox. Trevino in 1979 would say about it, "The book says the 'v' of the thumb and forefinger should point to your right ear. Hell, my 'v' points out of bounds! Sure, I am way left and take the club outside, but I win with it. . . . The key is sliding the hips to start the downswing; the legs have to move faster than the club."

He served in the Marine Corps for four years from the age of 17 to 21. Out of the service in 1960, he got his first job working as an assistant professional at a club in El Paso for $30 a week. He made most of his money hustling, winning bets from fellow golfers.

He made his debut on the Tour at the 1966 U.S. Open and earned his Tour card in 1967, but this top-20 golfer almost didn't have the funds to keep going and get established. He had to borrow $400 for transportation to Springfield, New Jersey, so he could enter the 1967 U.S. Open. He finished fifth and won $6,000. He was on his way.

At the 1968 U.S. Open, in Rochester, New York, Trevino won his first professional tournament and his first major. He won by four strokes, with a 275, tying Jack Nicklaus's one-year-old U.S. Open record. Trevino became the first golfer in U.S. Open history to shoot four consecutive subpar rounds.

To say he shocked the golf world would be an understatement. This was not a college-educated sophisticate like Bobby Jones. Nicklaus was born the same year as Trevino, but they seemingly had nothing in common. Trevino was a fast-talking, hard-living man; Nicklaus came from money. The Merry Mex proved that someone with a hardscrabble background could make it in the country club world of golf. He proved that someone from the wrong side of the tracks could compete.

After winning his U.S. Open in 1968, 28-year-old Trevino told the press that he had been married twice before. "I get rid of them when they get to be 21," cracked Trevino. He was a comic as well as a great shot maker. "I come from such a poor family, my sister was made in Japan," he said. Trevino also bragged that he was the only guy who ever won the U.S. Open who wasn't under contract to another soul. "I think that was real smart of me and my financial manager," he remarked, patting himself on the back.

I'm no psychologist, but it seems to me that the wisecracking Trevino used his sense of humor to convey pride in his background and to cover up his insecurity. It appears he took on a persona that worked for him, since off the course he was known as a private, quiet person. The media portrayed him as happy-go-lucky. He was probably anything but.

He may have played to the gallery and always appeared to be joking, but he had a steely determination and he never forgot where he came from. "God gave me this gift and He can take it away just as quick. I don't want to tempt Him by not practicing. There's nothing else I'd rather do than play golf," Trevino said when asked about practicing. To that he would add, "There's no such thing as a natural touch. Touch is something you create by hitting millions of golf balls." He may have had a god-given talent, but he nurtured it.

Trevino bypassed the Masters in 1970. He took some criticism for not playing Augusta and, though he never felt comfortable there, returned to the tournament after missing it for two years. Here was a player in the prime of his career passing up the most prestigious tournament in the world. It was Trevino who called the shots in his life.

Trevino's attitude may have been his greatest strength, but his ability to perform under the pressure brought on by the game is a close second. For instance, take the 18-hole play-off in the 1971 U.S. Open in which Trevino beat Nicklaus. In that play-off it was Nicklaus who double-bogeyed the third hole, had trouble in a sand trap in another early hole, and never led. Nicklaus would say afterward that the bad shots were not due to pressure but rather "bad execution." Trevino was humbled over beating someone of Nicklaus's caliber and of repeating his earlier U.S. Open victory. Trevino quoted Walter Hagen, saying, "Anyone can win one U.S. Open, but it takes a real champion to win two."

Nicklaus was the first to admit that he had lost to an opponent who was his age but who had much less experience than he did. Trevino had been playing tournament golf only from 1967. Nicklaus had pretty much been playing tournament golf since his teens in the mid-1950s.

So knowing the difference in experience they had, did Trevino feel pressure before the play-off? Well, as he and Nicklaus were ready to tee off on the first hole, Trevino pulled a rubber snake from his bag and tossed it toward his opponent. Some of the stuffier golf people felt that Trevino had gone too far with the snake. Jack didn't appear to show any displeasure or be distracted by it.

Trevino won the 1971 British Open at Royal Birkdale and then repeated the following year at Muirfield in a memorable final round. It was at the '71 British Open that Trevino won over the English fans. He survived a double-bogey on the 17th hole of the final round but held on for a one-shot victory.

In 1972 the first two majors of the year both went to Nicklaus. Entering the British Open at Muirfield, Nicklaus's quest for a Jones-like Grand Slam was the overriding storyline. But Trevino entered the final round six strokes ahead of Nicklaus. Jack did his part, by shooting a 65 in the final round. He put the pressure on Trevino by making birdie on 6 of the first 11 holes, gaining a share of the lead with Trevino and Tony Jacklin. The pressure would get to former champion Jacklin, who went bogey-bogey on the last two holes. But as demonstrated in the past, Trevino was immune to such pressure. He sank a 30-foot chip shot to save par on 17, after Nicklaus had bogeyed the 16th, and Trevino won the British Open for a second consecutive year.

Nicklaus had given the fans rooting for a Grand Slam everything he had. He said afterward that shooting 279 like he did would be enough to win 19 times out of 20. Trevino would say afterward that it would have been great for golf if Nicklaus could have won the Grand Slam. He may have pulled rubber snakes from his pockets at times, but he knew his manners.

As great and talented as Nicklaus was, his competitors were a big help in making him shine. Muhammad Ali isn't Ali without Joe Frazier. Nicklaus isn't Nicklaus without Arnold Palmer, Gary Player, Billy Casper, Lee Trevino, and, finally, Tom Watson. They brought out his greatness, and he brought out theirs.

Trevino, in the peak of his career, won the PGA Championship in 1974. Brandishing an old putter he had found in the attic of his rented home, he won the championship on a rain-soaked course. During the third round, Trevino had moved out in front with a 68 to get a one-stroke lead over Nicklaus. In the final round Nicklaus shot a 69, but he couldn't overtake Trevino, who matched Nicklaus's performance for a one-stroke victory.

He became Nicklaus's chief thorn in the side after first beating Jack in a play-off for the 1971 U.S. Open and then ending his hopes for a 1972 slam.

And then there were Trevino's lean years. It took him another 10 years to win his sixth major. At the 1984 PGA Championship in Birmingham, Alabama, the 44-year-old Trevino shot four consecutive rounds in the 60s. Trevino, wielding a hot putter he had purchased a few weeks earlier in Holland, shot 67 on Saturday and 69 on Sunday. His 15-under par 273 was easily enough to win, overcoming Gary Player's 277, which featured a record 63 among his rounds.

Trevino was always philosophical about his putter. "When a golfer changes his putter, things might go well for about a week because having something new gives him confidence. But then the new putter gets to know him, and things turn sour again. It's the Indian, not the arrow."

Trevino did finally stop winning majors for many reasons. Unlike Nicklaus, who would take three weeks off to prepare for a major, Trevino played as many tournaments as he could, which took a toll. Trevino, of course, chased the money more than the history books, no matter how many dollars he earned. He wasn't the longest hitter, which is one of the reasons that he never felt comfortable at the Masters. At Augusta it helped to be a great driver. He preferred the "bump and run" courses, as he called the British Open.

The time he was hit by lightning didn't help his game either. He was one of three golfers struck, along with Bobby Nichols and Jerry Heard, at the 1975 Western Open. Trevino required a back operation in 1976 for a herniated disc. He had to overcome several subsequent operations and several divorces.

The chance of someone being struck by lightning is roughly one in 700,000. The chance of someone from Trevino's background rising to the top of the golf world has to be even more of a rarity. His life was a one-in-a-million success story.

Before he left the game to pursue television, he had 29 wins on the Tour, which is still ranked among the top 20 of all time. Casper's 51 victories in roughly the same time period is the reason that he ranks ahead of Trevino, despite three fewer majors. Trevino was the PGA Tour Rookie of the Year in 1967, the PGA Player of the Year in 1971, and the leading money winner in 1970. He collected five Vardon Trophies for lowest scoring average in a season.

Trevino was also a member of six Ryder Cup teams and was captain of the 1985 squad. He would have won more (and improved his ranking), but in his 40s he preferred to be an analyst for NBC. His one-liners played well on television, but once he turned 50, the hustler needed the competition, so he returned to playing golf. He attacked the Champions Tour.

He won 29 times in his 50s and dominated the Tour in the early 1990s. In 1990, in fact, he was the leading money winner in golf and became the first Champions Tour player to earn more than $1 million in single-season earnings. He won seven times in 1990 alone. He would say that the only thing wrong with the Champions Tour is there is too much sitting-around time. "I wish we played two tournaments a week, one on Monday, Tuesday, and Wednesday, and the other on the weekend."

He was one of the greatest characters the game has ever known. Once saying, "If you keep your mouth shut for too long, you get bad breath," Trevino has never kept his mouth shut long enough to find out.

Who's Better, Who's Best
Lee Trevino or Nick Faldo?

Trevino and Faldo are the only male golfers with six majors. Trevino is ranked ahead of Faldo and here's why. The two greatest golfers in history are Tiger Woods and Jack Nicklaus. Either Woods or Nicklaus was a competitive threat from 1960 to 2005, with the exception of about eight years beginning in 1987. Faldo squeezed in his six majors between 1987 and 1996. Trevino, on the other hand, was smack in the middle of Nicklaus's prime.

A Better Analogy

Lee Trevino and Joe Frazier Trevino's life has more in common with boxer Joe Frazier's than golfer Faldo's. Frazier was born less than three years after Trevino to sharecroppers and worked in the fields during his youth. Frazier left school after ninth grade and married by the age of 15. He had a child a year later and moved his family from South Carolina to Philadelphia. Frazier began boxing to lose weight.

Frazier went on to win the World Heavyweight Title in 1970, defeating Jimmy Ellis in the fifth round. It was his three epic bouts with Muhammed Ali that cemented Frazier's reputation as one of the greatest boxers in history. Similarly, Trevino's career was defined by his contemporary, the great champion Nicklaus.

18

NICK FALDO
Europe's Greatest?

Nick Faldo grew up with a stage mom who didn't drive her son to become a legendary golfer. She wanted Nick to become a fashion model, because, she said, "he had smashing legs."

It turns out he had a smashing will to win golf tournaments as well. Nick didn't even begin playing the game until he was 14 years old, when he saw Jack Nicklaus on television and decided that he wanted to try and take up the game. On the first hole of his first-ever round, he hit a driver, followed by a 3-wood, and reached the green of a 450-yard par-4.

After playing golf for all of four years, he won the 1975 British Youths Amateur and English Amateur Championships. At the age of 20, he was the 1977 European Tour Rookie of the Year. He developed into one of the better players, though he had a reputation for folding down the stretch at big events (and was thus sometimes called Nick Foldo). The rep was undeserved and actually given to nearly every top golfer who didn't start out of the chute with a big major championship. Tom Watson was similarly tagged early in his career.

Faldo won five times on the European Tour in 1983, leading the Tour in money and scoring average. He knew he needed to improve to win the majors. He totally rebuilt his swing. It took some work (with the help of David Leadbetter), and he went three years without a single win. But he accomplished his goal. His rebuilt swing carried him into the biggest tournaments in the world.

Along the way, he played some of the greatest golf in history, including his final-round 65 to make up five strokes on Scott Hoch at the 1989 Masters. That would be a walk in the park compared with his comeback at the 1996 Masters, when he trailed by six strokes early in the final round and not only caught Greg Norman with a 67 but routed the Shark, who shot a 78.

It was in that tournament that Faldo had one of the greatest shots of all time. By the time he had reached the par-five 13th hole on the final day of the 1996 Masters, he was already two strokes up on Norman. He was looking at his second shot, 228 yards away over water. This was the hardest shot in golf, with the ball above his feet. After studying the possibilities, he used his 2-iron to hit a shot that, considering the stakes and the mounting pressure, was the greatest shot of his career and one of the greatest clutch shots of all time. Although there were five holes to play, Faldo could have tried on the green jacket after the 13th.

There was the 1987 British Open, which started his string of majors. On the final day of that tournament in Muirfield, Faldo plodded his way to a one-stroke victory over Paul Azinger and Rodger Davis. He had 18 consecutive pars on the final day. His game was marked by that. He was the first to have the word *grinder* attached to his game. He wasn't the flashiest of players. He didn't hit the ball the farthest, nor did he take the most chances. What he did, though, was grind out pars—relentlessly.

Faldo rarely made mistakes. At the 1990 British Open, at St. Andrews, Norman shot 66 and 66 in the first two rounds. He was tied for the lead with Faldo, who had shot 67 and 65. In the third round, playing together, Norman blew up with a 78. Faldo never did and even withstood a Payne Stewart charge on the final day to bring home his second British Open.

In 1992, back at Muirfield, Faldo won his third British Open. He had a four-stroke lead over John Cook with nine holes to play, squandered the lead, and then played the final four holes as well as he ever played four consecutive holes in his life. He needed a 4 on the final hole, and put himself in position to tap in his fourth shot on the 18th hole to defeat Cook by a shot.

Lanny Wadkins, CBS golf analyst and PGA pro: "Faldo would not rate as high as Tom Watson. He could have used more wins in the United States. But he was a great Ryder Cup player. He was one player who reminded me of Hogan. Faldo was very reminiscent of him—not a lot of outward motion. He played through his strength."

Faldo is ranked among the top 20 golfers of all time for his career. He didn't have the longest reign on top—he was basically a top player from 1984 to 1996. After 1996, at the age of 39, he was basically done.

He had his memorable comeback in the 1996 Masters, and after that, his good karma was all used up. He won only once in 1997 (at the age of 40), dropped to 163rd on the Tour rankings in 1998, and was even passed over in 1999 for a spot on the European Ryder Cup teams. And Faldo was, if nothing else, one of the great Ryder Cup players of all time.

His slump coincided with the arrival of Woods and the technology that allowed players to drive the ball with much more distance. Faldo couldn't or wouldn't adapt to the new game.

Peter Alliss, former player (eight-time Ryder Cup player for Europe) and television commentator, on Faldo's ranking among players he's seen: "I would certainly put Nick Faldo amongst the all-time greats, although he was only at the very top of the tree for a relatively short time and seemed to 'lose his game' at the highest level very quickly. I dislike placing players who didn't compete in the same generation but I think, on overall balance, Faldo might just be ahead of Thomson and Locke on points."

Faldo won 30 times on the European Tour and had a handful of PGA Tour victories to go with his six majors. If all we had to grade his career on were the majors, it would be impressive. He finished in the top five in 19 different major championships, winning six of them, of course. He finished in the top 10 in 26 different majors. But then there is the Ryder Cup competition as well.

Nick Faldo at the Ryder Cup
Faldo competed on 11 different Ryder Cup teams (1977, 1979, 1981, 1983, 1985, 1987, 1989, 1991, 1993, 1995, and 1997). That's a record for either side of the Atlantic. He has the Ryder Cup records for most matches played (46), most points won (25), and most matches won (23). He was only 20 when he competed in it for the first time. Only Sergio Garcia (who was 19 on the 1999 Europe team) was younger.

Nick Faldo in the Majors
Faldo came so close to a career Grand Slam. In 1993 he finished one stroke back of Paul Azinger, who shed his title as "the best player never to win a major." Faldo shot a closing-round 67 at the 1992 PGA Championship to get within three strokes of winner Nick Price, but the tie for second place was as close as he got at the PGA.

He got even closer to winning the 1988 U.S. Open when he tied Curtis Strange on the final two holes of regulation. Strange three-putted from 15 feet on the 17th green, which moved Faldo into the 18-hole play-off the next day. In the extra round, however, it was Faldo's putter that deserted him. He lost two strokes on 13, went on to bogey three of the last four holes, and lost to Strange by four strokes.

After playing in the 1992 Grand Slam of Golf, Faldo flew to Fort Worth, Texas, to meet with Hogan. Faldo held him in awe. Faldo asked politely if Hogan would watch a few of his swings. Hogan declined. Then Faldo asked if Hogan would share a secret with him. Hogan said, "What secret?"

Faldo responded, "I really want to win the U.S. Open, and I'd like you to share the secret of it."

Hogan said, "Shoot a lower score than everyone else."

Faldo laughed and then kept going. "No, really, what's the secret?"

Hogan said he wasn't joking. "Just score lower than everyone else."

Faldo never did win the U.S. Open.

He did win nearly everything else, including 42 worldwide titles. If he wasn't Europe's greatest golfer ever, he was on the very short list.

Who's Better, Who's Best
Nick Faldo or Harry Vardon?

If you believe his website, nickfaldo.com, you would read that he is Europe's greatest golfer ever. He is the greatest European golfer since Harry Vardon, but Nick, you mustn't forget Vardon.

I mean, Vardon played in three U.S. Opens (two way past his prime) and about 20 British Opens. He won just as many major championships in 23 majors, then, as Faldo, who entered 65 consecutive major championships in his prime.

Vardon won six British Opens to Faldo's three. Faldo won his last British Open five years after his first. Vardon won his last British Open Championship 18 years after his first. Vardon won the British Open in three different decades. It would only be a slight exaggeration to say that Faldo won his with three different wives (which, actually, upon further review, is probably more difficult).

Faldo would win six majors: three British Opens and three Masters Championships. While it's not more than fellow European Vardon, it is more than every other golfer besides Jack Nicklaus, Walter Hagen, Tiger Woods, Gary Player, Ben Hogan, Tom Watson, Sam Snead, Gene Sarazen, and Bobby Jones, and it's as many as Lee Trevino won.

19

KATHY WHITWORTH
The Female Sam Snead

I can't rank Kathy Whitworth any lower than 19th overall, and certainly, among the women, only Didrikson, Wright, and Sorenstam can be ranked ahead of her. With a 40-foot putt on the last hole at the 1983 Women's Kemper Open, Whitworth tied Sam Snead's record of 84 official professional golf victories (which she went on to break 16 months later). In 1985 she recorded her final tournament victory, her 88th win—a record among both men and women.

Even 20 years later, the record 88 professional golf victories stands. When Annika Sorenstam breaks the record, it will have stood for nearly a quarter-century. That says a lot for Sorenstam, who is, like Tiger Woods being ranked ahead of Nicklaus, ranked ahead of Whitworth in this book.

Kathrynne Ann Whitworth was born September 27, 1939. She was raised in Jal, New Mexico, which is in the southeastern corner of the state, not far from Texas. It was a small town of about 6,000 people. Her father ran the hardware store and after retirement became the mayor.

Although she played tennis growing up, Kathy was a stocky girl, standing at 5'9" and weighing 215 pounds by the time she finished eighth grade. It was an impromptu nine-hole course she played with her friends around the age of 15 that made her begin taking golf seriously. Golf took her seriously as well. Whitworth captured the New Mexico State Amateur title two consecutive years (1957 and 1958) before turning professional in December of 1958, a major feat for an overweight woman. But by 1959, her rookie year on the LPGA Tour, she was down to 170 pounds. Three years later, she was down to 145.

Her first golf instructor was local pro Hardy Loudermilk. Once Whitworth had won the New Mexico women's amateur titles, Loudermilk said he had taken her as far as he could go and drove her to Austin, Texas, where he introduced her to Harvey Penick, the legendary golf instructor and coach at the University of Texas. Penick was a lifelong friend and tutor, and she would call on him even late in her career, if a part of her game was off.

She didn't take the women's Tour by storm. In her rookie season, she entered 26 tournaments and her highest finish was ninth. In the two majors she entered, she finished tied for 18th at the LPGA and tied for 32nd at the U.S. Women's Open.

It was a different life than the LPGA stars lead today. The total prize money for the 26 events of the 1959 Tour totaled only $202,500, less than one-half of 1 percent of the 2004 prize money of $42,875,000. In the '50s, women didn't become rich by playing professional golf. Betsy Rawls in 1959 won a then-record $26,774, a mark that would stand until 1963 when Mickey Wright broke the $30,000 mark.

Whitworth's father loaded up the back of the car with her suitcases, and she drove herself from tournament to tournament. There was no glamour involved. She would spend three or four days of traveling, followed by three or four days of playing. For all the traveling, she earned just $1,217 in 1959. It wasn't until her 11th tournament in 1959 that she finished in the money: a tie for 15th place good for $71. The next year, she entered 22 tournaments and finished as high as second place. She earned a grand total of $4,901. She played in every LPGA event there was, giving the Tour her best shot.

So in her first two full years, she entered 48 tournaments, didn't win any of them, and earned a total of $6,118. That's an average of $127 a tournament, or $59 a week for two years. It's a wonder she played in 1961, rather than packing it in. She still couldn't crack the winner's circle because seven other women dominated the LPGA that year: Louise Suggs, Mickey Wright, Mary Lena Faulk, Kathy Cornelius, Betsy Rawls, Ruth Jessen, and Judy Kimball. Whitworth had entered 63 tournaments by the end of 1961 and hadn't won any of them. She ran home and almost left the Tour, but her supportive parents convinced her to stick it out.

Eventually, she would win a tournament, but it wouldn't be until the 16th LPGA event of 1962 and the 79th tournament of Whitworth's career. In July of 1962, at the Kelly Girls Open, Whitworth cashed a first-place check. Even in that tournament, there wasn't elation. Whitworth was already in the clubhouse when Sandra Haynie three-putted the 18th hole.

The early 1960s were Mickey Wright's time in history (she won 10 times in 1962). But in mid-October, at the Phoenix Thunderbird Open, Whitworth came from behind and defeated Wright by a stroke for her second Tour win. In the coming years, Whitworth would plan her games—she never overpowered golf courses, winning instead with planning and a solid all-around game.

At the Phoenix Thunderbird Open, Whitworth earned $1,300 for a week's work, winning her second tournament. Her scoring average improved each year from 80.3 to 77.1 to 76.1 to 74.3. Her earnings jumped like this:

1959: $1,217
1960: $4,901
1961: $6,853
1962: $17,044

Her playing improved exponentially. In 1965 Whitworth won 8 of the 30 LPGA events to lead the women, led the LPGA in earnings with $32,000, and was voted Female Athlete of the Year in the Associated Press poll—an honor Mickey Wright had held the year before. (Wright was in semiretirement and only played 11 of the 30 events that year.)

In 1966 Whitworth led the money standings again. During one memorable week in June at the Milwaukee Jaycee Open, she shot rounds of 68–71–69–65 to set an all-time women's scoring record of 273 for 72 holes, breaking by two strokes the old record held by Mickey Wright.

That record is now held by Annika Sorenstam, who shot a 261 for 72 holes (27 better than par) in Phoenix in the 2001 season. Karen Stupples actually shot a 258 score for 72 holes at the Dell Urich Golf Course in Tucson, Arizona, in 2004, but it was only −22 in relation to par.

The Whitworth era was upon us in the late '60s. She won 8 times in 1965, 9 in 1966, 8 in 1967, and 10 in 1968. And Wright was still around, though playing much less than Whitworth and the others.

1965–68

Kathy Whitworth: 35 victories in 119 tournaments
Mickey Wright: 19 victories in 66 tournaments

So both players won nearly 30 percent of the tournaments they entered in those four years. Now for a variety of reasons, it was hard to market Whitworth to the American public. Nationally known and syndicated columnist Jim Murray wrote this in 1963 about Wright:

Mickey Wright travels from town to town in a Starfire Oldsmobile with a rack full of dresses in the back seat. She tries to keep her nails up, her weight down, and her mind on her game at all times. Time was when a woman golfer was a kind of leathery old harpie with a face that looked like an old shag bag, a voice that came out of a bottle, and a swagger that made you think she chewed tobacco. She was about as feminine as the Smith Bros. . . . But Mickey Wright is a girl you wouldn't be ashamed to take to the Cotillion. A beautiful blond with soft skin and a quiet voice . . .

Women's golf was beginning to get television contracts. Although Wright shied away from any publicity as much as she could, it was a lot easier to market her than it was Whitworth. The prevailing theory at that time was that men would watch attractive women play sports. Whitworth would be upset in the early 1970s when Jan Stephenson began to get a lot of attention. It was a much easier "sell" to the majority of fans to watch some of the more eye-catching golfers.

In 1966 the LPGA Player of the Year Award was added to the roster of year-end honors. Whitworth was the first to win the prestigious award and won it seven of the first eight years it was awarded.

The Vare Trophy was awarded to the player with the best scoring average. Whitworth won the Vare in 1965, 1966, 1967, 1969, 1970, 1971, and 1972. Carol Mann had a 72.04 average to win the Vare in 1968, interrupting Whitworth's streak. Whitworth had a stroke average of 72.16 in 1968, a number that was just narrowly defeated by Mann.

In 1967 Whitworth won her 30th career LPGA title at the Raleigh Ladies Invitational at the age of 27½. She became the second-youngest player to win 30 LPGA tournaments. Wright was the youngest at 26 years, 11 months, and 7 days.

When the 1967 LPGA Championship was played in Sutton, Massachusetts, Whitworth upped her number to 31 career victories and 3 major titles, which included the 1965 Titleholders Championship and 1966 Titleholders Championship. The victories kept piling up, and so did the money; but the majors—in particular, the U.S. Women's Open—were more difficult. In this regard, she is the female Sam Snead. Snead never did win his U.S. Open, and Whitworth never did win her U.S. Women's Open. Her closest finishes at the Open were in 1969 (third), 1970 (tied for fourth), 1971 (second), 1974 (tied for fourth), and 1981 (third).

Whitworth only finished second once at the Open, and it was in 1971, when JoAnne Carner won by a whopping seven strokes. It wasn't like Snead, who finished second in 1937, 1947, 1949, and 1953, among these a couple of play-offs, which, had he won even one, would have given him his elusive Open.

In 1981 her third-place finish at the U.S. Women's Open made her the first player in the history of the LPGA to surpass the $1 million mark in career earnings. She made her money by dealing in volume, volume, volume.

The reason Whitworth doesn't rank higher in this book is her record at the major championships. Patty Berg had a women's record 15 majors (7 Titleholders, 7 Western Opens, 1 U.S. Women's Open). Wright won 13 majors, including 4 U.S. Women's Opens. Suggs won 11 majors, and Didrikson won 10. Sorenstam has 9 and counting. Even Rawls with 8 and Juli Inkster with 7 have more than Whitworth.

Whitworth won only six majors. She won the LPGA Championship three times, the Titleholders twice, and the Western Open once (1967). Of course, it doesn't mean she isn't a great LPGA legend. But she wasn't Babe Didrikson, who won three U.S. Women's Opens and 10 majors in a shortened career.

Whitworth holds the LPGA record for winning a tournament in 17 consecutive seasons (1962–78). She holds another record for winning at least once in 22 different seasons. No one else has won in even 19 different seasons.

One of the reasons for Whitworth's longevity is that she had no ties to marriage. She never married nor had children, which certainly interrupted the careers of many golfers, including Nancy Lopez.

Who were the youngest LPGA golfers to accumulate 40 victories? Wright was 27. Whitworth was 28. And Sorenstam was 31. They were also (in successive order) the three youngest to accumulate 50 wins.

Whitworth finished first on the season-ending money list eight times, a record she now shares with Annika, who finished first in 2005 for the eighth time. Whitworth reached $1 million in earnings in 1981, in her 22nd year on the Tour. Sorenstam was the first to reach $20 million in earnings, in her 12 years on Tour.

Who's Better, Who's Best
Kathy Whitworth or Sam Snead?

Whitworth didn't have the drama that Didrikson had or the charisma that Lopez had. She didn't have the instant success that others had. Snead didn't have the drama of Hogan, either. He took awhile to win big and (like Whitworth) never did win the U.S. Open. Their longevity is unparalleled, however.

In March of 1983, Whitworth won the Women's Kemper Open, which tied her with Snead for 84 professional golf victories. For a long time after that, she couldn't buy the additional victory to surpass Sam. Finally, after 16 months, in July of 1984, it happened. The 44-year-old Whitworth won a sudden-death play-off with Rosie Jones to capture the Rochester International Tournament and broke Sam's record.

She was asked about breaking Snead's record 10 to 15 times a day by reporters for the better part of a year. Whitworth had accomplished the goal of a lifetime. No one had won more golf tournaments than her.

When Snead was contacted after Whitworth's record-breaking win, the rascal replied that he should be credited with 160 official victories. He liked Whitworth, having played with her a bunch, and told reporters that he wished that she would go on and win 100.

Snead's victory total—whether 160 or merely half that—still rates ahead of Whitworth's, but they have parallels. Snead felt his game and his records often went disrespected, in favor of Nelson and Hogan. He countered that by outlasting his contemporaries and just kept on winning until he could not be ignored. Whitworth did the same. She was the female Sam Snead.

She won more than anyone else in the past, and even Tiger Woods might not reach 88 wins in the future.

A Better Analogy

Kathy Whitworth and Martina Navratilova Kathy Whitworth and Mickey Wright isn't exactly a perfect analogy of Martina Navratilova and Chrissie Evert, but there is a parallel. A decade after Whitworth and Wright competed, the women's tennis tour featured an attractive girl (Evert) who was dubbed by television and print journalist Bud Collins as "America's Sweetheart." Navratilova was once given a very different nickname by Bud: "the Great Wide Hope." Martina would wind up with 167 top-level singles titles—the most of any player, male or female—since tennis's Open Championship truly became open in 1968. After losing early in her career to Evert, Navratilova won a majority of her matches against her. Clearly, Navratilova was a better player.

I do not think that Whitworth was a better player than Wright (or Annika Sorenstam). I do, believe, however, that Navratilova was not given the recognition outside her sport that she should have received, and neither was Whitworth. They both received every award there was to be given in their respective sports.

20

HALE IRWIN
The Defensive Back

Hale Irwin was a marketing major at the University of Colorado. I find this kind of interesting because the one thing that he failed to do in his 30 years on the Tour was market himself effectively.

Irwin was born June 3, 1945, in Baxter Springs, Kansas, not far from the borders of Missouri and Oklahoma. His dad, Hale Irwin Sr., a salesman, cut down a set of golf clubs for his son and took him to the nine-hole public course when he was four. The Irwins moved to Boulder, Colorado, when Hale was 14. By that time he was already shooting in the 60s. He was an outstanding high school athlete (shortstop, quarterback, golfer). The 180-pound Irwin was recruited to play football by many schools but stayed home and chose the University of Colorado, where he played quarterback before switching to defensive back. At the same time, he was the 1967 NCAA golf champion and a two-time All–Big Eight selection as a football defensive back. He played alongside Dick Anderson, who would be an All-Pro for the Miami Dolphins and the 1973 Defensive Player of the Year. But Irwin wasn't quite that good on the gridiron. He didn't have the speed, so instead of spending his future chasing O. J. Simpson, he decided he'd chase Jack Nicklaus.

The former quarterback had settled for a less glamorous position on the gridiron in college and wasn't one of the glamorous stars on the golf courses either. "I didn't have blond hair. I was nondescript," he told the *St. Louis Post Dispatch* in 1995. "The only flair was that I'd played college football. Still, I could only be what I was. When I came on Tour, the names were Arnold Palmer, Jack Nicklaus, Gary Player. The gods were with me in that I had the fortune to play with those guys. Lee Trevino was a fledgling star. They all had a niche: Nicklaus was the Bear, Arnie had his Army, Lee his Fleas. Player did pushups. I had my glasses."

Irwin was the greatest player to, what, wear eyeglasses? In a word, yes. His large frames, shades, specs, or whatever you wanted to call them made his look geeky and uncool. This was the big football player? Wait, the geekiness gets worse. Besides the rimmed glasses, when he was 34 years old, in the prime of his career, he started wearing braces on his teeth. He explained the extensive orthodontic work this way: "I want to be able to eat a roast beef sandwich without getting it in my lap." As a golfer he never bit off more than he could chew.

One would think that because of his build and his football background, he would be a big hitter on the golf course. After all, this was a six-footer who had played college football. But he wasn't the longest hitter on the Tour. He hit a fade that almost looked like an out-and-out slice. He was always a good putter, with his short game always one of his major strengths.

Rick Reilly, *Sports Illustrated* **columnist:** "Hale is one of the greatest long-iron players of all time. He's also one of the most competitive. What a 3-wood player! No one could hit the ball straighter. He could do things with his clubs . . . he could make that thing do the rumba."

Besides his success on the Champions Tour, Irwin is remembered for a few things aside from his glasses. He will forever be remembered for his three U.S. Opens, and (to a lesser degree) his 86 consecutive tournaments without missing the cut.

Most Consecutive Events Without Missing Cut

1. 142 Tiger Woods
2. 113 Byron Nelson
3. 105 Jack Nicklaus
4. 86 Hale Irwin

Irwin missed the cut in January of 1975, in a tournament in Tucson, Arizona. He then made the cut at the Bing Crosby National Pro-Am in January of 1975, for the first of what would turn out to be finishing in the money in 86 different events, until he missed the cut in the first start of 1979 at the same Bing Crosby National Pro-Am. He went four years without missing a cut. Only Tiger Woods, Byron Nelson, and Jack Nicklaus can say the same thing.

Now it's an amazing achievement to go 86 tournaments over four years without missing the cut, but this was more true in Irwin's case than with the others. When Woods, Nelson, and Nicklaus were in the midst of their consecutive-cut streaks, they were winning a good percentage of those championships. It makes sense that they made the cut all the time. On the other hand, Irwin won twice in 1975, twice in 1976, and three times in 1977. He didn't win a single tournament in 1978. So Irwin won only 7 of those 86 tournaments in which he made the cut. Consistent? You bet. Excellent? Well, not compared to Woods, Nicklaus, or Nelson.

The Three U.S. Opens

Irwin's first major had come at the 1974 U.S. Open at Winged Foot, maybe the hardest course to host a U.S. Open. He didn't shoot in the 60s (only Hubert Green shot as low as 67, and that was in the second round), but he never blew up in a round either. Of the 72 holes, he hit 46 holes in regulation, ranking him third in the field in percentage. Irwin shot 73 (with three birdies) in the first round and 70 in the second (with four birdies). That put him in a tie for the lead. In the third round a 23-year-old Tom Watson took the lead with a 69, putting him a stroke ahead of Irwin. Finally, in the fourth round, Watson shot himself out early, and a duel developed between Forrest Fezler and Irwin. Hale's 2-iron on the last hole helped him win his first major despite a score of 287.

In 1979 Irwin had become 1 of 13 men to win the U.S. Open twice. He won with a score of 284, which was only even par. But he was the only competitor to even shoot that. He carried a much-needed three-shot lead into the final round. He finished double bogey, bogey on his final two holes. But he had a five-stroke lead going into the final two holes, so he didn't need to finish much better. On the 16th hole of the third round, Irwin hit a marvelous 2-iron that placed the ball just three feet from the cup. The 225-yard shot gave him an eagle and opened the gap to four strokes.

In 1990 Irwin got into the U.S. Open at Medinah outside of Chicago by special invitation from the USGA. In the final round he made five birdies on the last eight holes to tie Mike Donald and forced a play-off when he sank a 45-foot putt on the final hole to tie Donald. The putt had to curl a good four feet on the way to the cup. Irwin began running around the 18th green and slapping hands with the spectators behind the ropes. Dave Anderson, the esteemed *New York Times* writer, told me that Irwin told him that his reaction changed the way the world looked at him. The gallery gave out a huge ovation. He wasn't exactly an overnight sensation. I prefer to call Irwin an "oversight sensation."

The next day provided the highlight of his 30-year PGA Tour career. Donald didn't fold under the pressure and was two strokes ahead of Irwin through 12 holes of the play-off. But Irwin came back and would win the tournament thanks to a shot on the 16th. Standing 205 yards from the pin and hitting uphill into the wind, Irwin nailed a 2-iron within six feet. He made the putt to close to within a stroke. Irwin caught Donald, and they were still tied after the 18-hole play-off. They needed a 19th hole to separate. Irwin trumped Donald with a 10-foot birdie putt to win his third U.S. Open. This victory made him (at age 45) the oldest player ever to win a U.S. Open as well as only the fifth player ever to win as many as three U.S. Opens, joining Willie Anderson, Bobby Jones, Ben Hogan, and Nicklaus.

The Majors Irwin Didn't Win

There aren't many golfers who can lay claim to three U.S. Open titles, but Irwin had a shot at a few more. In 1978 the U.S. Open was played in Englewood, Colorado, at the Cherry Hills Country Club. Irwin had moved to Colorado when he was a teenager, so he was surrounded by family and friends. He led after the first round with a 69. But he must have pressed too hard, for he followed with disappointing rounds of 74, 75, and 70 and finished fourth. The loss in Colorado perhaps provided the impetus for Irwin to win the following year. He got his second Open in 1979 at Inverness in Toledo.

In 1984, when the U.S. Open returned to Winged Foot, Irwin went there with a heavy heart. From his home in Boulder, his dad was watching the Open on television while dying of cancer.

"I knew this would probably be the last tournament Dad would ever see," Irwin commented later. "Something that would give him a measure of pleasure." But Irwin tried too hard. His father died a week after the tournament had concluded. Irwin's inability to win that '84 title for his dad remains his biggest disappointment on the Tour. He would say after his final-round 79, which saw him go from first place to sixth, "I am befuddled. I have no explanation. It was a total disaster."

There were some other missed opportunities to win additional majors, including one unbelievable British Open. Irwin blew a two-inch tap-in at the end of the third round of the 1983 British Open at Royal Birkdale, costing him a chance at a play-off for the major championship. A 25-foot birdie putt at the par-three 14th hole rested just inches past the cup. Irwin whiffed the easy putt and eventually finished in a tie for second place, one stroke from a play-off with Watson.

Irwin won the Heritage Classic in 1973. Twenty-one years later he won the same event for a second time. That's the longest time between victories in the same event with no wins in that tournament in between. Irwin won his first Tour event in November of 1971 and his last one in April of 1994. That's a stretch of more than 22 years. Irwin turned 40 in 1985. Following his victory at the 1985 Memorial Tournament, his 17th tournament victory, he fell off the charts. He didn't win another tournament for five years.

So why do I place Irwin so high in the rankings? He won more major tournaments than Greg Norman or Phil Mickelson, two players seriously considered for the final spot in the top 20. Irwin played in a very competitive era, and his longevity and success on the Champions Tour places him over the others.

	Top-Five Finishes in Majors	Wins in Majors
Hale Irwin	11	3
Phil Mickelson	13	2
Greg Norman	19	2

Since joining the Champions Tour in June 1995, Irwin has won 16 times in his first 70 starts. He won four times in 2005, despite turning 60 in June. He has 44 Champions Tour victories. No other golfer has as many as 30 wins. Trevino is next with 29 victories.

Dan Hicks, golf announcer for NBC Sports: "[Irwin] is absolutely unbelievable. He is blessed with great genes. What a competitor he is! He wakes up in the morning, and must say, 'Who can I beat today?' I believe that what he has done on the Champions Tour is parallel to what Tiger did on the regular tour in 2000."

How about 11 consecutive years with multiple victories on the Champions Tour? He's won well over $20 million on the Champions Tour, after having won $6 million on the PGA Tour. Some experts feel that his Champions Tour success isn't as worthy as that of others. Johnny Miller wrote in his book *I Call the Shots* that being the greatest player in Champions Tour history "is a great accomplishment, but in a way it's like being remembered as the world's tallest midget."

Dave Anderson, *New York Times* columnist: "Hale is one of the great competitors in sports. He was a very good football player and he brings that football mentality to the game of golf. He has the same mental preoccupation that football players have. Of course, his record on the Champions Tour affects his historical ranking. These are not exhibitions that he is winning."

Irwin is still beating the likes of Watson and Larry Nelson and everyone else on the Champions Tour. It's not like he's playing guys 10 years older than him. If anything, he's playing younger athletes now. Irwin is a tough competitor who wants to win so badly that he'll move from quarterback to defensive back. He'll move from PGA Tour to Champions Tour.

Who's Better, Who's Best
Hale Irwin or Greg Norman?
Greg Norman had 19 top-five finishes in majors, compared to Irwin's 11. Shouldn't Norman be ranked ahead of Irwin? I asked two experts who had up-close observations for the entirety of both Norman's and Irwin's careers.

Lanny Wadkins, CBS golf analyst and PGA pro (winner of the 1977 PGA Championship): "Hale was one of the toughest competitors—more so at the end of his career. If he had the tenacity and the confidence early that he had late—which carried into his seniors play—he would have won a great deal more. He became a better putter as he got older, which not many guys do. If he's not a top-20 player of all time, he's right on the cusp. Norman is not a top-20 player. He had a lot of wins, and two majors. But he'll be remembered more for his failures, not his successes. Most of his big successes are overseas; he was a world player before it became fashionable."

Dave Anderson: "Irwin is definitely ahead of Norman. Norman blew too many big tournaments, it detracts from his ranking. Put it like this: if I had to bet a lot of money on Norman or Irwin to win one tournament—with both in their prime—my money would be on Irwin."

NBC Sports commentator Dan Hicks thinks "we'll never see a 2000 season like Tiger Woods had, and we'll never again see it from Tiger. We'll never see a single tournament dominated like Tiger dominated that U.S. Open." Jamie Squire/ Getty Images

The classic golfer (Tiger Woods) on the classic Old Course at St. Andrews, the site of Woods's 2005 British Open win. Richard Heathcote/Getty Images

Lanny Wadkins goes with Jack Nicklaus as the greatest player of all time. "If he became a great chipper and wedge player earlier, it would have been scary—wait, even scarier—what he could have accomplished." David Cannon/Getty Images

Sam Snead and Ben Hogan combined for 146 PGA Tour victories and 16 majors (while rarely competing at the British Open). Donald Uhrbrock/Getty Images

Lanny Wadkins views Ben Hogan as a workaholic. "He didn't have a game that worked. He worked until he had a game. He set the standard for golfers who practiced and practiced and finally figured it out." Time and Life Pictures/Getty Images

This 1922 photo captures four champions who divvied up 17 British Open championships. From left to right: J. H. Taylor, Harry Vardon, James Braid, and Ted Ray.

Golf commentator Jim Nantz feels that in Bobby Jones's day the best golfers were the amateurs—not the pros. "Forget the mere 52 tournaments—check out his record in *just the majors*. He was totally dominant. You have to take a look at those numbers."

Former professional
wrestler George Zaharias
says, "I got you, Babe." His
wife, Babe Didrikson
Zaharias, was one of the
great athletes of all time,
and if she had been born in
a later era, she would have
concentrated on golf from
a young age. Hulton Archive/
Getty Images

Walter Hagen was the antithesis of Bobby
Jones. He was the furthest thing from
an amateur that one could be. Hagen was
the player who psyched out opponents.
He played anyone, anytime, for money.
Hulton Archive/Getty Images

Byron Nelson, 30 years prior to Johnny Miller, had a peak that surpassed Miller's and almost everyone else's. The classy Nelson is one of the 10 greatest of all time.

Gary Player probably has logged more air miles than any other person in history. His physical fitness and mental outlook have been a marvel for more than 50 years. Bob Gomel/Getty Images

According to Brent Musburger, "The thing that Tiger [Woods] shares with Arnold [Palmer] is that television ratings went up when either of them was in the hunt. Palmer had great sex appeal. He could flick a cigarette and people wanted to watch. He had that unusual, powerful swing." Focus on Sport/Getty Images

Billy Casper's career spanned the same time as Arnold Palmer's, and Buffalo Bill actually won more after 1965. He wasn't *quite* as telegenic, however. Time and Life Pictures/Getty Images

The "Duel in the Sun" at Turnberry in 1977 was a showcase between two of the greatest players in history at the top of their game—Jack Nicklaus and Tom Watson.
Brian Morgan/Getty Images

Lee Trevino, seen here in 1971 when he was named the PGA Tour Player of the Year, was one of the game's greatest characters and competitors. Hulton Archive/Getty Images

In 1985 Kathy Whitworth recorded her 88th, and final, tournament victory. When Annika Sorenstam breaks Whitworth's record, it will have stood for nearly a quarter-century. Hulton Archive/Getty Images

Golf analyst and former LPGA champion Dottie Pepper points out "The best of Annika's game is that she has no weaknesses. She has not one glaring weakness. Put it like this: If Tiger Woods drove the ball with the accuracy and distance that Annika does, they would just hand him every trophy without playing it out." Doug Pensinger/Getty Images

PGA Tour veteran Roger Maltbie feels, "Quite simply, Seve Ballesteros was the most gifted player I've ever seen. What he could do, before technology became a greater issue in the game, was amazing. Seve could make it curve, dance, whatever he wanted. He was a magical shot maker and an unbelievable competitor." Brian Morgan/Getty Images

Ray Floyd won majors in the 1960s, 1970s, and 1980s. He was tough to beat once he got the lead in a tournament.
Rusty Jarrett/Getty Images

It's too bad that three-time Masters champion Jimmy Demaret couldn't give a makeover to three-time U.S. Open champion Hale Irwin.

Hulton Archive/Getty Images

According to *Sports Illustrated* columnist Rick Reilly, Hale Irwin "is one of the greatest long-iron players of all time. He's also one of the most competitive. What a 3-wood player! No one could hit the ball straighter."

Steve Powell/Getty Images

According to Roger Maltbie, Greg Norman was unquestionably the player of the day. "The cloud that hangs over Norman was that he couldn't get it done. Ultimately, the measure of a player's greatness is playing great at the appropriate times."
Stephen Dunn/Getty Images

Phil Mickelson celebrates the shot that put him a tap-in away from his 2005 PGA Championship at Baltusrol.
William Philpott/Getty Images

Vijay Singh of Fiji became the number one player in the world in 2004 for a brief period. When his putter didn't let him down, he was as good as anyone ever. Paul J. Richards/Getty Images

For a three-year period in the 1970s—during which Nicklaus, Palmer, Player, and Trevino were not far from their prime—Johnny Miller was the best player in the world. Focus on Sport/Getty Images

In 1935 Lawson Little repeated as the British Amateur and U.S. Amateur champion, earning what became known as the "Little Slam." Here he receives the trophy from USGA President Prescott Bush.

Hulton Archive/Getty Images

Patty Berg was one of the founders of the LPGA and dominated the Tour in her 30s, winning 44 professional titles between 1948 and 1962.

Hulton Archive/Getty Images

21

SEVE BALLESTEROS
The Arnold Palmer of Europe

Severiano Ballesteros was born on April 9, 1957, in Pedrena, a village in the north of Spain. If he wasn't born to be a great golfer, I don't know who was. His uncle, Ramon Sota, was one of the best European golfers in the 1960s and finished sixth in the 1965 Masters. Uncle Ramon was the pro at the local club when Seve was growing up, and Seve began caddying at a young age. Seve had three brothers who all turned professional.

When he was 10 years old, he took part in his first caddies tournament. Two years later, when Seve was 12, he won the tournament with a score of 79. He turned professional in March of 1974. He was only 17 when he came in fifth in the Italian Open. He was on the accelerated track to glory.

He began making a real name for himself in 1976, when, at the British Open at Royal Birkdale, he led the major for three days. In the first two days, he shot 69 and 69, which included a 33 on the last nine holes of the second round. The next day, with windy and rainy conditions, scores were higher, and Seve shot 73, which left him with a two-stroke lead over 29-year-old American Johnny Miller.

The Spanish teenager lost the lead for good by the sixth green of the final round and dropped five strokes back of Miller after nine holes. But over the next five holes Ballesteros picked up four shots, including an eagle on the 17th. On the 18th hole his chip shot with a 9-iron got him out from between two bunkers. He produced a magnificent shot that rolled four feet past the flag. He holed the putt for a birdie to finish in a tie for second with Jack Nicklaus. Sometimes you win more by losing. Especially when you're 19 years old and in your first major tournament.

The shot epitomized everything that had made Arnold Palmer so wildly popular two decades earlier. Most golfers would have used a sand wedge in Ballesteros's spot. Most would have given in once they lost their lead. Most wouldn't have been so stubborn and would have used a 1-iron instead of a driver off the tee to reduce the inaccurate tee shots.

No one knew at the time that Ballesteros would do for the European Tour what Palmer did for the American one. People were captivated by the teenager from Spain, but no one realized that he had the charisma that galleries would flock to, in stages around the world, and be known, like Arnie, by just one name. Seve went on to become a one-name superstar.

Dave Anderson, *New York Times* columnist: "On talent, Seve was ahead of Faldo and many others. He was the Arnold Palmer of Europe. But he didn't endure."

Roger Maltbie, PGA member and winner of five PGA tournaments: "Quite simply, Seve Ballesteros was the most gifted player I've ever seen. What he could do, before technology became a greater issue in the game, was amazing. Seve could make it curve, dance, whatever he wanted. He was a magical shot maker and an unbelievable competitor. His obvious flaw was that he could not guide the ball straight."

Brent Musburger, ABC and ESPN broadcaster: "At his peak, he compares with Tiger Woods. Seve was the best at recovery shots—the best I ever saw until Tiger came along. Ballesteros was remarkable in his ability to be off in the pines and hit great shots. It's a shame he couldn't keep it going."

Later in 1976 Ballesteros would win his first tournaments—the Dutch Open and the Lancome Trophy, where he made up the four shots Palmer had him by with nine holes to go. How did Ballesteros do it? On the 10th hole he made a long putt to save par. He was in the zone. He caught the 47-year-old Palmer by the 15th hole. He passed him with another birdie on the 17th. He shot birdie-5 on the final nine holes, scored a 31, and beat Palmer by a stroke.

In early 1977 Ballesteros served his country in the military, mainly by giving exhibitions and teaching golf to Air Force officers. He was given leave to play in the Masters. Although he finished well out of the pace, he would show great improvement with each year until he won in 1980.

Ballesteros at His First Four Masters

Year	Age	Score	Place
1977	20	291	33rd
1978	21	287	18th
1979	22	287	12th
1980	23	275	1st

No European golfer had ever won the Masters until Seve did it in 1980. Meanwhile, he was winning regularly on the European Tour. He won three tournaments in 1977 and four in 1978. He did this while making unpredictable shots that amazed everyone, including himself. One of his most famous came in 1978 at the Belfry. He used his driver to get a shot nearly 300 yards, with the wind helping a fade around trees and over water. That shot helped him defeat Nick Faldo.

In 1978 he won his first PGA Tour match in America, the Greater Greensboro Open, with a 66 in the final round. He was the first foreign non-Tour member to win an event in 13 years (when South African Harold Henning won the Texas Open). Ballesteros still wasn't 21 years old. That victory was his fifth in his last five tournaments.

Ballesteros had quite a year in 1978. He won four tournaments, including the Swiss Open, on the European Tour. He won the Japanese Open, the Kenya Open, and the PGA Championship in Greensboro, earning more than $1 million in an age when no one else approached that kind of money. It was no wonder that he turned down the opportunity to play regularly on the U.S. Tour in 1979.

Known as one of the longest hitters in the game, he won the 1979 British Open, at Royal Lytham and St. Annes, becoming the youngest winner of the 1900s. His driving was erratic, to say the least, but his play from the rough was something to behold. He was the first European champion at the British Open since Tony Jacklin had won in 1969. He held off Nicklaus and Ben Crenshaw by two shots apiece.

The very next major was the 1980 Masters Tournament at Augusta. That tournament, played the week of Ballesteros's 23rd birthday, was a blowout. Seve had a 10-stroke lead over the field with nine holes to play and would win by five strokes. This was two majors in a row for Ballesteros. That was ahead of Palmer's pace, Watson's pace, and Player's pace—and anyone else you can think of. Nicklaus won his second major, the 1963 Masters, when he was 23 years and 3 months. Tiger Woods won his second major, the 1999 PGA Championship, at 23 years and 8 months. He became the youngest Masters champion in history, younger than the 1963 Nicklaus.

The next major was at Baltusrol, in Springfield, New Jersey, site of the U.S. Open, where Ballesteros would try to win his third consecutive major. He didn't get off to a great start in the 1980 Open, shooting a 75 in the first round. The next morning his scheduled tee time was 9:45 A.M. He was staying at a suburban hotel just three miles from the golf course. Apparently not knowing his tee time was so early, he showed up late for a ride. Seve arrived seven minutes late and was disqualified.

Perhaps he was pissed that he was 12 strokes back of Nicklaus and Tom Weiskopf after the opening round. Maybe he didn't realize the traffic would mean that he needed to leave earlier than 9:25 for a 9:45 tee time. Maybe he really thought he was teeing off at 10 A.M. In any case, he stormed off.

Ballesteros never did come close to winning the U.S. Open (in 1987 he finished in third place, five shots back of Scott Simpson) or the PGA Championship (finishing as high as fifth and six strokes back). He would use excuses, saying that the PGA Tour, by not allowing him to play more in the United States in the weeks before the majors, put him at a disadvantage.

According to Al Barkow, in his 1989 book, *History of the PGA Tour*, sometime in the late 1960s, it became incumbent on all PGA Tour players to play in at least 15 tournaments a year. At the same time, with the growth of the foreign tours in the 1980s and individual events with large purses in Europe, Australia, and Japan, it became enticing for players to play in these tournaments, especially because the golfers were given appearance fees (not allowed on the American PGA Tour). Foreign players had a special dispensation to play in the United States. They did not need a release from the American tour to play in a date-conflicting tournament in their own country.

In the 1980s the most compelling and most popular player in the world was Spain's Seve Ballesteros. He felt that he should not be required to get a release if he wanted to play *anywhere* on the European Tour because there were not enough tournaments in his home (Spain), so the entire continent of Europe was his "home country."

The PGA went along with Ballesteros's contention, as long as he played the minimum of 15 PGA Tour events. In 1986 Ballesteros didn't play in enough events and was banned from the PGA Tour for a year.

Roger Maltbie: "It was kind of like Terrell Owens, the NFL star with the Eagles, in that Seve made a deal but then wanted more soon after the deal. So he developed kind of a rocky relationship with the U.S. players and was suspended from playing here for a while. But I'll tell you, he was wildly popular in Europe, and if I were paying to see a player from that time, I would have bought a ticket to see Seve."

Ballesteros would play in the majors—he had exemptions from winning the Masters— and played precious few PGA Tour events, aside from the U.S. Open, the Masters, and the PGA Championship. He did play for Europe in the Ryder Cup in every competition from 1979 to 1997, with the exception of 1981. And as much as he feuded with the PGA Tour, he was brilliant most Aprils at the Masters. In the 1980s he had seven years when he placed in the top five.

Ballesteros at the Masters in the 1980s
1980 first place
1982 third place (tie)
1983 first place

1985 second place (tie)
1986 fourth place
1987 second place (tie)
1988 fifth place

In 1982 Seve finished just one stroke back of getting into a play-off with Dan Pohl and Craig Stadler. The final round for Ballesteros in 1983 began with a birdie, an eagle, a par, and a birdie. In 1985 Ballesteros was tied after three days with the German Bernhard Langer, who defeated Seve by two strokes. The 1986 Masters might have been the most frustrating of all. In the final round he led by a stroke when he hit a 4-iron into the water on the 15th hole. Nicklaus then took the lead and won the tournament. In 1987 Seve and Greg Norman lost a three-way sudden death play-off to Larry Mize. In a six-year period, Ballesteros finished four or five shots away from winning four or five Masters.

If you're wondering how this compares with Tiger's and Jack's best 10-year stretches at the Masters, it looks like this:

Nicklaus from 1963 to 1972: four wins, seven top-five finishes
Ballesteros from 1980 to 1989: two wins, seven top-five finishes
Woods from 1996 to 2005: four wins, five top-five finishes

However, Nicklaus and Ballesteros both began their 10-year stretches at the age of 23, later than Woods, who was only 20 at the 1996 Masters.

Woods had the Masters in 1997, where he shot the tournament record 270. Nicklaus shot his then-record 271 in 1965. Ballesteros shot a 275 in 1980, when he had a big lead; he probably could have bettered his score by a stroke or two had he been more seriously challenged.

The point is, Ballesteros was certainly the best at Augusta in the 1980s. Faldo, the same age as Seve, won three Masters, but he didn't win his first until 1989. Those would be the only top-five finishes at Augusta for Faldo.

Ballesteros won at St. Andrews in 1984 for his second British Open. He won at Royal Lytham and St. Annes in 1988 (with a final-round 65) for his third British Open and his fifth major championship. He shot that 65 on a Monday, as gale-force winds forced the tournament to go an extra day. During his record-tying 65, Ballesteros missed only three fairways and three greens.

Seve was only 31 years old when he won his fifth major, but after that he never won another major. His great success as a member of the European Ryder Cup (20–17 overall) came in the 1980s, particularly in 1985, on American soil.

Although he was only 32 when the 1990s began, he didn't win much after that. He took only one European tournament in 1990 and just two in 1991 and 1992. His last win came in 1995. As soon as Faldo became dominant, Seve's game declined to the point that there was no rivalry. When Faldo passed Ballesteros with his sixth major (and third Masters), he earned the right to be ranked ahead of him. Faldo also came closer to winning the other two majors that had escaped both of them.

Ballesteros was never the most popular golfer in the United States, preferring to play elsewhere. The pinnacle of his career came in 1997, when he captained the winning European team played on the Costa del Sol. That Ryder Cup is remembered by many as "Seve's Ryder Cup."

Who's Better, Who's Best
Seve Ballesteros, Nick Faldo, or Bernhard Langer?

1. Faldo (six majors)
2. Ballesteros (five majors)
3. Langer (two majors)

Ballesteros was the best golfer Spain ever produced, and Langer was the best German golfer. All three had lots of European Tour victories (Langer had the fewest). Faldo didn't have as many European Tour victories as Ballesteros and wasn't nearly as exciting a player. But Nick won a few more PGA tournaments and a few more Ryder Cup matches, and he had more top-5 and top-10 finishes at the four major championships. They were the same age, yet Faldo won his final major eight years after Ballesteros won his final one. It's very close, as one can tell by their overall rankings.

A Better Analogy
Seve Ballesteros and Gabriela Sabatini The world was introduced to Seve when he was a teenager. In 1976, at the age of 19, he finished second at the British Open, one of the four Grand Slam events.

The world was introduced to Gabriela Sabatini in 1985, when she became the youngest-ever player (at 15 years and 3 weeks old) to reach the semifinals at the French Open (a Grand Slam tournament).

Three years after his strong British Open debut, Seve broke through and won the championship. Three years after her early semifinal appearance at the French Open, Gaby reached her first Grand Slam singles final at the U.S. Open. In 1990 Sabatini defeated Steffi Graf in the U.S. Open.

Two European players kept each from reaching the number one ranking in the world. In Gaby's case it was Graf and Monica Seles. In Seve's case it was the European Faldo and the Aussie Norman who kept him from the world number one ranking. After winning five tournaments in 1992, Sabatini had a 29-month period in which she failed to win any titles. She retired from tennis in 1996.

Sabatini, like Ballesteros, had worldwide fame and popularity, and they were both good-looking and had all the shots. Both looked like they would dominate their sport for years. Instead they were both finished at a very early age. Maybe they burned out from playing so much and so competitively in their teen years.

22

RAY FLOYD
The Stare Master

Born at Fort Bragg in Fayetteville, North Carolina, the son of a career Army man, Ray Floyd is known for many things. He is known for winning the PGA Championship twice. He is known for winning the Masters in record-tying fashion. He is known for winning the U.S. Open. He is remembered as a man who stared down his opposition with a steely-eyed glare that intimidated them. Call him the Stare Master.

Floyd learned the game of golf from his father, who was his first teacher. Ray, an outstanding baseball player, was forced to choose between sports by his high school coach. Floyd put the bats down.

At the age of 17, Ray won the 1960 International Jaycee Junior Championship. He joined the PGA Tour three years later, in 1963. For the first four months he spent playing on the Tour, he didn't earn a single dollar.

That changed in March, in the St. Petersburg Open, when he beat Dave Marr by one stroke and earned his first victory, as well as his first golf paycheck (for $3,500). At 20 years, 6 months, and 13 days, Floyd was the youngest winner of a PGA Tour event since Horton Smith in 1928. No one younger has won a tournament since Floyd's 1963 victory (Phil Mickelson was 15 days older than Floyd when he won a 1991 PGA tournament as an amateur).

That didn't exactly start a Floyd stampede through the PGA Tour, however. In his first six years on the Tour, he entered 119 tournaments and won exactly one besides the 1963 St. Petersburg tourney. In those six years (1963–68) he finished in the top 10 just 19 times and finished out of the top 100 a hundred times. He averaged less than $30,000 per year.

In 1964 he played the final two rounds of the U.S. Open with Ken Venturi, who somehow overcame heat exhaustion to win at Congressional, in Bethesda, Maryland. Floyd won the 1965 St. Paul Open, for which he earned $20,000 of the $36,000 he made that year.

In the late 1960s, Floyd's lack of success was blamed on women and too much drinking. "I'm single. Sometimes I take girls out. I like to go to a nice place. If it's a nice place, you usually find liquor around."

How well known was his playboy reputation? When he won the biggest tournament of his career—the 1969 PGA Championship in Dayton, Ohio—the PGA president needled Floyd about it during the presentation ceremony. Floyd was presented with a medal for winning and told not to give it to "one of those people in your little black book."

Floyd would admit that he spent five years on tour without goals or taking golf as seriously as he perhaps should have. He played golf with Rat Pack king Dean Martin. The Hollywood crowd loved him. Sometimes his game even made as many headlines as his curly hair or the women draped on his arm.

In 1969, at the PGA Championships, his mind was on golf, as he won his first major championship. In the minds of the public, however, the action on the field took a backseat to the political action going on around. Demonstrators forced the tournament to conclude under heavy police protection. ABC opened its telecast with films of fighting on the 10th green. There was rioting because of the presence of South African Gary Player. Floyd was paired with Player. Player would finish one stroke behind Floyd.

Floyd won two other times in 1969 and made more than $100,000 in a year for the first time. After the 1969 PGA Championship, Floyd went nearly six years without a tournament victory, until the 1975 Kemper Open.

In the early 1970s, Floyd attempted to change his image. The man who helped turn his golf career around was Jack Grout. Grout was the man who taught Nicklaus how to play. Grout worked with Floyd for eight months, helping him to retool his game and straighten out his swing.

Grout worked endlessly with Floyd but wouldn't accept any money from his friend. Also in the early 1970s, Floyd got married. He and his wife, Maria, had two sons, born in 1974 and 1976, and then a daughter a few years after that. Suddenly, he was a family man.

The victories started coming in regularly. He won the 1975 Kemper Open, his first win since 1969 and only his sixth win in 12 years. So began a decade that vaulted Floyd into the golfing elite.

The 33-year-old Floyd played the 1976 Masters about as well as anyone in history, winning by eight strokes. Over the first three days, he played 12 par-5 holes, birdieing 11 of them and eagling the other. He had an eight-stroke lead after 54 holes. His 70 on the final day of the tournament gave him a record-tying 271. (Nicklaus had shot 271 in 1965.) In the 29 years since Floyd's 271, it has been bettered only once. (Woods shot his 270 in 1997.) Only Woods (by 12 strokes in 1997) and Nicklaus (by 9 strokes in 1965) won the Masters by a bigger margin.

Floyd loved playing from ahead and won some of his biggest tournaments that way. In 1982 Floyd opened the PGA Championship at Southern Hills Country Club in Tulsa with a 7-under par 63 and led wire to wire. He shot 63–69–68–72 to hold off Lanny Wadkins by three strokes. The 39-year-old Floyd set the PGA Championship record for 18 holes (63, since tied), 36 holes (132, since broken), and 54 holes (200, since broken). Floyd's five-stroke lead in the 1982 PGA Championship after 54 holes tied his own 1969 PGA Championship record (which had also been tied by Tom Watson in 1978) for the largest 54-hole lead.

Floyd now had three majors: one in the '60s, one in the '70s, and one in the '80s. He still hadn't done anything in a U.S. Open, however. In his first 21 U.S. Opens, he had not finished higher than his fourth-place finish in 1971, at Merion. That changed in 1986. One round of golf—the final round of the 1986 Open at Shinnecock Hills—elevated Floyd over Greg Norman in this book.

Norman was at the height of his powers in June of 1986. He hadn't won the Masters in April, because Nicklaus shot a 65 in the final round to nip him by a stroke. Norman, the man they call the Shark, led the U.S. Open after 54 holes as well. Once again, however, Norman let one get away. He shot a final-round 75, compared with Floyd's 66. Floyd had an error-free round, getting four birdies and no bogeys.

If Norman had held on at Shinnecock Hills, he would have finished with three majors, as would have Floyd. But Floyd's fourth, coming at the age of 43 and augmented by a number of Champions Tour victories, moved Floyd ahead of Norman in the overall rankings.

It was hard for anyone to get super–charged up about Floyd's victory, however. The sports world was still in awe of a 46-year-old winning an 18th major in April. Two months later, a 43-year-old man winning his fourth major didn't seem as inspiring.

If one round of golf vaulted Floyd over Norman, then one play-off hole separated Floyd from Nick Faldo. Faldo and Floyd finished in a tie for first place at the 1990 Masters. Faldo won the green jacket by defeating Floyd on the second hole in sudden death. If Floyd had won that hole, he would have finished with five majors, the same as Faldo. A second Masters—with the second one coming at the age of 47—would have been enough to put Ray ahead of Nick.

Floyd had other close finishes at the majors. In 1992 he missed a couple of shots, allowing Fred Couples to defeat him by two strokes at the Masters. In 1978, at St. Andrews, Floyd finished two shots back of Nicklaus. Had he won, this would have given Floyd a career Grand Slam and a fifth major.

As it stands, Floyd won four majors. Only 18 men in the history of golf have topped that. The others with four majors are all from much earlier eras (Willie Park Sr., Willie Anderson, Tom Morris Sr., Tom Morris Jr., Jim Barnes, Bobby Locke). Floyd faced deeper fields and tougher competition than those earlier stars who had four majors.

In 1992, nearing the age of 50, Floyd won the Doral-Ryder Open. He became the sixth oldest to ever win a PGA Tour event. Remember, this is the same man who won a tournament in 1963, as one of the youngest ever.

He finished with 22 PGA tournament victories across as many seasons. He has 15 more Seniors titles. And one stare, which has worked across more than 40 years of competitive golf.

His beloved Chicago Cubs haven't made it to the World Series since he was three years old. Floyd, an old friend of the late Leo Durocher, worked out with the Cubs late in the summer of 1969, when they had an 8$\frac{1}{2}$-game lead over the New York Mets. Durocher should have activated the young Ray Floyd. He never would have let a big lead dissipate down the stretch.

Who's Better, Who's Best
Ray Floyd or Julius Boros?

There isn't much that separates the 13 place rankings between Floyd and Julius Boros. Boros won his first major at the age of 32, winning the 1952 U.S. Open over Ben Hogan. He then went 11 years without winning another major. Boros became a better golfer as he got older.

	Julius Boros	Ray Floyd
Wins on Tour	18	22
Majors	3	4
Top-five finishes at majors	16	13

Boros won majors at the ages of 43 and 48. Floyd won a major at 43 as well. Boros finished seventh at the 1973 U.S. Open (at the age of 53), and Floyd finished seventh at the 1992 U.S. Open (at the age of 50).

Floyd was just a little better than Boros at comparable points in their careers. Boros entered the British Open only once (in 1966) and won a greater percentage of the major championships that he entered (3–58, compared to Floyd's 4–97). That's not enough to tip the scales toward Boros, however. He had only one Masters Tournament where he finished in the top three. That was 1963, when he was third, two strokes back of Jack Nicklaus. Boros was otherwise never a factor at Augusta. Plus, Boros had three majors and was runner-up in just one other major (the 1956 U.S. Open), while Floyd won four majors and was runner-up in five others. Floyd finished two strokes back of Fred Couples, finishing 11-under par. He lost a sudden-death play-off to Nick Faldo at the 1990 Masters.

Boros is deserving of his ranking, but he wasn't the golfer that Ray Floyd was.

Field-of-Dreams Baseball Team Made Up of Legendary Golfers

SS Ben Hogan	The Wee Ice Mon leads off in the mode of Pete Rose.
2B Gene Sarazen	The Squire capably moves runners along and plays good defense as well.
3B Tom Watson	Like George Brett, he comes through in the biggest at-bats.
RF Sam Snead	He excels in this sport, where he doesn't play his long fouls.
1B Ray Floyd	This 6'2" 200-pound slugger worked out with the Cubs in the 1960s.
LF Arnold Palmer	His booming bat is a valuable commodity on this team.
C Billy Casper	He has the body to catch, as well as the management skills to call a game.
DH Walter Hagen	The Haig, a good athlete, was offered a contract with the Phillies.
CF Tommy Armour	There is no way he wouldn't have taught himself to be a good hitter.
P Jack Nicklaus	His long career, like Roger Clemens's, got better with age.
P Phil Mickelson	He would be starting Game 2 of the World Series, after Jack. He probably wouldn't be a great closer, though. (A few years ago, he gave baseball a serious shot, trying out with the minor-league Toledo Mud Hens as a right-handed pitcher.)
P Johnny Miller	You know there would be days when he would be untouchable, and other days where he would be wild.
RP Tiger Woods	He is the closer who comes in when the game is on the line.

This mythical baseball team would have done all right. Let's face it, golf and baseball have many transferable skills. Although the power on this team would have been supplied by Snead, Floyd, and Casper, you know that in the late innings of a seventh game it would be an unlikely hero—perhaps the little man Sarazen—who would come up with the big hit, the "shot heard around the world." The scrappy Lanny Wadkins would fill in for the aging Sarazen or Hogan on occasion.

23

PHIL MICKELSON
Lefty

T he toughest players to rank in any sport are the ones in midcareer. If I had written a book ranking golfers in 1976 instead of 2006, I would have wrestled with the ranking of Johnny Miller in the middle of his career. Miller was the best player behind a legend and young enough and talented enough to win a lot more. Even if he wasn't going to break Nicklaus's records, he was certainly going to win more than Casper and Trevino had. Would I have ranked Miller in the top 10 of all time in 1976, being that he was 11th on the all-time money list and winning tournaments by 14 strokes and in contention at the majors every year? Yes, I would have. Did Miller win much after 1976? Nope.

I asked PGA Tour veteran Roger Maltbie how he would rank Phil Mickelson compared with his contemporaries aside from Tiger. He ranks Ernie Els and Vijay Singh ahead of Mickelson. I rank Mickelson ahead and, using a casino term, am betting on the come that Mickelson will roll more major tournament victories before he eventually craps out.

Let me make my case for this great player in midcareer. I have to look into the crystal ball. What I want to try and do is project Mickelson to the end of his career. His four tournament victories in 2005 pushed his career total to 27.

Phil Mickelson Tournament Wins
Wins in his 20s (1990–June 15, 2000): 16 (1.6 wins per year)
Wins in his 30s (June 16, 2000–2005): 11 (2.0 wins per year)

He had three early wins in 2000 while still in his 20s and one after his 30th birthday. He had two wins in 2001, two more in 2002, none in 2003, two in 2004, and four in 2005.

If you make a projection based on his results from the last six years, he could get another 9 to 10 victories by the 2010 U.S. Open—around his 40th birthday. That brings him to 37 or so wins total. He's averaged three wins a year in the last two calendar years. Give him that average for the next five years. That puts him at 42 wins by the end of 2010.

Once Mickelson turns 40, it's a different ballgame. There have only been two male golfers who have won more than 10 tournaments after their 40th birthdays. Those two are Sam Snead and Vijay Singh.

Snead had a need for money. When he was 35 years old, he finished second at the U.S. Open and won $1,500. When Mickelson finished second at the U.S. Open at the age of 34, he won $675,000. Snead was literally hungrier to win tournaments in his late 30s and 40s than Mickelson will ever be.

And Singh didn't spend his youth winning college championships and dating cheer-leaders and making millions of dollars in his 20s. Instead, he was banished to the out-skirts of civilization, where he developed a craving to get back and make up for lost time. Singh has the personality and the Hogan-like practice routine to win deep into his 40s. I'm not sure Mickelson—who, in 2005, added to his record 13th consecutive year with $500,000 in earnings—will have the same drive.

By the end of 2005 Mickelson had made more than $35 million, more than anyone but Woods and Singh. Mickelson will surpass Singh in the next year or two. He's not playing the history books like Woods or playing with a chip on his shoulder like Singh. Mickelson has compared himself frequently with Hogan, who didn't win his first major until he was 34. Fine, but then realize this: Hogan won only six tournaments in his 40s.

So I'm not going to project anything more than five to seven more wins after Mick-elson turns 40. And I'm figuring on a total of 46 to 48 wins.

He has won two majors in two years and has a briefcase full of top-10 finishes at the majors. I am going to project three more majors by the end of 2011. My guess is that he'll wind up with five majors and 48 wins. Remember, even the great Jack Nicklaus didn't win many after his 35th birthday. Jack was born in 1940 and won his 14th at the 1975 PGA Championship. He won four more. It's hard to see Mickelson winning more than that.

That would still place him in the general foursome of Billy Casper (51 wins, 3 majors), Tom Watson (39 wins, 8 majors), and Gene Sarazen (39 wins, 7 majors). Casper, of course, rarely played all four majors like Mickelson does. My projection then puts Mick-elson (who was not ranked by *Golf Magazine* in 2000 in the top 50) at 23rd best at the end of 2005 and probably ranked 15th or so when he's all done.

What helps Mickelson is an amateur career that few golfers can put on their résumé. He won three NCAA Championships, a U.S. Amateur title, and an event on the PGA Tour as an amateur when he was only 20 years, 6 months, and 28 days old.

He started out his pro career with Nicklaus-like expectations. Tiger also won like crazy as an amateur. Nicklaus won the U.S. Amateur in 1961 and then won the U.S. Open in 1962. Woods won the U.S. Amateur in 1996 and then won the Masters in 1997. Mickelson won the U.S. Amateur in 1990 and then won his first major in 2004. Phil Mickelson won his first major championship at the age of 33 years, 9 months, and 26 days. It came on his 47th attempt at a major.

Along the way, he became the "people's choice." Woods became almost so good that the public needed someone to (a) pose competition to him and (b) connect with on a personal level. Mickelson was not physically intimidating. He signed autographs by the score. He loved pro football, same as most fans. He even made preseason bets on the 2000 Baltimore Ravens to win the Super Bowl (which they did) and the 2001 Arizona Diamondbacks to win the World Series (which they did).

Mickelson, a sports historian, put his money on teams that played great defense. But in his first 46 majors, he was strictly an offensive machine, going for broke and taking risks, which cut down his chances.

He was popular in the New York area, where he first made fans at the 2002 U.S. Open in Long Island. He couldn't defeat the great Tiger Woods, but he made 10 birdies in the final 30 holes to put a scare in him. Really, that's all anyone could ask. Mickelson has had so many of these "close, but no cigar" tournaments. Consider the following:

- **1999 U.S. Open:** Mickelson had a one-shot lead over Payne Stewart, with three holes to play at Pinehurst No. 2. Mickelson was also ready to leave the tournament at any moment if his wife, Amy, had gone into labor. Mickelson bogeyed 16. Stewart birdied 17. Stewart made a long, 15-foot par putt to win the Open. Mickelson became a father the next day. Stewart would die in a plane crash a few months later.
- **2001 PGA Championship:** Mickelson finished one stroke back of David Toms. Toms hit a 5-wood tee shot 243 yards into the hole for an ace on the par-three 15th at the Atlanta Athletic Club. Mickelson made a birdie chip from 45 feet on the same hole. They came to 18 tied. Toms made a 12-foot putt. Mickelson just missed a 25-foot putt that would have sent the tournament into a play-off.
- **2002 U.S. Open:** Mickelson finished three shots back of Woods.
- **2004 U.S. Open:** Mickelson finished two shots back of Retief Goosen.
- **2001 Masters:** Mickelson finished third, three shots back of winner Woods and one back of David Duval. It's Tiger's world.
- **2002 Masters:** Mickelson finished third, four shots back of winner Woods and one back of Goosen.
- **2003 Masters:** Mickelson finished third, two shots back of Mike Weir and Len Mattiace.

Being tagged as the best player never to win a major was put to rest at the 2004 Masters, when Mickelson birdied five of the last seven holes and outlasted Els. Mickelson shot a 31 on the final nine holes at Augusta to win his first major.

Mickelson was born in San Diego, and at the age of 18 months, he was swinging a cut-down golf club, mirroring his father in the backyard. The right-handed Mickelson became a left-handed golfer by looking at his father instead of standing behind him.

There are only a handful of left-handed golfers who have ever won a tournament on the PGA Tour. Mickelson has won 27. The next closest is Weir, who has won seven. Besides Mickelson, only Weir has won a major golfing from the left side.

Left-handedness is such an advantage in baseball and tennis but apparently not in golf. Rod Laver was the greatest lefty tennis player and maybe the best ever, period. Jimmy Connors, John McEnroe, and Martina Navratilova are also left-handed, as well as being among the top-10 players of all time. Monica Seles needed help from her right side for her powerful two-handed backhands, but she was a lefty. So were Roscoe Tanner, Goran Ivanisevic, and Tony Roche. Most baseball batting champions are left-handed. Some of the greatest pitchers in history were left-handed (Lefty Grove, Sandy Koufax, Randy Johnson, Warren Spahn, Steve Carlton, and Whitey Ford, to name a few). While being a southpaw is important in some sports it isn't in golf, where players compete against the course. They can't affect other players' shots.

When the man they call Lefty won his second major, the 2005 PGA Championship, he won the tournament with a beautiful chip shot from the deep rough to two feet away for a tap-in. When asked about the shot in the press conferences following, Mickelson said, "I tried to remember some of the shots I hit as a kid in my backyard." It paid to have a dad like Phil's, who built a putting green complete with a bunker in the backyard.

The best thing about Mickelson's game is that he is absolutely fearless. Of course, that has probably been his downfall at several of the close losses. He hits the ball as far as anyone and has a beautiful touch around the greens. He is a streaky putter, at times one of the very best.

In 2003 Mickelson didn't win a tournament. But he won six in the next two years, including his first two majors. Here's a big reason why:

Year	Driving Distance	Rank	Greens in Regulation
2003	306.0 yards	3rd	64.8% 107th
2004	295.4 yards	30th	69.5% 10th
2005	300.0 yards	26th	66.9% 46th

Sometimes it's best not to hit the ball as far as you can.

Mickelson really has had a storybook life. His biggest disappointments in golf have been in dealing with a bunch of majors that he contended in but didn't win. He's really a sensational player. He's playing in an era where 50 to 60 golfers could win on any given week. Aside from Woods, Els, and Singh, the 2005 leading golfers include a strong list, among them Toms, Goosen, Jim Furyk, Chris DiMarco, and Bart Bryant. That wasn't the case in other eras, when Byron Nelson played, for example. Mickelson would be better appreciated in another era, away from the large shadow that Tiger casts.

Tiger's goals have all been about major championships. Mickelson has played second best to him for nearly a decade. It's not like Mickelson played Dan Marino to Tiger's Joe Montana. Tiger had all the regular-season touchdown passes and yards *and* the Super Bowls. Mickelson has everything else life has to offer and gobbles up the tournaments—now, even the majors—that Tiger doesn't. Will he make that next leap in the next five years, to get into the top 15 or 20 of all time?

Who's Better, Who's Best
Phil Mickelson or Johnny Miller?

I started the chapter by saying how difficult it would have been to rank Miller in midcareer and pointed out the obvious pitfalls in doing so. Mickelson has never approached the peak of Miller's 1974 season. He has never won as many as five tournaments in a year. He's not a racecar, but a fuel-efficient vehicle that lasts a long time.

I'm partial to players that dominate tournaments, years, and eras. That isn't Mickelson. Yet he has performed well early in his career as an amateur, in the middle of his career (winning majors in his mid-30s), and needs only to add a third act to finish in the top 20 of all time. He's better than Miller and better than contemporaries Retief Goosen, Ernie Els, and Vijay Singh as well.

24

GREG NORMAN
Shark Tales

Greg Norman was born in Queensland, Australia, on February 10, 1955. If you look at him in his early 50s, you can understand how he was a top athlete as a teenager. He looks like the Crocodile Dundee movie character that can take on the muggers and anyone else. Norman was a rugby player and played Australian Rules football. He was brought up by a stay-at-home mother who was an excellent golfer herself and a father who was an engineer.

Norman took up golf at the age of 15, when he caddied for his mother and borrowed her clubs following the round. Within two years he was a scratch golfer. His first ambition was to become a pilot in the Australian Air Force, but golf proved a nice fallback. Six years after taking up the game, he turned pro. It took just four tournaments before he recorded his first title (the 1976 West Lakes Classic, in Australia). It would be the first of 68 international victories and 88 overall (including 20 on the PGA Tour). But Greg Norman is an athlete who will forever be known more for his failures than for his incredible success.

Norman was labeled the "Great White Shark" by a newspaper reporter during the 1981 Masters Tournament, his first Masters. The real great white shark is an apex predator, meaning it is at the top of the food chain and has no natural predators. It must have seemed like there could be no predator golfer who had the capability to victimize or destroy Norman's golf abilities. One reason is that this guy just drove the ball better than anyone else. Before technology made a big hitter out of everybody on the Tour, there wasn't anyone who could drive the ball like Norman. In 1990, when the average driving distance on the PGA Tour was 262 yards, Norman's average was 282 yards. (For comparison, Tiger Woods—another big driver—averaged 302 yards in 2004, but the PGA Tour average was 287 yards. Tiger was only 15 yards better than average, not 20 as Norman was.)

In 1980 the 25-year-old Norman won six international tournaments, including the Australian Open, the French Open, and the Scandinavian Open. He finished fourth in his first trip to Augusta in 1981 and followed that up with a fourth-place finish at the

1981 PGA Championship. He had plenty of time, it seemed, to make his haul of major championships.

He joined the PGA Tour in 1983 at the age of 26. At the 1984 U.S. Open, he finished second at Winged Foot when he merely made par on the 72nd hole to tie Fuzzy Zoeller, who defeated him in an 18-hole play-off. There would be time.

At the 1986 Masters, on the final hole, Norman make bogey after his approach shot went into the stands. Of course, he birdied four consecutive holes before the 18th. That one was decided by fate anyway. Pretty much everyone was rooting for Jack Nicklaus to win that tournament. No one wanted to see 46-year-old Nicklaus shoot a 65 on the last great day of his career and have him walk away with another runner-up finish. The crowd at Augusta was—no offense, Norman—almost unanimous in wanting Nicklaus to win that day.

One of the great collapses of all time came in Shinnecock Hills, in Southampton, New York, site of the 1986 U.S. Open. Norman led after 54 holes. On the final day, however, he shot 75 while Ray Floyd, Chip Beck, and Lanny Wadkins all shot 65. Floyd won the Open.

Many great golfers have to shed the image of not being able to win the big one. Norman won a major, his first, at Turnberry, the site of the 1986 British Open. The jinx was over, or at least appeared to be.

Later that summer, at the PGA Championship at Inverness Club in Toledo, Ohio, Norman shot 65–68–69 in the first three rounds to lead after 54 holes. Bob Tway became the first player in modern history to win the PGA Championship with a birdie on the 72nd hole when he holed a seemingly impossible shot from a greenside bunker.

You want to talk about being *this close* to a Grand Slam that, as of this writing, even Tiger and Jack never reached? In the 1986 calendar year, Norman led all four majors after the third round of each.

Norman's next major was the 1987 Masters Tournament. It seems hard to believe, but someone named Larry Mize chipped in from 140 feet to beat him on the second hole of sudden death.

In between these majors, Norman's career was skyrocketing. He was the number one player in the world for 62 consecutive weeks, from September 14, 1986, to November 15, 1987. Two weeks later he was back on top for another 48 consecutive weeks. A few months later he was number one in the world for 54 more weeks.

But except for his second and final British Open in 1993, Norman couldn't win a major. Worse, he was so close on so many occasions. The 1993 PGA Championship saw Norman tied with Paul Azinger after 72 holes. On the second play-off hole, Norman's par attempt from four feet above the hole rimmed in and out of the hole.

At the 1996 Masters he took a lead into the final round of a major and lost for the sixth time. It's hard to believe that a golfer could lose majors to incredible shots by Tway and Mize—but at least it wasn't because Norman himself choked under the pressure. At the 1996 Masters he let a big one slip away for the worst defeat of his career.

Norman took a six-stroke lead into the final round and had a four-stroke lead after seven holes. It was the biggest collapse in a major championship. Although Nick Faldo shot a 69, it wasn't some record-breaking performance. Faldo, for the most part, plodded along with pars. Norman made bogeys and shot 78 on the day. Faldo won by five strokes after trailing by six to start the round.

When the match ended, Faldo didn't know what to say, telling Norman, "I just want to give you a hug." Amazingly, so did everyone else. Losing had humanized the Shark. Although he made more than $10 million a year, he was seen as a sympathetic figure to everyone. He was the underdog that his opponents wished well. He didn't hide from reporters. He didn't go off in an angry tirade. He didn't cry. Norman was old school. He was beaten, pure and simple, and handled his losses the way older athletes like baseball's Ted Williams could admire.

The next year, Norman—willing to try anything—sat down with motivational speaker Anthony Robbins. What happened? Norman failed to make the cut at the Masters, and Robbins lost all confidence in his motivational skills (only kidding).

Why couldn't Norman seal the deal and finish some of these major championships? The only other golfer who had so many near misses was Nicklaus, who finished second in 19 majors—but, of course, he won 18. (Compare this to Tiger, who has never lost a major when leading after 36 holes.)

Tom Weiskopf was a lower-case Norman, someone who won the British Open once but should have had several more major championships. Weiskopf finished second at the Masters in 1969 (one shot back of George Archer), 1972 (three shots back of Nicklaus), 1974 (two shots back of Gary Player), and 1975 (one shot back of Nicklaus).

Norman, however, became the poster boy for excruciating losses. He never won the Masters Tournament, having finished one stroke behind the winner in three different years. He's the only person to lose all four majors in a play-off. He's finished in second place in eight different majors.

Greg Norman—Second-Place Finishes in Majors

1984 U.S. Open (in a play-off)
1986 Masters
1986 PGA Championship
1987 Masters (in a play-off)

1989 British Open (in a play-off)
1993 PGA Championship (in a play-off)
1995 U.S. Open
1996 Masters

So he never won the Masters, U.S. Open, or PGA Championship. In 1996, however, he became the first to surpass $10 million in career earnings. He won three Vardon Trophies for lowest scoring average. He spent 331 weeks as the number one player in the world.

Norman was one of the greatest players of all time. He had longevity (he was fourth at the 1981 Masters and third 18 years later, at the 1999 Masters). He won only those two British Opens, but he did have eight top-five finishes at the Masters.

Lanny Wadkins, CBS golf analyst and PGA pro: "Greg Norman is not a top-20 player. He had a lot of wins and two majors. But he'll be remembered more for his failures. Most of his big successes are overseas—he was a world player before it became fashionable."

Obviously, if Norman had won a few of those majors in which he held a late lead, he would be ranked as high as one of the top 15 golfers of all time. Some of his friends speculated that the well-rounded Norman didn't have the killer instinct needed. If he didn't have that killer instinct to close out opponents like Woods and Ben Hogan and (in another sport) Michael Jordan and Larry Bird, then it would help explain how Norman managed to cope with those toughest of defeats.

Who's Better, Who's Best
Greg Norman or Nick Faldo?

Nick Faldo was the greatest player to come out of Europe since Harry Vardon. He won 42 professional tournaments, including the six majors (three British, three Masters). Greg Norman is the best player ever from Australia. He had more career victories than Faldo: 88 (20 on the PGA Tour and 68 international). And during his career Norman did hold the number one world ranking for 331 weeks. They played in the same era, often against each other for all the marbles. Fellow pro Johnny Miller has called Norman the most compelling golfer of the last 40 years, while he says that Faldo was not particularly inspiring to watch, explaining, "His game was grinding, inexorable, and utterly devoid of dash." But Miller also wrote that given one guy to play a head-to-head match on a tough course for all the marbles, he would take Faldo.

Faldo was the Hogan of his time—someone who worked and worked on his game. Norman's failures at the Masters, meanwhile, mirror Snead's failures at the U.S. Open. Norman was one of the longest hitters on the Tour at a time when not everyone was able to drive the ball the great distances. In the 1996 Masters the Australian blew a six-stroke lead. It was Faldo who took away the green jacket, which was within Norman's grasp. Faldo did shoot a 67 and put the pressure on Norman. Under the pressure of the majors, Faldo was clearly superior. But Norman had his moments. In the 1993 British Open at Royal St. George's, it was Norman who trailed by one stroke entering the final 18 holes, and it was Norman who closed with a 64 to win the major over Faldo. Those moments, however, were rare. Faldo gets the pick over Norman.

A Better Analogy

Greg Norman and Pat Day At the age of 52 the great jockey Pat Day retired in August of 2005 after 32 years. He won four Eclipse Awards (in 1984, 1986, 1987, and 1991) as the nation's best jockey and retired as thoroughbred racing's career money leader, having won purses totaling $297,941,912. His 8,803 career wins (fourth on the all-time list) include his share of Triple Crown races. He won the Preakness Stakes five times and the Belmont Stakes three times, and he recorded 12 Breeders' Cup wins. Day rode 22 times in the Kentucky Derby—more than anyone except Bill Shoemaker—and won only in 1992, aboard long-shot Lil E. Tee.

Here's why Day is one of the few people who know what Norman went through. Before he won his lone Kentucky Derby, Day finished second at the biggest horse race in America for three straight years. In 1988 he was aboard Forty Niner. In 1989 he rode favorite Easy Goer. And in 1990 he finished second on Summer Squall. Day, by virtue of his lone Derby win in '92, answered most of his critics. Norman, by failing to win the Masters, has to live with questions and second-guesses about his performance. Day was 1–22 at the Kentucky Derby, and Norman was 0–22 at the Masters. Day and Norman were two of the best athletes in their respective sports, but Day missed several Derbys by a precious few seconds and Norman missed some green jackets by a few inches.

25

JIM BARNES
The Forgotten Champion

T he PGA Championship is one of the four major championships in golf and dates back to 1916, well before the Masters. Yet the man who won the first PGA Championship—heck, he won the first two ever played—is barely remembered, even among golf fans. Jim Barnes may have won the first four PGA Championships had the tournament been played in 1917 or 1918 (it was canceled due to World War I).

He was a great golf champion whose accomplishments rank him a place still among the top 25 ever in his sport. He won all the majors that existed in his day and finished close in the ones that he didn't win. This golfer became quite the instructor—giving lessons and hanging out with presidents, the Duke of Windsor, Perry Como, John D. Rockefeller, and Babe Ruth, among others. A Baseball Hall of Fame member was his caddie for his U.S. Open victory in 1921.

Why doesn't anyone remember and celebrate "Long Jim" Barnes? There are several reasons, including the time he lived in, the fact he played in the shadow of Walter Hagen, and his quiet, reserved personality. When he is remembered, it's usually for a boastful quote on the order of "I always do better after lunch."

It seems that sports began in this country in the mid-1920s. The nation (finally) had leisure time to follow professional sports. The inventors had made communication easier with the advent of radio. There were larger-than-life stars in nearly every sport—think of Babe Ruth, Red Grange, Jack Dempsey, and Walter Hagen. It was the golden age of sports, and these guys were show-stealing heroes. Prior to the 1920s there weren't a lot of celebrities. The few sports celebrities prior to the '20s (like Harry Vardon) needed to seek out fame.

Barnes's lack of ink aside, he deserves to be remembered as one of the greatest ever. *Golf Digest* named their 50 Greatest Golfers of All Time in July of 2000 and ranked Barnes number 39. This ranking was way too low. Barnes should be ahead of international players like Peter Thomson and Bobby Locke, and he certainly should be ahead of Americans Gene Littler and Payne Stewart, who didn't dominate their eras. They were all great, but they don't deserve to be ahead of Barnes.

The 6'4" Barnes (hence, Long Jim Barnes, or Big Jim Barnes) won the British Open in 1925 (and finished seven times among the top eight). He won three Western Opens (considered a major tournament at the time). He won the U.S. Open in 1921. And he won the PGA Championship in 1916 and 1919—the first two times the championship was held.

Unless your name is Billy Casper or Kathy Whitworth or Greg Norman and you compensate for a lack of majors with volume, volume, volume, you better win the major championships in your era to earn a spot in the top 25 of all time. It's not like Barnes competed in the British Opens of the 1860s, when the fields were filled with just a dozen men, most of them local residents. He played against the Sarazens and Hagens and other professionals.

Just when fame was becoming a marketable commodity, Barnes left the scene. By 1925 the inventors had done their job, and the public was "inventing" celebrities. Barnes's prime ended in 1921, and he won only a handful of times after that.

He didn't win the Masters because it wasn't played until he was 47 years old. He didn't win the PGA Championship prior to 1916 for a simple reason: it wasn't played before then. Barnes finished second to Hagen in the PGA Championships in 1921 and 1924. He finished second in the British Open in 1922. Those are awesome achievements.

In researching a book on the greatest golfers of all time, I realized that I had to learn about Barnes. Besides his record, what did anyone really know about him? He was tall, right-handed, and slim. He was known for always golfing with a stalk of clover in his mouth. It became his good-luck charm.

Barnes was born in 1887 in Cornwall, England. He was a caddie as a youngster and immigrated to the United States in 1906. He had a job lined up as a greenskeeper in San Francisco, but the big earthquake destroyed the country club and his job prospects. He took a job as a club pro in Spokane and Tacoma, Washington. Club pros were actually encouraged in those days to take time off and enter prestigious tournaments, as it would give status to their club. By 1913 Barnes had won several minor tournaments and was on his way.

You want to talk about lurking in the shadows? Barnes finished in a tie for fourth at the 1913 U.S. Open in the "Greatest Game Ever Played." Everyone knows that local caddie Francis Ouimet defeated the great English champions Harry Vardon and Ted Ray. Even more disheartening for Barnes, the flamboyant Hagen showed up on the scene and tied Barnes for fourth place in that '13 Open.

Clover Jim broke through in the majors in 1914, when he won the Western Open. In 1916 he won the first PGA Championship. In the finals of the match-play tournament, he was up against Jock Hutchison.

Hutchison shot 37 to Barnes's 39 in the morning, in the match-play championship. On the back side Barnes reduced the lead to one. After a break the match resumed with Barnes telling the crowd, before his drive on the first hole (here it comes), "I always do better after lunch."

Barnes squared the match on the 21st hole and took the lead for the first time at the 25th hole, with an 18-foot putt. Barnes wasn't out of the woods yet. He needed to make a 35-foot birdie putt on the 27th hole to halve the hole. On the final green both Hutchison and Barnes had five-footers for fours. Hutchison missed the putt and Barnes made his, winning 1-up. For his efforts Barnes won $500.

In 1919 Barnes defeated Fred McLeod in a 6-and-5 victory. Barnes nailed a 40-foot birdie putt on the 31st hole to seal the win.

Barnes was most proud, however, of his 1921 U.S. Open victory. A few months prior to the June victory, Barnes was in southern Florida for the winter. A friend, former U.S. Open champ Fred McLeod, introduced him to President-elect Warren G. Harding. With a few months to go before the inauguration, Harding was on vacation. Barnes played golf as a partner to Harding against McLeod and one of Harding's friends. Harding promised to attend the U.S. Open a few months later to watch Barnes.

It was played at Columbia Country Club, in a suburb of Washington, D.C. A week before the championship, a combination of blight and drought severely damaged the greens. It seemed that everyone—save for Barnes—had trouble with it. Barnes shot 69–75–73 in the first three rounds, opening up a seven-stroke lead.

His caddie was a 17-year-old black youth. Following the national championship, Barnes was rewarded with his $500 winner's check. He gave $200 to his caddie for his good work. When the caddie went home, his mother accused him of stealing the money. Barnes had to go to his caddie's house and explain the situation to his mother. The caddie was Sam Lacy, who went on to become a legendary sportswriter and editor. Lacy, who died in 2003 at the age of 99, was a pioneer in baseball journalism and elected into the Baseball Hall of Fame in 1997. Working mostly for the *Afro-American* in Baltimore, Lacy in the 1930s and '40s was a crusader who did much to end the practice of segregation in baseball.

Barnes shot a 72 on the final round of the '21 Open and played the final holes before the president and vice president of the United States. Newsreel crews surrounding the final green asked Barnes to hold off on the final putt while they repositioned the president.

After Barnes sank the final putt, President Harding said to him, "Congratulations, partner." Of course, President Harding himself was one of the least-remembered presidents. He was in office from 1921 until he died of a heart attack in 1923.

What was Barnes's game like? In 1924 many were calling him the greatest shot maker in the game. In 1919 he published the first instructional book on golf that featured pictures. According to a 1924 British Open preview by Ray McCarthy in a syndicated column:

> In chipping to the pin from just off the green, probably the hardest shot of all, Barnes is an artist. He will get dead to the cup eight out of ten times, where others will do well to get a fifty-fifty break. He has power, unusual ability in playing the irons, and a grand putting touch. Others may excel him in certain departments, but none can match him for all-around shot-making.

Barnes, at the age of 39, won the British Open in 1925. Having now won every title of consequence in the golf world (now called a career slam), Barnes took his rank alongside Hagen.

Barnes was known as a straight arrow. "He is very careful of his diet at all times, never has dissipated in the slightest degree, he does not even drink coffee, and has always been 'early to bed, and early to rise,'" said McCarthy (who covered Barnes on an exhibition tour of the West Coast in the mid-'20s) in 1925.

In some respects Barnes was very much ahead of his time. Gene Sarazen told a story in the late-1990s about Barnes. By 1929 Sarazen was at the peak of his career, while Barnes was semiretired. They were both living in Pelham, New York, and shared a commuter train into New York City one day. It seems they discussed portfolios.

"Sell them all. Stocks, bonds, everything," Barnes said to fellow commuter Sarazen.

Sarazen said that he took Barnes's advice and he sold it all. Two weeks after, everything broke with the stock market crash. "We got along better after that," remembered Sarazen, who had thought Barnes was rather cold before that.

A Better Analogy

Jim Barnes and Forgotten Movie Stars Do movie fans remember the early Academy Award–winning actors Emil Jannings, Warner Baxter, or George Arliss? They were the first three Oscar winners for Best Actor. Jannings (from Switzerland) and Arliss (from England), like Barnes, were born overseas. The first *famous* actor to win Best Actor was Clark Gable, who won in 1934 for *It Happened One Night*. Gable was the Walter Hagen of movie stars. They were larger than life. Barnes was the equally (or just less) talented actor who didn't last long enough—or have the looks or heritage to star in *Gone with the Wind*.

Soon enough Barnes was gone with the wind. In his later years, Barnes moved to West Orange, New Jersey, with his wife, Carolyn Mary, and raised his two daughters, Carolyn and Jean.

A man named Joe Manda married Carolyn in 1949. Having met her sister, Jean, in 1939 in junior high school, he had known the Barnes family well before that. Manda was close to his father-in-law until Barnes's death in 1966.

"Mr. Barnes never bragged about his accomplishments. He talked to me about my business—the orchid business—or traveling. He wanted his girls to play golf but never competitively. He never regretted missing out on the big money in golf. He didn't need a lot of money. He didn't buy a new car every year, for instance."

The 80-year-old Manda's house is a golf collector's dream. There are golf clubs and golf balls. There are books, written by and about his late father-in-law. There are newspaper clippings, pictures, and memories.

All are fading.

26

PETER THOMSON
King of the British Open

Peter Thomson was known as the Melbourne Tiger long before Eldrick "Tiger" Woods was born. Even Woods hasn't been able to conquer the British Open more than twice, as of this writing. Peter Thomson won it five times, which is as many as Tiger Woods and Jack Nicklaus combined! The Australian Thomson was born on August 23, 1929, which put him out of harm's way in World War II. Thomson had an uninterrupted career free of military duty, crippling accidents, and damaging injuries. Did he use the time wisely? Well, his singular ambition in life was to win the British Open. He accomplished the feat five times, which has been bettered only by the great Harry Vardon.

There is no rags-to-riches story here, as Thomson took up the game of golf in 1941 at the age of 12. In the mid-1940s he entertained thoughts of becoming an industrial chemist. Chemistry's loss was golf's gain when Thomson turned pro in 1949. What type of golfer was he?

Peter Alliss, eight-time Ryder Cup player for Europe and three-time winner of the British PGA Championship: "The way Bart Bryant played and won two very prestigious events in 2005, I think, in a modern way, personifies Thomson's style—hit the fairways, find the greens, and don't do anything stupid. That mode of play is as valid now as it ever was and will continue to be so for generations to come."

Thomson had a rhythmic, seemingly effortless swing. He didn't believe in overpracticing. At some events, instead of spending hours on the practice range getting used to conditions, he would sightsee.

That style worked very well for Thomson. He won nine New Zealand Opens and three Australian Opens. He won the national tournaments in Germany, the Netherlands, Spain, Italy, India, Hong Kong, and the Philippines, as well as one PGA tournament in Texas. His life's ambition was to win the British Open, and he accomplished that five times, while playing very little in the United States.

Peter Alliss: "He was more at home in Europe and Britain, in particular. He was very much an Anglo-Briton-Australian, a Commonwealth man."

In Peter Mitchell's 1991 book, *The Complete Golfer: Peter Thomson*, Thomson is quoted as saying, "The British circuit just seemed to me to be more friendly and more intimate than America's. There wasn't the hype that went with the U.S. scene, and I enjoyed that."

So the Open Championship became the focal point of Thomson's year and his yearly goal. No one in the last 100 years has been more successful (Tom Watson also won five British Opens).

Thomson first played the British Open in 1951, when he was a 22-year-old unknown. He shot a 70 in his first round at Royal Portrush, in Ireland, and was in second place after the round. After his great start Thomson finished eight strokes back of winner Max Faulkner, which was good for a sixth-place tie.

The following year, at Royal Lytham and St. Annes, there were ferocious whipping winds on the final day that made it easier to score well going out but terribly difficult to score well coming in. Bobby Locke used his remarkable short game to finish his final round and ended with 287. Thomson, after playing the front nine in 37 strokes and playing several groups behind Locke, knew he needed a 68 to win and a 69 to tie. It seemed highly unlikely for him to shoot a 31 under difficult conditions to surpass Locke.

But Thomson made a 30-foot putt on the 11th hole. He had a terrific pitch on the 13th to get to within two feet of the hole. He came to the final three holes, needing birdies on each to win his first Open. He birdied the 16th, fell short on the 17th, and didn't eagle the last hole. He wound up one shot short of Locke in the 1952 Open.

The next year 40-year-old Ben Hogan shot a 68 on the final round at Carnoustie, Scotland, to defeat Thomson by four strokes. This was Hogan's only British Open.

After consecutive runner-up finishes, Thomson's first British Open Championship came in 1954. He won by a stroke, thanks to a shot on the 510-yard par-five 16th, when he got out of a bunker 30 yards from the hole with a great shot that came within inches of holing in.

At 24 Thomson was the youngest Open champ since 1926, when Bobby Jones won the British Open. He repeated in 1955 at St. Andrews, with a two-stroke margin. He won for the third consecutive year in 1956 at Hoylake, this time by three strokes.

After Locke won his fourth British Championship in 1957 (with Thomson again finishing second), Thomson won his fourth in five years with a win in 1958 at Royal Lytham and St. Annes. In that tournament he posted his best—a 278, including a 66 on the first round. But it wasn't an easy victory by any means. Although his score broke by one stroke the record that Locke had set in 1950, it was tied by a 22-year-old named Dave Thomas. The rules of the day required a 36-hole play-off. After the first 18 holes of the play-off, Thomson's 68 still couldn't shake Thomas, who hung in with a 69. On the 11th hole of the final 18, Thomson made birdie to open up a lead on Thomas, and Thomson had his fourth British Open.

That completed a seven-year stretch at the British Open where Thomson finished 2–2–1–1–1–2–1. That he would go on to have 10 more top-10 finishes at the British Open—including a 1965 victory at the age of 36—showed his true greatness.

In many of these years, Thomson played in the United States as a tune-up for the British Open. He played the Masters seven times, without much success (he finished as high as fifth in 1957, six shots back of winner Doug Ford).

Who's Better, Who's Best
Peter Thomson or Billy Casper?

Thomson is just two years older than Casper, yet they almost never competed against each other until the Champions Tour, when both were in their 50s. Casper played in only five British Opens and didn't make the trip until 1968, when he was 36 years old. His highest finish at the Open was fourth in 1968 at Carnoustie. Thomson played in only four U.S. Opens, and his highest finish was a fourth-place tie, four strokes back of winner Cary Middlecoff, in 1956.

To choose between the two is very difficult. In Thomson's case we show two more majors over Casper. A 55-year-old Thomson won the 1984 PGA Seniors Championship, finishing eight strokes higher than the 52-year-old Casper. The Aussie then won nine times on the 1985 Champions Tour. And, in his prime, Thomson won the Australian Open three times, the New Zealand Open nine times, and other titles around the globe, although he had only one win on the U.S. Tour.

Casper won 51 times on the PGA Tour. He won only three majors: a Masters and two U.S. Opens. To win Casper had to fend off Palmer, Hogan, and Snead in the 1959 U.S. Open; he had to stage a remarkable comeback against Palmer in the '66 Open (with Nicklaus finishing third); and in the '70 Masters he had to nudge past the Big (Player and Nicklaus in the top five) and the (Gene) Littler in an 18-hole play-off. But Thomson didn't compete against the best players in the world in his five British Opens, and Casper's three majors are therefore better than Thomson's five.

Thomson won 26 times in Europe and 30 more times in Asia and Australia, plus his lone PGA win in the United States. That's a number similar to Casper's PGA victories. But Casper won overseas tournaments as well, and his competition week-in and week-out was superior to Thomson's.

Thomson faced a top international field, but in four of his five British Opens, the top Americans did not make the trip:

- Ben Hogan played the British Open only once (and won), in 1953.
- Sam Snead did not play at the British Open in the 1950s. (He won in 1946 and didn't return until '63.)
- Cary Middlecoff played only once, in 1957.
- Julius Boros did not play at the British Open in the 1950s.
- Lloyd Mangrum played only once, in 1953.
- Arnold Palmer did not play at the British Open until 1960.

Thomson finished ahead of South African Bobby Locke and English golfer Syd Scott in 1954. He finished ahead of Scottish golfer Johnny Fallon and Englishman Frank Jowle in 1955. He completed the three-peat with a victory in 1956 over Belgium's Flory van Donck and Argentina's Robert de Vicenzo.

In 1958 Thomson defeated Wales's Dave Thomas in a 36-hole play-off. Scotland's Eric Brown and Ireland's Christy O'Conner finished third and fourth.

After Palmer's first trip in 1960, the top U.S. golfers began playing in the British Open. It also became doable financially in the '60s. Thomson did win in 1965, with Nicklaus and Palmer in the field.

The skill level of Casper's competition leads me to place him well above Thomson. I made a conscious decision to avoid jingoistic feelings about the United States and its Tour being of a higher caliber when deciding my rankings. But the success of Snead (who won the first time he played), Hogan (who won the first time he played), Palmer (who won two of the first three years he played), and Nicklaus (who had a win as well as a second-place and a third-place finish in his first five British Opens) leads to me to conclude that Thomson played against much weaker fields. Casper was the PGA Tour Player of the Year in 1966, when he finished ahead of Arnold Palmer and Jack Nicklaus, and again in 1970, when he won as many tournaments as Nicklaus and Lee Trevino combined. Casper should be ahead—and is ranked well ahead of Thomson—in this book.

Thomson—after a failed first marriage that produced a daughter—married for a second time in 1960 and fathered three more children. In his mid-30s, with a young family, he wasn't going to start leaving Australia for months at a time to play in the United States (which he never enjoyed much anyway). He played in national tournaments in other countries and became involved in local politics. After his playing days he ran for a seat in his country's Parliament but lost by a narrow margin in 1982. Following that he returned to the United States for a triumphant tour in late 1984 and 1985 and dominated the Champions Tour.

There are many golfers who are unimpressed with success on the Champions Tour, because the players are not beating the best players at the peak of their careers. In Thomson's case the only time he defeated the top Americans with any regularity came when they were past their peak on the Champions Tour.

Peter Alliss: "Peter Thomson ranks very highly in golfing history. How difficult were the [British Open] fields in the '50s? Well, he was beating all the good players of his time. What more can you do? All things being equal, he may well have won at least one U.S. Open (had he played in the States regularly). I don't think the setup at Augusta suited his style of play, although historically quite a number of relatively modest hitters won the event.

"I don't believe whatever a player does on the Champions Tour will affect his overall place in history. Why? Well, some very successful players remained amateurs until certainly they hit their 45th birthday, some waiting as long as their 50th. On the other hand, Thomson, Hale Irwin, and a number of others have played remarkably well on that tour, and I'm sure, for the successful ones, it's been a very enjoyable and profitable journey."

27

BOBBY LOCKE
The Greatest Putter of All Time

The greatest golfer from South Africa was Gary Player. But Player had to surpass the first great golfer from his country, Bobby Locke. If you look up the word *player* in a dictionary, one definition you'll find is "an active participant." The description fits Gary Player. And if you look up the word *lock*, one definition you'll find is "a sure thing." This fits Bobby Locke's short golf game, where he may have been the greatest putter of all time.

The putter that Locke used during his career has often been called his magic wand. It was given to him in 1926, when he was nine years old. It was a long wooden-shafted rusty club with a small, upright iron blade. Locke thought so much of this putter that on his first visit to the United States, he slept with it at night. When he was involved in a terrible automobile accident in February of 1960 (when he was 43), he was unconscious for several days and it was a month before he could open his left eye. He would suffer from double vision for the rest of his life. Yet when he awoke he was concerned first and foremost about his putter, which had been in the car with him during the accident and was flung backward 30 yards down a bank. Locke was tossed through the back window, and his putter was lost. Someone actually returned it to him a few days later, although its magic would not be needed again.

Player once said, "One six-foot putt, for my life? I'll take Bobby Locke. I've seen them all, and there was never a putter like him. In the 100 or so competitive rounds I played with him, I saw him three-putt just once. . . . You had to see it to believe it." Locke himself said, "You drive for show, but putt for dough." He realized early on that no matter how far he could hit the ball, he would not be a consistent winner unless he could putt.

Arthur D'Arcy "Bobby" Locke was born November 20, 1917, in Transvaal, South Africa. By 1936 he had made a name for himself, beating everyone in South Africa. He made his first trip to England at the age of 18.

While in England he became a friend of Harry Vardon, and his talks with the grand master of the game were priceless to the young Locke. Vardon saw greatness in the 18-year-old South African and invited Locke to compete in the Harry Vardon Cup, a tournament comprising the best amateurs in Britain. Locke was an easy winner. When Vardon presented the cup to Locke, he told the crowd that they had just seen driving and putting equal to anything he had ever seen. Locke was the last player to receive the Vardon Cup from Vardon, who died three months later.

Locke stayed overseas to compete in the British Amateur (which he lost) and the 1936 British Open at Hoylake (in which he finished eighth, seven strokes behind the winner, Alf Padgham). Locke may have finished eighth in the British Open, but the seven ahead of him were all professionals; he had the best finish among the amateurs. Great things were expected of him in future years.

He developed a reputation as the world's slowest putter. On one occasion it took him longer than 2 minutes and 10 seconds to strike one putt. It worked for him. J. H. Taylor, a great player from the 1910s, said, "Locke I regard as one of the greatest golfers I have ever seen, and I have had a lifetime of experience in international golf for the last 40 years."

Locke returned to South Africa and turned professional at the end of 1936. In 1938, at the age of 20, he won the South African Open, the Irish Open, and the New Zealand Open. He won 38 tournaments on the South African Tour.

In June of 1940 he enlisted in the South African Air Force. The 22-year-old played little golf over the next six years. In the prime of his career, he wasn't thinking about birdies; rather, he was flying more than 2,000 hours on bomber missions.

It wasn't until January of 1946 that he was able to return to golf. He won the South African Open, as expected, and flew to Britain to play the 1946 British Open. Sam Snead won the British Open that year, but Locke finished second. And toward the end of 1946, Snead was guaranteed a fee of $10,000 to visit South Africa for a series of matches against Locke. It pitted not only the top South African against the top American but the two best finishers in the most recent British Open against each other. It was a surefire financial success.

In 16 matches most sources credit Locke with winning 12 and losing 4. *Sports Illustrated*, in a 1999 article about Locke, reported that Snead won only 2 of the 16 matches, with 2 others halved. Ronald Norval's 1953 biography of Locke (*King of the Links: The Story of Bobby Locke*) says that Snead won 3 and 1 was halved.

By any account, Locke dominated the series of matches. It was time for Locke to come to the United States, as it had to be obvious to Locke and everyone else that he had to look there to find meaningful competition that could challenge him.

Locke arrived and went straight to Augusta to play in the Masters. He played the course for the first time in the tournament, never having spent a minute in a practice round at Augusta. He finished 14th.

The next week he won his first U.S. tournament. He won four of the next five he entered. In short he started dominating the Tour. Jimmy Demaret was the leading money winner of 1947, but Locke (who played only half the season) was just shy of Demaret's total.

In 59 events in the United States, Locke won 11 times and finished second 10 times, third 8 times, and fourth 5 times (34 out of 59 tournaments in the top four). The Norval biography discounts this and says that of the 59 tournaments, he won 13 (not 11) and finished in the top four in 35 of the 59 tournaments. In 1948 he won the Chicago Victory National by 16 strokes, which remains the PGA Tour record for margin of victory. Even Tiger Woods, as of this writing, never won a tournament by 16 strokes (although he won a major—the 2000 U.S. Open—by 15).

It was alleged in the summer of 1949 that Locke failed to appear in certain tournaments to which he had made commitments. Huh? For that he got a lifetime ban (which was later lifted)? Locke called the move to bar him "a disgrace." He packed his bags and said he didn't have to play again in the United States.

The U.S. golfers didn't have much use for the man they called Old Muffin Face. He had filled out considerably and looked much older than he was. When Locke was playing in the United States in 1948, he overheard two golfers discuss the "old guy from South Africa." When Locke asked them what his age was, they said he must be 43. Locke replied that they were 12 years off. "Impossible, you can't be 55," they replied. Locke was only 31 at the time.

It's not that they disliked Locke for appearing old. They disliked him for coming to their country and winning all the prize money and pocketing even more in exhibitions and endorsements.

Snead liked him and called him Old Baggy Pants, and I wonder if the two would have staged a long, fierce rivalry had Locke not been banned. The ban was lifted in 1951 (as other Tour golfers skipped tournaments themselves), but Locke saw no reason to play on the U.S. Tour again, except in some U.S. Opens.

Locke competed in the 1947 U.S. Open in St. Louis and finished third. The next year, at Riviera Country Club, he finished fourth. And in 1949 he finished tied for fourth at Medinah, outside Chicago.

His greatest international success would come at the British Open. In 1949 Locke won the first of his four British Opens, after an epic battle with Harry Bradshaw that resulted in a 36-hole play-off. Locke blew Bradshaw away by 12 strokes in the play-off. Locke repeated the British Open Championship in 1950 and 1952. Then in 1957 the 39-year-old Locke won his fourth British Open in a record-tying 279 at St. Andrews, in Scotland. He became the first since James Braid in 1910 to win a fourth British Open.

You would have to believe that Locke would have won a huge number of tournaments if he had been allowed to play regularly in the United States. He finished third at the U.S. Open in Oakland Hills in 1951 and fifth at the 1954 U.S. Open at Baltusrol. So he entered seven U.S. Opens and finished in the top five in five of them.

Locke was an interesting man. He became a close friend of Bob Hope and Bing Crosby and would be invited to watch the shooting of Hope's movies. He never felt pressure playing golf and remained laid back in his game. While others anxiously awaited their tee times, Locke would find a place in the clubhouse and nap. He would ask to be wakened five minutes before he had to go to the tee. Sometimes he would pass the time by strumming his banjo and singing. Until he lost a match in 1955, Locke went 20 years without being beaten over 72 holes on South African soil.

There weren't too many happy days in the later part of Locke's life, which ended in 1987. He had been married in 1943 and had a daughter. He met someone else, a woman from Vermont, and told her to wait for him. Locke would divorce in 1953 and marry the woman from Vermont in 1958. It was reported that Locke had married someone else in between. A daughter, Carolyn, was born in February of 1960, days before the car accident that took Locke's career (and almost took his life).

Locke's remaining years were spent drinking and spiraling downhill. After he died from meningitis in 1987, his daughter from his second marriage went to England and auctioned off most of her father's trophies to get some much-needed money for herself and Locke's widow. It still left them in a desperate financial situation. A few years later the 80-year-old widow and the 40-year-old daughter committed suicide. In the end there is another definition of the word *lock* that applies to Mr. Locke. It is this: "an interlocking or entanglement of elements or parts."

He was a character who liked to sing and have a few drinks, like Hagen or Snead or Demaret. He was a war hero, like many others of his generation. There was some glitch in his personality that made him great on the links, but the entanglement with others caused problems. He didn't bond with his fellow golfers, his family, or in this country. He was seen as an outsider. He is likely to be dismissed among the greatest of all time. Yet in a competitive era, he might have been the equal of—or just short of—Hogan and Snead.

He lost his six prime years due to World War II and then suffered the car accident at age 43. In four attempts he never won the Masters. In seven attempts he never won the U.S. Open. But he won four British Opens, albeit against weaker fields than seen in the Open fields of the last 45 years.

But Arnold Palmer and Billy Casper have gone on record saying that Locke was the greatest putter they ever saw.

Best Putters of All Time

1. Bobby Locke
2. Billy Casper
3. Ben Crenshaw
4. Tiger Woods
5. Jack Nicklaus
6. Paul Runyan
7. Horton Smith
8. Bob Charles
9. Johnny Revolta
10. Ben Hogan, Sam Snead (tie)

He probably was the greatest putter of all time and his domination of the PGA Tour in the mid-1940s is enough proof to place him among the top 30 golfers of all time.

28

J. H. TAYLOR
His Life's Work

Virtually every one of the top golfers in this book, not to mention many other golfers, have written their own books. J. H. Taylor, England's first great professional golfer, was arguably the finest writer among the golfing legends (à la Bobby Jones). His 1943 classic, *Golf: My Life's Work*, is a definitive source for golf historians. That it was written solely by Taylor—who left school when not quite the age of 11—is as impressive as his five victories in the British Open.

John Henry Taylor was born on March 19, 1871, the second oldest child of Joshua Taylor, who died at 46. John Henry's life reads like a Dickens novel:

> Courage that nothing could daunt was mother's chief characteristic. There were the illnesses of my father, which meant that the weekly wage came to a full stop, and the five children and she had to subsist on parish pay and the few shillings earned by work at the wash-tub.

He was born in Northam, North Devon, near the first seaside course in England. J.H. began to caddie when he was young and became a full-time caddie when he left school before his 11th birthday (only six years of grade school were required, and the Taylor family needed money). At age 15, caddies at Westward Ho in Devonshire needed to find something permanent, so J.H. became a gardener's boy for three years at a house overlooking Westward Ho. After a few years working as a mason's laborer for 15 shillings a week, he took a job as a groundskeeper at the Westward Ho.

He tried to enlist in the British Army but was rejected six times because of his poor eyesight. He was too short (5′8″) to become a policeman. The one thing he was able to do well, it seemed, was golf. In his spare time as the groundskeeper, he was able to play against British Amateur champ Horace Hutchinson—and Taylor defeated him 3 and 2.

In 1888 he won second prize in a competition and was given the choice of a golf club from the shop. He selected a new type of club, a "mashie" (today's 5-iron). Taylor recalls in his autobiography:

I visualized that it could be used for getting out of bunkers or playing the delicate chip shots from just off the green, or greatly daring, used for approaching play. . . . As a matter of downright fact, the majority of us working men possessed only one iron which circumstances compelled us to use under all conditions and play all kinds of strokes.

A new club had been established at Burnham-on-Sea, and Taylor, not yet 20, became its groundskeeper and pro. His first professional job included sole responsibility for the keeping of the course, including building tees with his own hands. And with his new job, he began making a name for himself. He entered the British Open at Prestwick in 1893. In his first round he shot 75, which led the field by three strokes. He didn't win, but he served notice that he was a player.

He won his first Open title the next year at the new Sandwich course. Taylor recounted what it was like in his autobiography:

I had achieved my life's ambition. I had won the Open Championship at the age of 23, the first English professional to do so, and the first time it had been played on English links. . . . My winning score, 326, has often been criticized by the unthinking as unworthy. Compared with present day scores it appears huge, but the critics cannot have the faintest conception of what the game was forty-five years ago and the conditions under which it was played. It is a waste of words to try and convince them, and I gave up trying a long time ago. But there is one indisputable fact that should set them thinking again. At Sandwich the best players in the world met, and if they could not return lower scores, it meant that existing conditions precluded lower scoring, and when that is realized there is nothing more to be said.

Taylor won back-to-back titles when he won the following year at St. Andrews. Just as is true in present-day golf, a second major championship made an even greater demand of Taylor's services. For an exhibition match of 36 holes, the fee was usually 10 pounds inclusive of traveling and hotel expenses.

In one of these exhibitions, Taylor met James Braid. Braid holed a difficult putt on the 36th green to halve the match. This put Braid on the map. In another exhibition, Taylor met Harry Vardon. The three men would become great friends and together be known as the Great Triumvirate.

The rise of Vardon came at Taylor's expense. Taylor finished seventh at the British Open in 1897 and finished only as high as fourth in both 1898 and 1899. Vardon, meanwhile, won three times in four years.

Taylor's third British Open victory came in 1900, also at St. Andrews. He defeated Vardon by eight strokes and matched Vardon's three British Open Championships. In August of 1900 Taylor went to the United States with Vardon to compete in the U.S. Open at Chicago Golf Club in Wheaton, Illinois. He finished second to his longtime rival by two strokes.

What makes Taylor's mark so astounding is that he adjusted from the gutta-percha ball to the rubber-core ball. Taylor was given a supply just before he played in the 1900 U.S. Open, where he finished second to Vardon. He was too set in his ways to play the Open with the new balls; but a short time later he tried one during a casual round at the Rockaway Hunting Club, on Long Island. Taylor's usual drives were about 175 yards, but with the new ball Taylor's drives covered around 240 yards. Taylor realized the old gutty ball was not long for this world.

It was the following year that Taylor helped form the British PGA. The pros "wanted more unity among themselves." Taylor was elected chairman of the London and Counties Professional Golfers. When Wales and Scotland wanted to join their organization, the name was changed to Professional Golfers Association.

Taylor finished second at the British Open for four straight years, from 1904 to 1907. He went almost a decade before capturing his fourth Open in 1909 at Deal, Kent. He posted a score of 295. Taylor added a fifth Open title in 1913, in impossible conditions at Hoylake. A full gale blew and the rain came down in blinding waves. One golfer, Michael Moran, who started the final day in second place, took 10 strokes on the first hole. Taylor not only won, but he won by eight strokes. The fifth Open tied Braid and Vardon, but Vardon would win his sixth the next year. The last victory by Vardon would mean 16 Opens between the Triumvirate in a 21-year span.

Following 1914, golf was suspended for six years due to World War I, but Taylor played the Open until 1926, when he was 55 years old. Taylor retired after that to the place of his birth, in a cottage overlooking Westward Ho, the course of his youth. He worked on the building of public courses in an attempt to bring the game to the masses. He died in 1963 at the age of 92.

My Favorite Golf Autobiographies
1. *Golf: My Life's Work* by J. H. Taylor
2. *Bobby Jones on Golf* by Bobby Jones
3. *My Autobiography* by Peter Alliss
4. *Getting Up and Down: My Sixty Years in Golf* by Ken Venturi
5. *One Magical Sunday* by Phil Mickelson

6. *A Fairway to Heaven: My Lessons from Harvey Penick on Golf and Life* by Tom Kite
7. *A Feel for the Game: To Brookline and Back* by Ben Crenshaw
8. *The Velvet Touch* by Horton Smith and Marian Benton

And Some Good Biographies

1. *Ben Hogan: An American Life* by James Dodson
2. *Byron Nelson: The Story of Golf's Finest Gentleman and the Greatest Winning Streak in History* by Martin Davis
3. *Jimmy Demaret: The Swing's the Thing* by John Companiotte

There are many terrific reads among the biographies of great golfers. James Dodson's *Ben Hogan: An American Life* tops the list. Among the autobiographies, Alliss and Venturi have countless firsthand stories and anecdotes about their lives in the game. However, it is Taylor and Jones who are head-and-shoulders above the rest.

Taylor's opinion on the greatest of all time, in his 1943 autobiography: "Vardon is the finest and most finished golfer that the game has ever produced. I have seen and watched every player of eminence during the past fifty years and taking into account everything they have done I still hold that my opinion is sound, and I am willing to uphold it even if the world should be against me. The test of who should be considered the best golfer, as I see it, must conform to this formula. He is one who over a length of years has played fewer bad or indifferent strokes than any other aspirant, and in addition has shown, during this period of time, consistent brilliancy. If this is conceded, and its logic appears to be irrefutable, then Harry Vardon stands alone in all the glory that his performances testify."

It would be a mistake, it seems, to rank Vardon so high and not list Taylor (and Braid) also among the top 50. Taylor had almost the same résumé (if not the influence) that Vardon did at the end of the 1800s. Taylor finished second in four consecutive British Opens and added (his fourth and fifth) titles in 1909 and 1913. But without those titles Taylor wouldn't be ahead of Scotland's Willie Anderson (who won U.S. Open titles in 1901, 1903, 1904, and 1905). Anderson finished 11th in 1900, when Taylor and Vardon competed in the U.S. Open. And while four U.S. Opens are a great achievement, it doesn't approach what Taylor did against tougher competition at the British Open each year. Taylor winning his final major in 1913 in England is miles ahead of winning a fourth U.S. Open, like Anderson did in 1905.

Who's Better, Who's Best
J. H. Taylor or John Ball?

John Ball was born in 1861, 10 years before Taylor was. Ball was the greatest amateur golfer of the time, winning eight British Amateur titles—a major championship at the time—in 1888, 1890, 1892, 1894, 1899, 1907, 1910, and 1912. In addition, he won the British Open in 1890 (becoming the first amateur to do so) and finished second in the 1892 Open. Ball was born and grew up in Hoylake, near Liverpool, where he died in 1940.

But here we go again, revisiting the Bobby Jones amateur debate while considering the level of Ball's competition versus Taylor's. Ball was masterful in his eight amateur victories, but he didn't face Vardon, Taylor, or Braid in any of them. Enough said.

29

ERNIE ELS
The Big Easy

Theodore Ernest Els was born in South Africa in October of 1969. His father, Neels, introduced him to golf and served in the same capacity as Earl Woods served for his son Tiger. Ernie, though, wasn't on the same single track that Tiger was on. He played cricket, rugby, and soccer. His mother, Hettie, was the more competitive parent, instilling in Ernie the desire to win. And it was she who forbade all sports other than golf around the time he turned 12. His parents even dug up their tennis court in the backyard and replaced it with a putting green.

The net result (pun intended) was to create one of the biggest worldwide celebrities that South Africa has produced. Of course, many of the other well-known South Africans became famous for activism, rather than athleticism.

Famous South Africans
Nelson Mandela—political prisoner who became president
Steve Biko—activist who died in police custody after being beaten
Desmond Tutu—Nobel Peace Prize winner
Christian Barnard—surgeon who performed first human heart transplant in 1967
Charlize Theron—Academy Award–winning actress for the movie *Monster*
Gary Player, Bobby Locke, Ernie Els, Retief Goosen—pro golfers

Els didn't change the world, but he did become one of the best in the world at the game of golf. Ernie was a scratch golfer by the age of 14. In 1984, still just 14, he won the Junior World golf title in San Diego over Phil Mickelson and Retief Goosen, among others. By 1985 he was competing against professionals. He turned down scores of scholarship offers from American universities and instead served a mandatory 22 months in the South African Army in 1988.

After his Army stint, Els turned pro at the end of 1991. In 1992 he won six events on the South African Tour. He joined Gary Player to become the only golfers to win the South African Open, South Africa PGA, and South African Masters in the same year. In

1993 Els became the first player ever to record four consecutive rounds in the 60s at the British Open. He finished in a tie for sixth.

His breakthrough victory at the majors came at Oakmont in the 1994 U.S. Open, when Els was still only 24. Els won a three-man play-off against Colin Montgomerie and Loren Roberts. In the play-off Els took a triple-bogey-7 and was 4-over par after two holes, but Montgomerie and Roberts didn't fare any better. It was Els's first professional victory in the United States, and he became the first foreign player to win the U.S. Open since 1981 and the first South African since Player in 1965.

This was one international star who didn't seem to upset many U.S. pros. Many of the top international stars (such as Nick Faldo, Seve Ballesteros, and Bobby Locke) seemed to upset, intentionally or unintentionally, the top U.S. stars. Not Els. He was likable to his fellow players, as well as to the press and fans.

Three years later, at age 27, Els won the U.S. Open for a second time. At this point in his career, he had won 2 of the 20 majors he had entered and finished in the top 10 in 9 of the 20. He won the 1997 U.S. Open at Congressional by hitting 52 of 72 greens, best in the field. Coming on the heels of Tiger's coming-out party at the 1997 Masters, it was reasonable to expect a Woods-Els rivalry for the ages over the next decade. It didn't happen.

Els challenged in other majors and won his third at the 2002 British Open at Muirfield. In that tournament Tiger shot an 81 in the cold and wet conditions in the third round to put himself out of contention. The leaders were bunched, but Els led after the third round.

In the final round of that 2002 British Open, Els made a costly mistake on 16 and finished with a score of 70 and a total of 278. Steve Appleby shot a 65 to tie Els. Thomas Levet and Steve Elkington both shot 66 to tie Els. That set up a four-man play-off. The four coleaders were fortunate that the play-off wasn't larger. Gary Evans (65 in the final round), Shigeki Maruyana (68), and Padraig Harrington (67) all finished with 279 scores, one stroke back of the coleaders.

In the four-hole play-off, Els made par on all four holes. Appleby and Elkington both were 1-over par, and Levet birdied the 16th hole but bogeyed the 18th, again giving new life to Els in the play-off.

Those four holes eliminated Appleby and Elkington, leaving a sudden-death format for Levet and Els. Levet found a fairway bunker at the 18th. Els found a bunker by the green but played a wonderful shot out of the bunker and found himself just four feet from the hole. Levet missed his seven-foot putt, and Els made his four-footer to give him his first British and third major overall. With Els still only 32 years old then, his three majors put him behind only Tiger Woods at the time (it is my contention that Mickelson has passed him but perhaps only temporarily).

Els's personality was described as laid back, and his nickname the Big Easy somehow fit. His game was known for its swing, as was Sam Snead's, a golfer with whom he has been compared.

Rick Reilly, *Sports Illustrated* **columnist:** "Ernie has one of the most beautiful swings I ever saw. Probably one of the five best in golf history."

According to Els's website, ernieels.com, an interview with his father, Neels, reveals that

> Ernie's idol at 8 years old was Seve Ballesteros. Ernie guided his swing on him. From day 1 Ernie's swing was natural, pure, easy. No coach ever really got hold of Ernie in the early days and I believe that is why his swing stayed natural. It was only later when he focused on more technical shots that a coach was brought in. At the time when Ernie was "winning everything" he did everything himself.

For someone so independent, he sure built up an entourage. In a different section of Els's website, he lists his team members. He has a personal assistant, a U.K. personal trainer, a U.S. personal trainer, a writer, and a mental coach.

If you're asking yourself why a mental coach, there are several reasons. First of all, perhaps to combat the psyche of Tiger Woods. Els brought on Jos Vanstiphout, a sports psychologist from Belgium. "What does Jos Vanstiphout do for Ernie Els? Well, in much the same way that David Leadbetter looks after Ernie's swing, Jos takes care of the mental side of the game," writes Steve Newell, the writer on Team Els.

Vanstiphout was brought on in 2001, just months after an article appearing in *Golf Digest* (February 2000) quoted Els saying this:

> I wish golf could be more like rugby. At the end of a match the teams shake hands, then the losing side forms a funnel and applauds the winners off the pitch. Afterward they probably have a couple of beers together. All after they've been knocking the hell out of each other during the match. I want to be able to tell you afterward, over a beer, that I think you were wrong to whip up the bloody crowd.

In the same article Els admitted that fellow South African Gary Player wasn't a particular idol of his, or his playing record a target. He said that if he had Gary's drive or his mind for golf, or his dedication, then he would be doing what Woods was doing. That's a pretty damning and honest assessment.

Not every great athletic talent is wired to be so fanatical. Els has the money, the toys, and the family that mean more to him than anything else. In 2005 Els missed the PGA Championship and four months of play because he twisted his knee sailing the Mediterranean on a vacation with his family. This isn't the way our obsessive sports stars suffer injuries. They suffer them the way Michael Jordan did—getting hurt in a pick-up scrimmage against a much younger Ron Artest. They suffer injuries the way Ben Hogan did in 1949—driving all night from one tournament to the next, fighting fatigue as well as weekly opponents.

Els isn't the only pro athlete with his own private plane, and he's not the only one to go to the resorts of the "rich and famous." He's not the only golfer with a mental coach. But at 6′3″, Els is certainly "the Big Easy." He is a big guy and has had things relatively easy. He grew up under apartheid with servants at his house and attended an all-white school. He had it easy in his military duties, mostly teaching golf. He never even had to face the pressures of never winning a major, as he won two before his 30th birthday. He has faced little pressure to win more, as Woods brings along a ready-made excuse. His swing is easy, is fundamentally perfect. If he chooses to, he can walk away from golf at a relatively young age. Does he have the inner drive to add to his three majors and push Tiger Woods from the number one spot?

If you are cycling behind another bicyclist and can move into the wind behind that bicyclist, you can gain an advantage. The low pressure moves you forward, and the eddies push you forward. In cycling it's called drafting. In golf it's called Ernie Els.

Who's Better, Who's Best
Ernie Els or Greg Norman?

For nearly 20 years there has been an official World Golf Ranking system. The official events from the six professional tours (U.S. PGA Tour, European Tour, Japanese Golf Tour, South African PGA, Asian PGA Tour, and the PGA Tour of Australasia) together with the Canadian, Nationwide, and Challenge Tours are all taken into account and points are awarded according to the players' finishing positions. Only 12 men have been on top of the World Golf Ranking system. Two of them (Tom Lehman on top for just 1 week and Bernhard Langer for 3) stopped on the penthouse floor for what seemed long enough to only get a cup of coffee. Tiger Woods, on the other hand, has been number one in the world for 367 weeks as of late November 2005. Greg Norman was on top for 331 weeks. Ernie Els was number one in the world ratings for just 9 weeks.

Now Norman was getting off the elevator just as Tiger Woods was pushing the button to get on. I have no doubt that if Els had been playing in Norman's era, Els would have been on top of the World Golf Ranking system for much more than 9 weeks (although it probably would have been fewer than 331).

Els has three majors to Norman's two. Norman, however, was 36 years old in February of 1991 and had more tournament victories than Els at a similar juncture in their careers. But if you lower the standard a bit (recognizing that these guys weren't Nicklaus or Woods), you can get a little more perspective as to how close they are to each other.

Number of Times Finishing First or Second in a Major

Ernie Els: 9

Greg Norman: 10

Runner-Up at a Major

Ernie Els

1.	1996 British Open	Winner: Tom Lehman
2.	2000 Masters	Winner: Vijay Singh
3.	2000 U.S. Open	Winner: Tiger Woods
4.	2000 British Open	Winner: Tiger Woods
5.	2004 Masters	Winner: Phil Mickelson
6.	2004 British Open	Winner: Todd Hamilton

Greg Norman

1.	1984 U.S. Open	Winner: Fuzzy Zoeller
2.	1986 Masters	Winner: Jack Nicklaus
3.	1986 PGA	Winner: Bob Tway
4.	1987 Masters	Winner: Larry Mize
5.	1989 British Open	Winner: Mark Calcavecchia
6.	1993 PGA	Winner: Paul Azinger
7.	1995 U.S. Open	Winner: Corey Pavin
8.	1996 Masters	Winner: Nick Faldo

Norman was runner-up to eight different players at major tournaments. Yes, he lost to great players (Nicklaus and, to a lesser degree, Faldo), but he also lost to Moes, Larrys, and Fuzzys. Norman wasn't in Nicklaus's shadow, except at the very tail end of Nicklaus's career. Els, on the other hand, has played all but his first three seasons in Tiger's enormous shadow. He has finished second to Tiger twice at the majors and at three other tournaments.

Norman is ranked ahead of Els, but not by much following the 2005 season. Els is young enough that he may yet win (or be runner-up at) more majors. Norman had 88 titles worldwide, including 68 overseas. Els has a good start on that total, but he's behind Norman's pace. If he wins one more major and gets close to Norman's worldwide victory total, then he'll pass the man known as "the Shark."

Ernie Els is still a force in golf. He hasn't "jumped the Shark" yet, however.

30

JIMMY DEMARET
The First Three-Time Masters Champ

Jimmy Demaret, one of golf's legendary characters, lived life to the fullest. Arnold Palmer once said that Demaret could play the piano all night and shoot 65 the next day. It's interesting that Demaret would be compared his entire career with Walter Hagen (because of their personalities), but Demaret was probably the best golfing friend of Ben Hogan, an odd couple of a seemingly fun-loving individual and a man who had a dour personality.

Demaret was a Hall of Fame golfer (like Hagen and Hogan) who led the PGA Tour in earnings in 1947 and won three Masters Tournaments. The fourth of nine children, he was born in Houston, Texas, on May 24, 1910, to a house painter and carpenter. He got his first job as a club professional in 1932 in Galveston, Texas. According to Al Barkow's 1989 *The History of the PGA Tour*, Demaret, "who had some talent as a singer of popular songs, was backed on the tournament circuit by bandleader Ben Bernie and Sam Maceo, who owned a nightclub in Galveston where Demaret got to croon now and again."

Demaret was a flashy dresser known for wild-colored clothing. There aren't many people who can pull off pink, purple, flaming scarlet, and hunter green golf outfits. He was such a good golfer, he would've still been noticed if he wore camouflage.

While growing up in Houston he caddied at several clubs. He won the Texas PGA Tournament five times in a row, from 1934 to 1938, before joining the professional tour full-time. He entered the PGA Championship in 1935 and began play in the U.S. Open the following year. His victories in the San Francisco match-play event in 1938 and the 1939 Los Angeles Open earned Demaret a spot in the 1939 Masters, then an invitational (not an "open") tournament. He didn't finish in the top five in a major championship, however, until the 1940 Masters, when he was 30 years old.

At the 1939 Masters he finished poorly, tying for 33rd place with Bobby Jones, the tournament founder. Demaret won five events in the first two months of 1940 leading into Augusta. By the time the tournament rolled around, the Texan was one of the favorites.

His game was tailor-made for the Masters because he hit the majority of the fairways. The greens were fast and Demaret was a streaky putter who could get on a roll.

Lloyd Mangrum made headlines with a then-record 64 on the opening 18 holes. Demaret shot 37 on the first nine but had a record-breaking 30 on the second nine. He punched in a 50-foot putt (after first removing his shoes and stepping into two feet of water to make the shot) on the 15th hole and made another long putt on the 16th for another birdie. Demaret caught Mangrum after the second day, but then a stomach problem put Demaret in the hospital after his round was finished, and he stayed there overnight. He went back to the course the next day and took the lead after the third round, after which he nursed his lead in an error-free final round to win the championship.

World War II interrupted the Masters for three of Demaret's prime years. By the time it resumed, he was 36 years old and had to deal with a declining game and a rising Nelson, Hogan, and Snead. That didn't mean Demaret couldn't compete with the slightly younger competition. In fact, he won the Masters in 1947 over one of the deepest fields ever. Demaret shot 281 for the tournament, which was two strokes better than Nelson and three strokes ahead of Hogan. Bobby Locke, having just arrived in the country, finished eight strokes back.

Back on the 15th hole at Augusta, Demaret's second shot in the first round of the 1947 Masters rolled back down the bank into the water. When Demaret got to the submerged ball, he had to again take off his socks and shoes to get both feet in the water to take a stance to try and hit it out. He used his wedge to take the ball within four feet of the hole. A birdie putt followed. Demaret played magnificent golf throughout the four rounds and had his second Masters.

He made news not only with his golf but with his clothes. "Dapper Demaret wore a stunning salmon pink sweater," wrote the Associated Press, as Demaret showed up for the first round of the 1950 Masters.

At that 1950 Masters he was handed a third victory when Jim Ferrier relinquished a huge lead late. Ferrier, with Demaret finished and in the clubhouse, needed only a 38 on the final nine to win. Ferrier finished with a 41 coming in and lost by three strokes.

The 1950 Masters field that was won by Demaret also had a star-packed leaderboard. Following Demaret and Ferrier, the rest of the top 10 included Snead, Hogan, Nelson, Mangrum, Lawson Little, Cary Middlecoff, and Gene Sarazen. If there is any question as to why Demaret places as high as 30th in this book, all one has to do is to look at the strength of competition he beat out.

Another reason Demaret places as high as 30th all-time was his fifth place finish at the 1962 Masters at the age of 51. By then a whole new generation of shot makers, including Arnold Palmer and Jack Nicklaus, had made their stamp on the Tour.

Demaret was great despite never winning the U.S. Open. It was canceled from 1942 through 1945, Demaret's prime. And in 1948 he set a U.S. Open record by shooting 279. It stood for a few minutes, until Ben Hogan finished his round with an even better mark.

At the PGA Championship, Demaret made the semifinals four times but lost each time in the semis, twice to Hogan (1946 and 1948), once to Snead (1942), and once to Chandler Harper (1950). A win in any of these PGA Championships would have vaulted Demaret into the top 25 of all time. Demaret didn't even enter the PGA Championship from 1952 to 1955. He made only one trip to the British Open, in 1954, finishing in a tie for 10th. Demaret's three Masters are more impressive than those of the players ranked below him: Tommy Armour, Cary Middlecoff, Julius Boros, and Vijay Singh. At this writing, all four of those players have the same three majors as Demaret, but not all majors are considered equal.

Demaret was one of the most popular golfers of his era, to both his fellow players and the general public. His appeal was enormous, and anything he endorsed—from golf balls to sporting goods equipment—was successful. He was a hit on the big-band radio shows that he appeared on. He could sing, he could act, and he could play golf. He put out *The Swing's the Thing* in 1959, a series of six 45-rpm records with accompanying golf instruction books.

He made an appearance on a 1954 episode of "I Love Lucy" that has run countless times over the last half-century. In the episode Demaret finds Lucy and Ethel playing golf ahead of him, and he joins them and instructs them. Of course, he plots with them to get back at Ricky and Fred, who have duped the women into doing everything wrong.

Another long-lasting image of Demaret comes through in the 1960s television series "Shell's Wonderful World of Golf," which Demaret cohosted with Gene Sarazen, beginning in 1966.

Demaret was 6–0 in his Ryder Cup matches and was named to four Ryder Cup teams. He most certainly would have been named to other Cup teams had the Cup not been canceled during World War II.

I don't believe that he was one of the four best golfers of his era. These were clearly Hogan, Snead, Nelson, and Locke. Demaret belongs in the next tier, but ahead of the Mangrums and Middlecoffs. If he had played in the 2000s, he would have played in many more majors and probably would have won five or six (instead of three). He would also have made zillions of dollars with his charismatic personality. He was an ambassador of the game after his playing days with his announcing duties and his contributions to creating what is now the Champions Tour.

He won nine tournaments in 1940 and seven more in 1947. I think it's reasonable to assume he would have won 15 more tournaments in the World War II years had tournaments not been canceled then, pushing his 31 up to the mid-40s. Hogan once described Demaret as "the most underrated golfer in history." When people thought of Demaret, they were more likely to think of his presence as a television commentator and his reputation for having a good time rather than thinking of him as a golfing great. And, of course, people remembered his taste in fashion.

However, in 1979 he gave the golfing world a gift that continues to thrive. He organized the first Legends of Golf Tournament, which grew into the Champions Tour. Golfers who compete in their 70s or older are now referred to as the "Friends of Demaret."

Who's Better, Who's Best
Jimmy Demaret or Hale Irwin?

Jimmy Demaret has to be considered a great player, but he was the Hale Irwin of his day. Demaret was underrated because of his charismatic personality; Irwin was underrated because of a lack of charisma. Both Irwin and Demaret were far more successful in their 30s than they were in their 20s. Demaret won three Masters but no U.S. Opens; Irwin won three U.S. Opens but no Masters Tournaments. Demaret is remembered for founding the tournament that sprouted the Champions Tour; Irwin is remembered for his domination of the Champions Tour.

Despite Demaret's contributions to the game, Irwin edges past him in the overall rankings based on performance.

A Better Analogy

Jimmy Demaret and Ralph Kiner At a time when Demaret was winning Player of the Year and the Vardon Trophy in 1947, Major League Baseball great Ralph Kiner was tearing up the National League. Kiner hit 51 home runs in '47, many of them over the left-field fence in Pittsburgh's Forbes Field, which was dubbed "Kiner's Korner." Although he was a great player, Kiner wasn't the baseball equal of contemporaries Stan Musial or Ted Williams. Kiner, who dated Hollywood actresses Elizabeth Taylor and Janet Leigh, was most known for his man-about-town image.

And like Demaret, Kiner became a broadcaster of his sport, and quite a popular one at that. He joined the Mets broadcast booth in 1962, and in addition to the games, he hosted a postgame show called "Kiner's Korner." Both Demaret and Kiner were responsible for introducing many colloquialisms into the lexicon. Demaret popularized *worm burners* and *white knucklers*. Kiner was famous for his "Kinerisms." He would say, for example, about a certain player, "He's going to be out of action the rest of his career." Or about the Mets, "All of the Mets' road wins against the Dodgers this year occurred at Dodger Stadium." And there's this one: "I think one of the most difficult things for anyone who's played baseball is to accept the fact that maybe the players today are playing just as well as ever."

Leave it to Demaret, who was quoted as saying, "Golf and sex are about the only things you can enjoy without being good at." You could do worse than sit by the television listening to Demaret and Kiner spin their tales. They were underrated broadcasters for the same reason that Demaret was an underrated golfer: he didn't look like he took it seriously enough.

The great golfer passed away in 1983, suffering a heart attack as he stepped foot into a golf cart.

31

TOMMY ARMOUR
The Silver Scot

Tommy Armour was born on September 24, 1894, in Edinburgh, Scotland. The Silver Scot was certainly one of the top three dozen golfers of all time. His life was filled with legendary tales. He was a war hero in World War I. He influenced some of the top professionals with his coaching and tutelage. His books helped millions play better. And his influence lives on today with his grandson Tommy Armour III, who set the all-time PGA record by shooting a 254 in the 2003 Valero Texas Open.

Hailing from Scotland, golf's birthplace, he was as authentic as the golf greats come. One of his high school friends was Bobby Cruickshank, another golf great. The two remained close for 60 years. Armour became serious about the game after seeing Harry Vardon, James Braid, and J. H. Taylor play in exhibition matches. Armour once even went to England to take lessons from Vardon.

Armour graduated from the University of Edinburgh. His life was interrupted when he went into World War I as a private. He rose through the ranks, making the rank of staff major. In a mustard gas explosion, Armour was blinded. During the six months he spent in the hospital, the sight in his right eye returned, which enabled him to resume golf. He needed a metal plate put into his head and left arm.

In 1920 he played in the British Amateur tournament and came to the United States, where he was a semifinalist at the U.S. Amateur. That year he won the French Amateur. In 1921, still as an amateur, he played for the first British Amateur team to compete against golfers from the United States.

Armour decided to move to the United States in 1924. He met Walter Hagen on the ship while sailing there and struck up a friendship. Hagen got him a job as a club secretary in Westchester, New York. Armour was close to 30 years old when he turned pro.

A team of American golfers arrived a few weeks early for the 1926 British Open in order to play against a team of British stars at Wentworth. Hagen and Ted Ray were the two captains. This series of matches—the first time the professionals played against each other (won by Ray's British team)—was so popular that the next year the first Ryder

Cup was played. These weren't the first official Ryder Cup matches, the reason being that several players on the American team (including Armour) weren't actually American. The following year only American-born players were eligible to compete on the Ryder Cup team. (In 2002, eligibility for the U.S. Ryder Cup team changed to include individuals who obtained U.S. citizenship prior to their 18th birthday.) So Armour played on a team against the United States in 1921, and in 1926 he played for the United States. You could say he was one of professional sports' first free agents.

His first pro tournament victory came in 1925 at the Florida West Coast Open. In 1926 he took only one tournament—the Winter Pro Golf Championship. In his early years he was plagued by poor putting. But he managed to become a good enough putter to put together a dominant nine-year period from 1927 to 1935.

In 1927 Armour had five victories, including the U.S. Open. In that tournament he defeated Harry "Lighthorse" Cooper ("Lighthorse" because he played so quickly) in an 18-hole play-off. That was the U.S. Open played in Oakmont that represented the only time in nine years that Bobby Jones (eight strokes back of Armour) failed to finish first or second at the U.S. Open.

In the summer of Bobby Jones's Grand Slam, there was one major that Jones didn't win—the PGA Championship, which was open only to professional golfers. The PGA took place that year in Flushing, New York, at Fresh Meadows Country Club. The finals pitted the two top pros of the time, Armour and Gene Sarazen. The match was close throughout, as neither golfer had more than a two-hole lead. They went to the final nine all square. Sarazen took the lead. On the 14th Armour squared the match again with a birdie. On the 18th hole Sarazen hooked his tee shot while Armour hit the fairway. Both men put their second shots into the bunker. Sarazen put his bunker shot 10 feet past the hole, while Armour's went 12 feet away. As Armour got over his putt, he was forced to back away as a spectator using his personal movie camera disturbed him. Fellow golfer Leo Diegel had to beg for quiet and consideration. Armour got back over the putt and his ball had just enough momentum to topple in to win 1-up.

The 1931 British Open was the first to be played at Carnoustie. After the third round, Argentinian Jose Jurado opened up a three-stroke lead over the field. Armour played before Jurado and signed his scorecard 296, the leader in the clubhouse. He matched the course record with a 71 in that round, overcoming a five-stroke deficit. Jurado needed to shoot only 75 in his final round to beat Armour. Needing to make a four on the final hole, Jurado missed his putt and instead finished one stroke back of the Silver Scot. This missed nine-foot putt would have given him the championship. There was some talk that Jurado didn't realize the score because of a language barrier and played too cautiously off the 17th and 18th tees.

Armour had won all three professional majors: the British Open, U.S. Open, and PGA Championship. The Masters would not begin play until 1934, when Armour was nearing 40 and the end of his career.

There were a few things that contributed to the end of Armour's playing days. His putting woes returned. He coined the term *yips* (nervous tension affecting the performance of crucial athletic actions such as putts), saying, "Once you've had 'em, you've got 'em."

Armour wasn't exactly the quiet do-gooder either. He was a big drinker, probably (like Hagen) a bigger drinker after his playing days were over. Armour drank with the best of them. Conservatively, there were many days when he would drink a scotch and soda, followed by a Bromo-Seltzer, then a chaser, then gin, and then he would repeat as necessary. Seeing this, one companion remarked, "That Bromo-Seltzer is going to kill that Scotch S.O.B. one of these days." Surprisingly, after living on that formula for close to 50 years, Armour quit drinking cold turkey in his later years.

He was the perfect man to endorse cigarettes, and the magazine ads from the 1930s were quite persuasive. "Camels are my brand and have been for years. I smoke a lot, but I must be sure that my nerves are healthy and my head is clear. That's why I prefer Camels."

Did his injuries from the war cost him his steady hand needed to putt effectively? Was it age? Was his drinking a contributing factor to the premature end of his career? It probably was a combination of everything.

During the 1930s he developed a reputation as being one of the best teachers of golf. His pupils included Lawson Little, Julius Boros, and Babe Didrikson. He was a link to Scotland and Vardon and the 1920s. He became best known as a storyteller and a teacher. He lost a fortune in the stock market crash of 1929 but made another fortune quickly enough. He did what he could to help the Allied forces in the Second World War and played exhibition matches with other famous golfers.

In a 1952 interview the 57-year-old retired golf star, who was a huge baseball fan, made this comment:

> You know, all games are based on timing. I've seen it with the batters like DiMaggio, Hornsby, Cobb, Williams, and Musial. Walter Hagen had the timing in golf. He was great. He was the greatest all-around golfer in history, but then again, maybe I shouldn't say that because it can't be proved.

Armour thought that anyone who played Major League Baseball could be taught to play fairly competitive golf. Although he never played baseball, he challenged baseball star Stan Musial one year. Musial, formerly a pitcher, threw to Armour, who proceeded to hit a bunch of line drives into the outfield. Perhaps Armour was right about timing.

He wrote three books, including the bestseller *How to Play Your Best Golf All the Time*. The books, and his professional-golfer grandson, were his legacies. Armour died in 1968, getting the most out of his 72-plus years.

This guy was some character. When he was the golf pro at Medinah Country Club near Chicago, he occasionally passed time while giving lessons by shooting at chipmunks with a .22 caliber rifle. Giving a lesson one day to a not-very-skilled player, he seemed to be doing more shooting than instructing. The member said, "When are you going to stop that and take care of me?" With the rifle at his side, Armour said, "Don't tempt me."

Who's Better, Who's Best
Tommy Armour or Jim Barnes?

Armour's books, pupils, and grandson combined to keep his name in the public eye a little longer than Jim Barnes's name. Barnes, like Armour, won the PGA, the British Open, and the U.S. Open. But Barnes won the PGA Championship twice (in 1916 and 1919), and might have won it more, had it not been temporarily canceled. Barnes also won the Western Open, a major championship at the time, in 1917 and 1919. Armour won the Western Open only once, in 1929. Barnes gets the nod.

32

JOHNNY MILLER
The Straight Shooter

The year was 1973, and the world was a crazy place. The headlines were dominated by President Richard M. Nixon, who was waging a war against hippies even as the nightly reports of the Watergate break-in consumed the country. In sports it was a Halley's Comet type of year, meaning we'll see things like this every 88 years, if we're lucky. In January the Miami Dolphins completed their 17–0 season by beating the Washington Redskins in the Super Bowl. In March, Bill Walton scored a record 44 points in the final game of the NCAA Championship, leading the UCLA Bruins to their seventh-consecutive NCAA Championship. In the spring, Secretariat won the Derby, the Preakness, and the Belmont to become the first horse since Citation in 1948 to win the Triple Crown. The horse set a track record at the Kentucky Derby and won the Belmont by 31 lengths.

And then, in the summer of 1973, Johnny Miller shot a record-low 63 on the final day of the U.S. Open at Oakmont, passing Arnold Palmer, Jack Nicklaus, and Lee Trevino in the process.

We'll never see anything like that year again. It's been more than 30 years, and there hasn't been anyone or any team to approach the Dolphins, the Bruins, Secretariat, and Miller.

In 1973 Miller was 26 years old. One of the original baby boomers, he was born in 1947 and raised in San Francisco. Far from his hippie contemporaries, Miller was a 6′3″ Mormon who didn't smoke, drink, or curse. He attended Brigham Young University. Yet Miller became known as a rebel for his 15 years of candor as a golf analyst for NBC Sports. His commentary, like his play on the golf course, was anything but conservative.

Although his prime wasn't long, he shot out like a comet, and he dominated the game in the greatest of all eras.

Roger Maltbie, PGA member and NBC golf analyst: "I would have to say, that for a short period of time, Miller deserves to be ranked among the best of all time. Miller, for the period beginning in the early to mid-1970s, was maybe the best player in the world. He was brilliant. I don't know if anyone ever played better golf, ever. He shot 61 on back-to-back weekends; he shot his record 63 at Oakmont at the U.S. Open. He was absolutely amazing. I didn't see the great players before me—the Hogans, Nelsons, and Sneads, so I can only guess—but they couldn't have played better. What made Miller great was how straight he hit the ball, and how close he hit it. . . . He hit the ball far enough, he was a good driver, but it was his iron play that was just spectacular. He hit a ball that didn't curve. He hit the ball ridiculously close to the hole. I never ever saw anyone play like that. I heard legendary stories about Byron Nelson, and how straight a hitter he was. But I never saw Byron myself."

Call Miller a straight shooter then, in his playing days and in his television days. He talked about players choking, which he described as being all relative to where your pressure point is. Everybody has a choking point. For some it's the last round of a major. For others it's well before that.

Miller helped win a couple of Ryder Cups as a player. He first began making a name for himself in 1964, when he won the Junior Amateur Championship. He played at BYU and turned pro in 1969.

He had the blond hair and the All-American image and was saddled with the tag of being the next Jack Nicklaus. In 1971, at the age of 24, he almost picked off his first major. He shot a 68–68 on the final two rounds of the Masters to tie Nicklaus for second place, two shots behind winner Charles Coody. Miller blew late chances to win the green jacket. Later that summer he finished in a tie for fifth place at the U.S. Open, just three strokes back of Nicklaus and Trevino. In September he won his first tournament, the Southern Open, by a whopping five strokes.

It was 1973 when Miller began his period of greatness. He finished in a tie for sixth at the Masters before his record 8-under par performance at the U.S. Open. In his final-round 63, he made nine birdies (including the first four holes) and one bogey. He began the final round six shots behind the leaders, before his stirring comeback. A few weeks later he was second at the British Open in Troon, Scotland, three strokes back of Tom Weiskopf.

In 1974 Miller became known as Mr. January for his dominance in the month. He won the first three tournaments of the year: the Bing Crosby National Pro-Am, the Phoenix Open, and the Tucson Open. No one had ever won the first three tournaments of the year before. (In fact, he won four in a row, if you go back to the final event of 1973.) The final round of the Tucson Open saw him shoot his 11th consecutive subpar round, averaging 68.3 strokes. He won five other tournaments during the calendar year to complete one of the greatest seasons a golfer ever had. He was the leading money winner in the year, the only person to lead the PGA Tour in earnings between 1971 and 1980 other than Nicklaus or Tom Watson.

The following year Miller captured three of the first four tournaments, adding to his mastery of the Arizona and California stage of the Tour. By early February he had won 11 tournaments in 14 months. For comparison, that's how many tournaments two-time U.S. Open champ Payne Stewart won in his career.

But at the 1975 Masters, Miller was 11 strokes back after the first two rounds. To get into contention he needed a record 13-under par the final 36 holes. He lost by one stroke to Nicklaus. The difference was Nicklaus making a long birdie putt on 16 and Miller missing a makeable birdie putt on the 18th green. At the 1975 British Open, Miller finished one stroke back of Watson and Jack Newton.

The following year Miller had a record-tying 66 on the final day of the British Open to easily defeat Seve Ballesteros and Nicklaus by six strokes. In contrast to Ballesteros, who used his driver in the high winds, Miller played more conservatively and used his 1-iron to win at Royal Birkdale. It was Miller's second major.

After that his putting deserted him. He didn't win again for four years. Then he won steadily, getting five more wins in the next four years. He finished second at the 1981 Masters.

Although he is known for his peak performance from 1973 to 1976, Miller did win tournaments 23 years apart, in 1971 and 1994. His win at the Southern Open came when he was just 24. His final win came when he was a grandfather.

I forget who said it, but someone once said, "Show me your sporting heroes, and I'll show you sixth grade." That's exactly where I was in 1973, when Miller was shooting his 63 at Oakmont. Miller won only two majors, and Walton won only two NBA titles. They defeated their Nicklauses and their Abdul-Jabbars and for a brief moment in history, when Jack and Kareem were in the full-fledged prime of their careers, were better than them.

Who's Better, Who's Best
Johnny Miller or Vijay Singh?

Vijay Singh did have a year (2004) that rivaled Miller's 1974 season and has three majors. Singh even shot a 63 in a major and has a handful more victories than Miller. Maltbie told me that if you take the putter out of the bag, Singh is a better ball striker than his contemporaries Ernie Els and Phil Mickelson.

What makes this a fascinating comparison is that most golfers play their best in their 30s. Miller played his best by far in his 20s. And Singh played his best by far in his 40s.

Miller challenged Nicklaus, and Singh challenged Woods. But I'm taking Miller in his 20s over Singh in his 40s. Not by much, though.

A Better Analogy

Johnny Miller and Bill Walton In this and my earlier books, I have made analogies to players from other sports and pop-culture figures. There isn't a closer analogy, in my opinion, than Miller in golf and Walton in basketball.

Bill Walton was from Southern California and Miller from Northern California. Walton was a great amateur in his sport and for a short period interrupted the domination of the NBA by Kareem Abdul-Jabbar, who won championships before Walton came into the NBA and after Walton left. Miller was a great amateur in his sport and for a short period interrupted the domination of professional golf by Jack Nicklaus, who won major championships before Miller came on the Tour and after Miller left.

I ranked Walton among the greatest in his sport and now Miller among the greatest in his. In 1976 it would have been inconceivable to believe that either of them would have such short careers. Walton had a myriad of injuries. Miller was bothered by injuries as well, and then his putting deserted him.

Walton, after missing most of five years, returned to the game in triumphant fashion, winning an NBA Championship as a sixth man on the 1986 Boston Celtics. Miller, at the age of 47, returned to win his 25th PGA Tour victory in 1994 at Pebble Beach. The last time he won before that, also at Pebble Beach, was in 1987.

Walton and Miller both brought a player's perspective but a fan's passion to the broadcast booth. Their credentials as players give them instant credibility. They both have said things that have made them unpopular with the current players. Walton, in 1999, called Knicks forward Larry Johnson a "disgrace to the game of basketball" and "a sad human being." Miller, later in 1999, called the first couple of days of the Ryder Cup as he saw them. At the time, the United States was getting beat and Justin Leonard (0–4–2 in Ryder Cup play to that point) was playing badly. Miller said, "Leonard needs to go home," which is far more polite but no less blunt than Walton's observation. Leonard wound up making a 45-foot putt, and the United States, using Miller's words to help motivate them, made a historic comeback.

33

CARY MIDDLECOFF
The Dentist

C ary Middlecoff, son of Dr. and Mrs. Herman Middlecoff, was born January 6, 1921, in the small western Tennessee town of Halls. The family moved to Memphis when Cary was still young, and he began playing golf at the Chickasaw Country Club at the age of nine. Cary showed much promise and by 1940 was easily the best amateur in the state.

After graduating from the University of Mississippi and then the University of Tennessee College of Medicine, Cary went into the Army Dental Corps, where he remained until 1945. He almost lost his dental career and his golfing career in one terrible moment. In 1944, while in the Army, he was assigned in South Carolina. There he started his brief dental career working on crowns and bridges. Unlike dentists of today, he failed to wear protective glasses. While Middlecoff was working on a patient, a bit of debris flew up and became embedded in his eyeball. Army doctors washed his eye out and then took the dentist to the hospital. The minute piece of debris was not detected. Middlecoff returned to his job, but his eye bothered him for days. He returned to the hospital, where he stayed for two months, with the eye gradually getting worse and the infection eventually spreading to the other eye. He was on the verge of total blindness; doctors doubted he would ever see again. Then specialists tried a new treatment, which worked. His vision returned to normal.

After the war Middlecoff began a career as a dentist in Memphis. But he had a vision of playing golf full-time. He won the 1945 North and South Open as an amateur and was then selected for the 1947 U.S. Walker Cup team. Although it was the highest accolade any amateur golfer could receive, the 26-year-old Middlecoff wrote a letter to the USGA, declining the invitation. It coincided with his wedding date and the date he had in mind to turn professional. "I know I would never be happy practicing dentistry without knowing for sure if I were a good player or a great one, and dentistry is too confining ever to offer me that opportunity," he wrote.

Middlecoff gave himself two years to prove himself. He had followed his father and uncle into dentistry, and his father, not pleased with his decision to turn pro, told him,

"If you stay out here and don't finish with any money after going to school for 20 years, you are an idiot!"

Since the majority of golfers at the time couldn't make a living at it, it didn't appear to be a wise move. For Middlecoff, however, it turned out to be a pretty good move. Besides, you could get hurt as a dentist, as he had already discovered. It was much safer playing golf, although there was a lot more anxiety involved in playing professionally than there would have been had he just been playing for fun on Wednesdays. Middlecoff, a chain smoker, was frequently described as nervous or fidgety.

He was an exceptional driver and one of the biggest hitters on the Tour in those days. He was very good with his short-iron game. It was his putting that often let him down.

Did he succeed and show his father that he could make it in golf? In the 1948 Masters, one year after he turned pro, he finished second at Augusta—ahead of Byron Nelson, Sam Snead, Ben Hogan, and Bobby Locke. For that he won $1,500. This was easier money than pulling teeth.

In 1949 he won the U.S. Open at the prestigious Medinah Country Club and put $2,000 in his bank account. Middlecoff led the Tour in victories in 1949, 1951, and 1955. When he was successful—and he was wildly inconsistent—it was because he could reach any green, even 500-yard par-5s, in a drive and a long iron. When Middlecoff didn't win, it was because of poor putting.

In 1955, at the Masters, he was at the peak of his game. He won at Augusta by a then-record seven-shot margin. (Tiger has since won there by 12 strokes over the next closest.)

Middlecoff had his short game working so well that after the final round he said, "I'm going to marry that putter," about the putter he had used since 1949. "She's the greatest thing since automatic starters." But even an automatic starter on an automobile couldn't roll in an 82-foot putt on the 13th green of the Masters like Middlecoff's putter did.

The player known as Doc was giddy about winning a major championship for the first time in six years. It wouldn't take long for his third, however.

In 1956, seven years after winning the U.S. Open for the first time, Middlecoff won his second by staying ahead of Hogan, who finished second. Hogan, the four-time Open champ, missed an easy four-foot putt on the 17th hole of the last round. With Middlecoff in the clubhouse, Hogan needed only pars on the final two holes to tie. He couldn't do it. Julius Boros couldn't catch Middlecoff either.

Middlecoff's game was marked by not only the jittery short game and tremendous drives but also the pace at which he played. He was the slowest player of his time. In 1955 Middlecoff played Doug Ford in the finals of the PGA Championship at Meadowbrook Country Club, in Northville, Michigan. Middlecoff was known for his slow, deliberate playing, while Ford was one of the fastest players. Before the '55 PGA finals pitting Middlecoff with Ford, Doc told the press, "I hope my game doesn't hold him up. I don't try to be slow intentionally, just cautious."

Despite his comments to the contrary, perhaps Middlecoff did use his slow play as a psychological edge against opponents. Or maybe his hay fever (Middlecoff took shots because he was allergic to grass) really acted up in the hot weather, and he needed the time to get around.

By his mid-30s, a bad back and a shaky short game were slowing down Middlecoff. He pulled his game together at the age of 35 and won the Vardon Trophy for the lowest stroke average in 1956.

In the post–World War II years, Middlecoff was the biggest winner until about 1960. These are the only golfers with more PGA Tour victories than the 40 won by the swinging dentist: Sam Snead, Jack Nicklaus, Ben Hogan, Arnold Palmer, Byron Nelson, Billy Casper, Tiger Woods, and Walter Hagen. If you added up Lanny Wadkins's 21 and Ben Crenshaw's 19, you would reach Middlecoff's total.

When he retired because of back surgery in 1963, he was among the biggest all-time leading money winners, with just under $300,000. Middlecoff continued playing into his mid-40s, eventually becoming a television analyst. He died in 1998.

Middlecoff gave up a promising career as a dentist in Memphis, Tennessee, in the late 1940s. Had he listened to his father and not selected what was behind "door number two," he might have treated the following Memphis residents in their youth: Morgan Freeman (born in 1937), Tim McCarver (born in 1941), Aretha Franklin (born in 1942), and Cybill Shepherd (born in 1950). But you couldn't get this dentist back in the office.

Who's Better, Who's Best
Cary Middlecoff or Sam Snead?
The younger Middlecoff actually was Snead's equal in 1949, smack in the middle of Snead's prime.

	Wins	2nd Place	3rd Place	Top 10s	Majors
Sam Snead	6	4	4	20	Masters, PGA
Cary Middlecoff	6	5	5	21	U.S. Open

Snead won bigger tournaments that year (aside from the U.S. Open, Middlecoff won the Rio Grande Valley Open, the Jacksonville Open, the Motor City Open, the Reading

Open, and the Miami Four-Ball). Snead's six wins included the Masters, PGA Championship, and Western Open. He was PGA Tour Player of the Year in 1949, won the Vardon Trophy for lowest scoring average, and was the leading money winner. Snead was one of the top-five golfers in history. Middlecoff would have been closer to Snead in the rankings if he would have had more years like 1949. There just weren't enough of them.

A Better Analogy

Cary Middlecoff and Warren Spahn They were both born in 1921 and began winning after leaving the Army, where they served during World War II. Spahn, a pitcher in the major leagues, finished his career with 363 wins, an amazing number for someone who spent four early years of his career in the Army. Middlecoff won 40 times on the Tour, despite also missing four years while in the service. They both were competing—though much less effectively—in their mid-40s.

These were the consistent players in their sport during the 1950s—the ones who were always among the league leaders in victories.

34

JAMES BRAID
One of the Great Triumvirate

James Braid was born in Scotland on February 6, 1870. That made him two months older than Harry Vardon, who was born on May 9 that year, and 13 months older than J. H. Taylor. Braid was the only one of the three from Scotland, where the game of golf as we know it originated.

Braid began playing when he was young and won his first local tournament in 1878, at the age of (yup) eight. While other kids were reading their Dickens novels, Braid was more interested in learning about club making. When he was 23 he took a job in London as a club maker. He didn't turn pro until he was 26 years old.

Before 1900 Braid had a well-deserved reputation as a long driver who couldn't win consistently due to his short game. Braid's putter kept him from joining the likes of Vardon and Taylor sooner. But when Braid switched to an aluminum-headed putter (from a wooden-headed model), his short game improved, and Vardon and Taylor had their hands full. Comparisons of the three are fascinating. Since there was only one Open that mattered then, it is easy to compare the records of the big three in their 21-year reign at the British Open (see table on page 208).

That is an incredible 21-year period that might have continued if not for World War I. Vardon, based on his U.S. Open success and his late-career comeback, has the clear edge. But it's close between Taylor and Braid.

Braid's first British Open victory, in 1901, got him going. But in that tournament he began by hooking his first drive over a stone wall and out of bounds. He rallied and came to the 72nd hole with a lead. Attempting to reach the green of the 18th, which was 200 yards away, Braid slashed at his ball and watched as the shaft splintered and the head went flying off toward the clubhouse. Despite the broken bat, the ball carried onto the green and he beat Vardon by three strokes.

Braid's long game was excellent, but his putting was not. That was largely corrected when he replaced his wooden putter with an aluminum-headed one. How excellent was his long game? In the Sunday, January 14, 1917, edition of the *Washington Post*, there was a headline entitled "Braid, Scotland's Great Golfer, Is Said to Be Longest Driver." In the

Year	Course	Taylor	Vardon	Braid
1894	Sandwich	1	5	10
1895	St. Andrews	1	9	—
1896	Muirfield	2	1	6
1897	Hoylake	10	6	2
1898	Prestwick	4	1	11
1899	Sandwich	4	1	5
1900*	St. Andrews	1	2	3
1901	Muirfield	3	2	1
1902	Hoylake	6	2	2
1903	Prestwick	9	1	5
1904	Sandwich	2	5	2
1905	St. Andrews	2	9	1
1906	Muirfield	2	3	1
1907	Hoylake	2	7	5
1908	Prestwick	7	5	1
1909	Deal	1	26	2
1910	St. Andrews	14	16	1
1911**	Sandwich	5	1	5
1912	Muirfield	11	2	3
1913	Hoylake	1	3	18
1914	Prestwick	2	1	10

* Notice that at this point, Taylor has three championships, as does Vardon, while Braid doesn't get his first until the following year. ** Vardon was stricken with tuberculosis after the 1903 British Open; his play in 1911 was remarkable.

article Braid is described as a "driver of extraordinary ability. Braid has a reputation, wherever golf is played, of being the longest driver, amateur or professional, in the whole golf world." The article said that he got his long drives "from skill, not strength, and it proves conclusively that efficiency in the handling of clubs means more than the shoulders of the swing behind them."

Braid's spectacular success came at the turn of the century. In 1901 he won his first British Open in Muirfield. Braid, Vardon, and Taylor all finished in the top three. Braid, a superior driver to Vardon, must have been special to defeat Vardon in his prime.

Within 10 years Braid became the first man to win the event five times. He was runner-up three times in those 10 years. (Taylor won five Opens, but only one between 1901 and 1910.)

Braid retired at the age of 42. His great passion after his retirement was course design. It is estimated that he designed or redesigned more than 200 courses around Great Britain. (Fear of flying and motion sickness on boat rides prevented him from ever working in the United States.) Among the courses he helped remodel were Carnoustie, Troon, Prestwick, and Ballybunion.

An article by sportswriter Chick Evans in January of 1922 told more about Braid and his place among the golf greats.

James Braid probably had the most uncanny ability any golfer ever possessed in placing his ball so it would be in the best position possible for the next shot. I want to give James Braid his place in my Hall of Fame because I don't think anyone will ever dispute that he originated the scheme of play by which the shot beyond the shot in hand was the play to be striven for.

Braid also gave a devotion to the game and a dogged determination for which his skill was a just reward. When Braid played, the world might have ended without his knowing about it. If the Scotch put golf just after religion, as has been charged, then "Jimmy" Braid is the best exponent of this theory of life that I have ever known. In his play, he is so absorbed that he neither sees, hears, nor speaks of anything but the shot in hand.

This country has seen a good deal of Vardon, Taylor, and Ted Ray, but Braid has always been "a poor sailor" and but few American and Canadian players have seen him in action. I first met Braid when I went to England to play in the 1911 Open Championship. Braid was then the holder of the title.

In action, Braid was the opposite of Vardon. I must say that I did not care for Braid's style of play, as I did for Vardon's. But this must be said. No one could watch him play and not pay him the fullest respect for his great skill, his determination, and his genius for taking pains.

As I often watched Braid studying his ball I was struck by the contrast between his rather rugged style of play and the easy, smooth play of Vardon. Both men were always mechanically perfect in their stance and swing and in the timing of their shots; but Vardon does it all with a wonderful grace, while Braid accomplished it with a kind of precision which got the result.

Who's Better, Who's Best
James Braid or J. H. Taylor?

There were three great golfers at the beginning of the 1900s. Vardon, Taylor, and Braid were known as the Great Triumvirate. They could have been nicknamed anything else—

for example, the Three Musketeers, Braid's Bunch, or the like—but the Great Triumvirate stuck.

It seems clear that Vardon, through his records and the recollections of contemporaries like Taylor, was the best of the three. James Braid won the same number of British Opens as Taylor. But Taylor was a better golfer through to 1900 (when he won Opens in 1894, 1895, and 1900) and after 1910. Braid won his five Opens in a 10-year period. I'll take Taylor for his longer period of brilliance (15 top-five finishes in the British Open, 11 of them in the first or second spot). But Braid (19 consecutive years in the British Open and 15 top-five finishes) wasn't far behind Taylor, and he earns a spot in the top 50 golfers of all time.

A Better Analogy

When Three Great Athletes Dominate an Era Golf's Great Triumvirate won 16 British Opens in a 21-year span. The NBA experienced a similar Triumvirate beginning in 1980. A run of 11 championships in 14 seasons was split between Magic Johnson's, Larry Bird's, and Michael Jordan's teams. In fact, one of those three won the NBA title in 14 of 19 seasons beginning in 1980.

Major League Baseball had a similar Triumvirate with Willie Mays, Mickey Mantle, and Duke Snider. Beginning in 1951, either Willie's, Mickey's, or the Duke's team won the World Series in 10 of the next 12 seasons. Unlike the golf or basketball trios, however, the baseball centerfielders didn't share the wins fairly. Mays played on only one World Series champion team, and Snider played on just two.

Beginning in 1974, the men's singles championship at Wimbledon was won 10 times in 11 years by either Jimmy Connors, Björn Borg, or John McEnroe. Only Arthur Ashe was able to break through and win during that run.

35

JULIUS BOROS
The Moose

Whenever a golfer in his 40s has a hot hand in a major, the name Julius Boros invariably comes up. Boros, known when he played as the Moose, won the PGA Championship in 1968 at the age of 48. He remains the oldest person to win a major—older even than Nicklaus was in 1986, when Jack won the Masters.

This was no one-trick pony (er, Moose). At the age of 43, Boros won the U.S. Open in 1963. That was 11 years after he won the Open for the first time, in 1952, when he hadn't even qualified to carry his PGA card.

Boros, the son of a Hungarian-born man who earned but $20 a week as a factory worker, was born on March 3, 1920, in Connecticut. Julius (at the age of seven) and two of his brothers would sneak over the fence onto the local golf course (located just behind their house). He later became a caddie at the country club in Fairfield, Connecticut. His mother would remind him often that golf was a sport for the rich.

In high school Boros played on the golf team and was a basketball star as well. He went to Bridgeport University and got a degree. He would be an accountant. Accounting and pro golf had to wait, however, as he went into the military for World War II. Boros was stationed at Biloxi for four years as a medic. Suddenly, in 1945, the Air Force discharged him with a rheumatic heart. A cardiologist told him that he could play "nine holes of golf now and then," but only if he were to "play slow and never take it seriously."

After that he went back to school and became an accountant. He still played a lot of golf, however. Boros spent a great deal of time with legend Tommy Armour, the professional at Boros's club in Connecticut. He received some tips from Armour. Armour always taught to "hit the hell out of the ball with your right hand," but Boros couldn't play that way. He tried Armour's way repeatedly yet kept shanking the ball. Boros began playing in the bigger amateur tournaments and the big pro-ams. When Boros told Armour that he was turning pro, Tommy predicted that Boros would never succeed. Admitting that Boros was exceptional from sand bunkers, Armour gave him this piece of advice: "Aim for the bunkers and you might make it."

Boros developed his great bunker shots by playing them with a 9-iron early in his career. He used it when he finished second (tying Sam Snead) in 1948 at Pinehurst in the North and South Open. Seeing Boros hit with the 9-iron, Vic Ghezzi, the 1941 PGA champion, told him that he would send him a sand wedge. Boros had gone down to Pinehurst, ostensibly to do accounting work. He wound up finishing second in the tournament. He desperately wanted to turn professional. It would be against his mother's wishes, as she wanted her son to have the financial security of an accountant.

In December of 1949 Boros became a golf pro at the age of 29. He got married in May of 1950. Marrying a woman who would allow a man of 30 to throw away an established career and income in favor of a dream meant that his accounting career was effectively over.

By 1950 the unknown Boros led the U.S. Open for much of the tournament, eventually finishing ninth to winner Ben Hogan. Julius and his wife, Ann (known as Buttons), had a son in 1951. During childbirth Ann went into a coma. Two days later Julius lost her to a cerebral hemorrhage.

His career was almost over just as it was beginning. His late-blooming career, already set back years, would be set back for another year as he got his life in order.

Then in Dallas, site of the 1952 U.S. Open, the unheralded Boros, called an "apprentice professional" in the papers, defeated Hogan and won his first major at the age of 32. Hogan had won the U.S. Open in 1948, 1950, and 1951 and went on to win again in 1953. He didn't enter the U.S. Open in 1949 because he was recovering from his auto accident. The only players to finish ahead of Hogan in the U.S. Open in the six-year stretch from 1948 to 1953 were 1952's winner Boros and runner-up Ed Oliver (who won in 1949).

Boros married an airline flight attendant named Armen, the daughter of a golf pro, in 1955 and had six more children. One of them, Guy, born in 1966, would grow up and win a tournament, making Julius and Guy one of only six father-son winners in pro golf. In addition there were Tom Morris Sr. and Jr., Willie Park Sr. and Jr., Joe Kirkwood Sr. and Jr., Clayton and Vance Heafner, and Al and Brent Geiberger. Maybe the fact that Boros had seven young kids was the reason that he never went to the British Open (well, except for 1966, when he finished 15th) and the reason he played so long on the Tour.

Boros never did much at Augusta. He had four top-five finishes but never finished higher than a tie for third place. In 1955 he finished fourth, behind Cary Middlecoff, Hogan, and Snead. In 1960 he came close, but that was Arnold Palmer's Masters. In 1963 he finished two strokes back of Nicklaus.

Boros swung easy, and it was written that it looked as if he was hitting the ball at half speed. He played at over 200 pounds, so opponents must have expected more length on his shots. Boros had a personality that responded well to pressure. He was a nice guy, both on and off the course.

In 1955, at the Western Open, Boros birdied two of the first five holes and appeared to be on his way to a great round. Then his young caddie touched the ball on the sixth hole, and Boros was forced to take a two-stroke penalty. He still finished with a 71. The boy cried. Boros refused to change caddies the next day and called the boy's parents after the tournament to tell them what a fine son they had.

Boros was the number one money winner in pro golf in 1953 and 1955. He didn't play the British Open but rather opted for more lucrative exhibition matches. His greatest success usually came at the U.S. Open.

Boros at the U.S. Open

1952 first place
1956 tie for second place—one shot back of Middlecoff
1957 tie for fourth place
1958 third place
1960 tie for third place—three shots back of Palmer, one back of Nicklaus
1963 first place
1965 tie for fourth place

Boros's 1952 U.S. Open victory caught everyone by surprise, but that would be his only major until he was 43 years old. In between his U.S. Open victories, he had two three-year stretches when he didn't win a single tournament. The Open in 1963 took place in Brookline, Massachusetts. When the 72 holes were played, there was a three-way tie between Jackie Cupit, Palmer, and Boros. Boros was playing against men 18 years and 10 years younger than him. In the 18-hole play-off, the father of seven prevailed to win his second major.

Big Julie survived the wilting summer heat in Texas and won the PGA Championship in 1968, defeating Bob Charles and Palmer by one stroke. Palmer made a tremendous shot to save par on the final hole and finished with 282. But Boros pitched in a long chip within two feet of the pin for a par, making him the oldest winner of a major, a mark that still stands.

Boros explained his success by saying he never tinkered with his swing. Unlike Woods, Faldo, or others who revamped their swing in midcareer, Boros stayed with the same swing that he had started with as a kid in Connecticut. After he retired he stayed busy, of course. He was seen on television hosting a show ("Outdoors with Julius Boros") where he hunted and fished with celebrity guests and then gave golf tips at the end of the show.

He helped form the Legends of Golf, which became the Champions Tour. The man who never had a formal golf lesson in his life began teaching golf in his later years. One of his pupils was tennis star Jimmy Connors.

Boros had ups and downs in his life. The former accountant, on balance, had the highest of highs and the lowest of lows. He made up for a late start with more success on the back end than almost any other golfer. He lasted long enough to make some real money out of golf.

Historically, he's tough to rank. Tiger Woods and Nicklaus had accomplished so much by their 30th birthdays; all of Bobby Jones's golf accomplishments were achieved by his 30th birthday. Boros, on the other hand, spent time in the Air Force and balancing books before his. Boros won his three majors over 16 years. He tasted success early, middle, and late in his career. He defeated Hogan in his prime and Palmer and Nicklaus in their prime.

Who's Better, Who's Best
Julius Boros or Cary Middlecoff?

Middlecoff was one year older than Boros. He was a dentist by trade, which trumps Boros's accounting degree. Middlecoff won 40 times on the Tour, compared to the Moose's 18 victories. Middlecoff won three majors (two U.S. Opens and a Masters) as did Boros (two U.S. Opens and a PGA). Middlecoff, like Boros, only played the British Open once.

One shot separates them, though. At the 1956 U.S. Open at the Oak Hill Country Club in Rochester, New York, Boros finished one stroke back of champion Middlecoff. Boros had a chance on the 72nd hole when his 15-foot putt lipped the cup and swerved around it. If that putt had found the cup, Boros would have had four majors and Middlecoff just two.

Cary Middlecoff gets the nod, though not by much. If you were hiring only one of them, you would be impressed with Dr. Middlecoff's "Masters" degree.

Who's Better, Who's Best
Julius Boros or Vijay Singh?

Boros and Singh were the most accomplished golfers after their 40th birthdays, with the singular exception of Sam Snead. Both Boros and Singh have three majors. In style and temperament, though, they are very different. Boros was easygoing and boasted that he rarely practiced. Singh is known as the hardest-working guy on the Tour. This is almost as close as Middlecoff and Boros. But Boros's pair of U.S. Opens and a major championship at the PGA when he was 48 narrowly better Singh's pair of PGA Championships and a Masters.

As of this writing, Singh has entered 17 British Opens without winning one. Boros entered the British Open just once. Boros, therefore, won a higher percentage of his majors than Singh has.

36

LLOYD MANGRUM
Pro Golf Isn't So Tough

Texas really is the cradle of golfing greats in the United States, and Mangrum is just one more from the Lone Star State to make the top 50. Mangrum was born in Trenton, Texas, in 1914, putting him in the era of fellow Longhorns Byron Nelson and Ben Hogan.

He went to California with his family as a child and learned golf from his brother, Ray. Lloyd caddied and was an assistant to Ray, who was the head professional at a country club. Lloyd became a golf pro himself at the age of 15. Then as an unattached professional at the Sunset Hills Golf Course, in Los Angeles, Lloyd hustled amateurs for $5 or $10 bets, which means the teen wasn't working at the club and he didn't tell the people he was making bets with that he was a golf pro.

Sometimes they competed brother against brother. There have been only three sets of brothers in history to each win at least five Tour events apiece: Lloyd and Ray Mangrum, Joe and Mike Turnesa, and Lionel and Jay Hebert. Ray won five tournaments in his career. His younger brother would win 36 times on the PGA Tour, as well as a number of international championships. In other words, Ray Mangrum was more like Charlotta Sorenstam (one LPGA victory and one international victory) to Lloyd's Annika. Lloyd needed the competition and the money. He married when he was 19 years old, the age when he played his first pro tournament—the Southern California Open.

The quick-witted Mangrum described his game this way: "I took Sam Snead's swing, Byron Nelson's drive, Johnny Revolta's short game, and Ben Hogan's concentration. But I didn't take my putting stroke from anybody but me." At the time, the theory was for players with small hands (like Mangrum, who was only about 145 pounds) to use a full right-hand grip. Mangrum used the interlocking grip—even while putting. He used only a modicum of wrist action, depending more on his forearms for his long shots off the tee and even for driving. Mangrum was considered a wizard in calculating distance and always seemed to use the right club. He became one of the best putters on the Tour.

Mangrum's first breakout performance came at the 1940 Masters, where newspaper reporters called him "Cinderella Man." There were two places left in the Masters—then an invitational—so tournament officials went back through the winter season's records and decided that Mangrum (who had won the Thomasville Open in Thomasville, Georgia, in March) should get one of the last two spots. He was still an unknown and was lucky to be in the field. He shocked the world when he shot an opening-round 64 at the Masters. At the time, it was the greatest round of golf ever shot in a major tournament.

On that eye-opening 64 performance, Mangrum made every green in two shots and made nine birdies. He was eight strokes under par. His record-breaking round at the Masters would stand for 46 years, until Nick Price broke it in 1986 with a 63.

The clock struck midnight for Mr. Cinderella in that tournament, and he finished second to Jimmy Demaret. But Mangrum quickly moved into the top-10 money winners by 1942.

World War II interrupted Mangrum's blossoming career. Sergeant Mangrum was injured while on reconnaissance as the 90th Infantry Division was on a mission. A jeep turned over on him as it swerved to avoid hitting a truck in a blackout. Surgeons advised Mangrum that his deltoid muscle was torn and that if he couldn't lift his right arm when the cast was removed, an operation would be necessary, in which there was danger that his arm would never be the same. The biggest thrill of his life came weeks later when the pro athlete, out of the cast, was able to lift his arm.

He returned to the front lines and was training for the D-day landings when he was offered the professional's job at the Army's Fort Meade golf course, which would have kept him out of combat. He declined the offer.

He was wounded in the Battle of the Bulge. He was nicked below the right knee by a sniper. Later he was struck under the chin by shrapnel, but he stuck with his men from the 90th Infantry Division reconnaissance group, which spearheaded the drive into Czechoslovakia. He won two Purple Hearts.

Fresh from the Army, he won the 1946 U.S. Open. He was 32 years old that year, when he outlasted Vic Ghezzi and Byron Nelson in 36 extra holes for the championship. (All three were tied after 72 holes, as well as after an 18-hole play-off.) In 1947, 1949, 1951, and 1953, he played the Ryder Cup for the United States (did you expect that he would not represent his country?).

Mangrum was different from his fellow-Texans Hogan and Snead. Mangrum was known for his relaxed demeanor on the course. He was described as sharp witted and an entertaining conversationalist. He was a chain-smoker on the course who was known to have a highball or two in the evening with a cigar.

In July of 1950 his personality got him into a little bit of trouble with Snead. Mangrum beat Snead by one stroke at the Motor City Open, in Detroit. Snead, never noted for his sense of humor, blew up when the jubilant Mangrum thanked him jokingly for missing an easy four-foot putt on the last hole that would have forced a play-off. Mangrum tried to console Snead with a friendly slap on the back, but Sam brushed him off and stormed away. Obviously, Snead had a reputation for blowing up under pressure, and Mangrum bore the brunt of it.

The *Saturday Evening Post* featured a 1956 article by Mangrum entitled "Why Pro Golf Isn't That Tough." Mangrum wrote in the article that the game is easy and there is no pressure in it. While it seems crazy to say that there is no pressure in golf or that it is easy, one must keep in mind that the article was written by a veteran who risked his life in dangerous missions for his country. Now *that* was pressure to Mangrum. By comparison, there was no pressure in golf.

Sportsmanship Personified

In 1950, Mangrum tied Ben Hogan and George Fazio at the Merion Golf Club, site of the U.S. Open. On the 17th tee of the 18-hole play-off, the USGA rules chairman informed Mangrum that he had sustained a two-stroke penalty for lifting his ball in play on the 16th green. Mangrum had just holed that putt to make a great recovery and was only one stroke behind Hogan with two holes remaining.

He was informed of the killer penalty as he prepared to tee off. "Do you mean I had a 6 instead of a 4?" The official replied yes. Mangrum didn't sulk, cry, storm about, or curse. "Well, I guess we'll all still eat tomorrow," he said.

Mangrum, perhaps because he had only one major championship in his possession (the 1946 U.S. Open), publicly professed that all tournaments were equal. He won 36 times, which was in the top 6 of all time when he retired and is still among the top-12 totals.

Why didn't he win more majors? Well, he only played in 45 majors, and that includes 11 when he was in his 40s, past his prime. He played the British Open only once, in 1953. He played the PGA Championship only nine times, going 19–9 in his 28 matches. Twice (in 1941 and 1949) he reached the semifinals. He lost that play-off for the 1950 U.S. Open to Hogan. He was second to Snead in the 1949 Masters. He finished third to Hogan at the 1953 U.S. Open. Mangrum did, however, have two wins at the Western Open, which was considered to be a major by most golfers at the time.

Mangrum was the leading money winner in 1951. That was no small accomplishment, as either Nelson, Hogan, or Snead were the money leaders in 9 of the previous 10 years (with Demaret leading in money in 1947) and Mangrum was not the golfer that those three were.

In November of 1973 Mangrum died of a heart attack in Apple Valley, California, where he had lived since the early 1950s. (When he retired, a writer had dubbed him "the Squire of Apple Valley.") Mangrum died at the age of 59, leaving a wife, a son, two daughters, eight grandchildren, and five great-grandchildren. I suppose that when one marries at 19, it is possible to have five great-grandchildren within 40 years. Do the math, folks—it's pretty impressive.

Mangrum faced and overcame a lot of pressure in his life. In addition to surviving the first 11 of his 12 heart attacks, he survived the Battle of the Bulge. He wasn't a conscripted teenager who went to fight for his country in World War II. Rather, he was a 28-year-old man with three kids, and not only did he serve, but he declined the cushy job that was offered. Now Mangrum wasn't the only top athlete to serve his country and certainly wasn't the only one of his generation. Another noteworthy example is Baseball Hall of Famer Ted Williams, who lost nearly five years of his career between stints for World War II and Korea. That doesn't take away from the heroic Mangrum. But he was right—pro golfers don't face pressure.

A Better Analogy

Lloyd Mangrum and James J. Braddock The story of heavyweight boxer Jimmy Braddock is fairly well-known thanks to the recent motion picture *Cinderella Man*. Braddock was a promising Depression-era fighter who initially failed to reach the top, in part because of a series of injuries, but who waged an amazing comeback against all odds. Mangrum was from the same era as Braddock. Although there were other golfers (including Hogan) who picked themselves up off the ground with little money and became success stories, Mangrum was the one referred to as "Cinderella Man" by sportswriters in 1940. In due time they could call him a war hero.

37

NANCY LOPEZ
Five Straight in '78!

On Easter weekend in March of 2005, Annika Sorenstam won the Kraft Nabisco Championship (a major tournament) by eight strokes. The victory was Sorenstam's fifth consecutive tour victory over two seasons, which tied the record held by Nancy Lopez, who had won five consecutive tournaments in the spring of 1978. Even the great Sorenstam could only match but not surpass Lopez, as Annika finished 12th in her subsequent tournament. There was much more to Nancy Lopez than the five straight in '78.

She was born on January 6, 1957, and started playing golf at the age of eight under the guidance of her father, Domingo. She grew up in Roswell, New Mexico (about 100 miles from the town where Kathy Whitworth was from), and it only took her a year to win her first tournament, at the age of nine. She was only 12 when she won the New Mexico Women's Amateur. Following that she won the U.S. Girls' Junior Championship twice (1972 and 1974). She won the Western Junior three times and the Mexican Amateur in 1975.

Also in 1975 she entered the U.S. Women's Open in Atlantic City as an amateur and finished in a tie for second. The 18-year-old Lopez three-putted the 18th green to lose sole possession of second place in the major that Sandra Palmer would win by four strokes. Lopez tied for second with JoAnne Carner and Sandra Post. It was there, in Atlantic City, where the galleries first connected with Lopez.

The 5'5" Lopez had a warm, radiating personality. Her Latina heritage brought new fans to the table. She was a feisty competitor and had, for lack of a better word, charisma.

Lopez enrolled in college, with plenty of opportunities still to come to capture a U.S. Women's Open. She matriculated at the University of Tulsa, where she was a 1976 All-American and the university's first Female Athlete of the Year.

In July of 1977, at Hazeltine National Golf Course, in Minnesota, Lopez entered her first tournament as a professional. She took aim at the U.S. Women's Open and five holes into the final round had a share of the lead, tied with Stacy Hollis. But a double-bogey on the 12th hole ended Lopez's chances of beating Hollis. Lopez finished in second place, two strokes back.

She was only 20 years old and had a pair of second-place finishes at one of the majors on the LPGA Tour. After earning her Tour card, she played six events in 1977 without winning. But it didn't take much longer before she won. In the fourth tournament of 1978, the Bent Tree Classic, at Sarasota, Florida, she was tied with Donna White for the lead going into the last round. After White fell off, Lopez found herself in a tie with JoAnn Washam with four strokes to go. Lopez made a 15-foot birdie putt on 17, made par on 18, and won her first tournament. At the presentation ceremonies she dedicated that victory to her mom, who had died a few months earlier of heart disease. Lopez followed up her first tournament victory in February of '78 with a second—the Sunstar Classic in Los Angeles—two weeks later.

Three months after that, in May, Lopez began her streak of five consecutive tournament wins. She won in Baltimore; Jamesburg, New Jersey; New Rochelle, New York; Kings Island, Ohio (where she took her first major, the LPGA Championship); and Rochester, New York.

By this point she had transcended the back of the sports pages and was front-page news. She was America's newest hero. In fact, all the interviews and appearances probably mentally wore her out by the time the Lady Keystone Open, at Hershey, Pennsylvania, rolled around. While losing, the 21-year-old Lopez met sportscaster Tim Melton; they were married within six months.

Her rookie season of 1978 was one of the greatest seasons any golfer, let alone a rookie, ever had. She won the Mickey Wright Award for most tournament wins (nine). She won the Vare Trophy for the leading stroke average (71.76). She won the LPGA's Player of the Year Award. The one thing she didn't win in 1978 was the U.S. Women's Open, finishing in ninth place. The U.S. Women's Open would remain elusive her entire career.

Lopez had almost as good a year in 1979, winning 8 out of 19 tournaments. In fact, she had a five-year period from 1978 to 1982 as good as just about anyone in the history of the game. She wasn't quite Kathy Whitworth from 1965 to 1968 (35 victories in 119 tournaments), but Lopez (25 victories in 115 tournaments) was close, especially if you believe that the level of competition was better in the late '70s and early '80s.

Even when Lopez lost she won. The crowds adored her, and she became the most popular and accessible athlete on the LPGA. Her marriage to sportscaster Melton, however, had deteriorated quickly, as it couldn't survive the pressure of her always being away. She would file for divorce after two years.

Melton, by the early 1980s, was a sportscaster in Cincinnati and had become friends with Reds third baseman Ray Knight, whom he introduced to his wife. After Lopez split with Melton, a friendship blossomed with the baseball player, leading to a second marriage, for both Knight and Lopez, in October of 1982.

This was a big sports marriage. This was before the Steffi Graf–Andre Agassi union a generation later. Even that later union didn't pose the problems that this one did. Graf didn't marry Agassi and have children until the end of her playing career.

Lopez was 25 when she married Knight. Both were in the prime of their careers. Lopez was willing to interrupt—or even end—her playing career to be with Knight. He never asked her to stop playing.

Knight, by the way, was no benchwarmer. When Pete Rose left the Cincinnati Reds, it was Knight who took over at third base. Knight made two All-Star teams. While Lopez had career earnings in excess of $5 million, it probably didn't outdo the career earnings of her baseball husband.

Lopez gave birth to a daughter, Ashley, in November of 1983. She played only 12 events that year, winning in February and April. When she was two months pregnant, she won the J&B Scotch Pro-Am Desert Inn, played in Las Vegas. She played into late June, at the Rochester Invitational, but she had gained a lot of weight and took time off before the baby was born.

A reduced schedule in 1984 saw two more tournament wins and six top-10 finishes in only 16 tournaments. In 1985 Lopez won five tournaments, finished second in five others, won her second LPGA Championship, and returned to number one in the rankings. She and Ray had figured out this baby business quite well by 1985. They added a second daughter, Erinn Shea, in May of 1986. Yes, the name sounds awfully Irish for a product of a Native American father and a Hispanic mother. No, the middle name, Shea, was not for the stadium where Daddy (having been traded to the New York Mets in 1985) played his home games that season. Lopez played in only four tournaments in 1986, finishing in the top three in three of the four.

While she never did win her U.S. Open, it was her husband who seized his one moment in time at his "major." In October of 1986 Knight's Mets made the World Series against the Boston Red Sox. With the Red Sox just one strike from winning their first World Series in 68 years, Knight singled in a run and would come around and score the winning run in Game 6 on a Bill Buckner error. Then in Game 7, with the score tied 3–3 in the seventh inning, Knight's home run gave the Mets the championship. Knight was named the World Series MVP.

Despite playing a reduced schedule in 1987, Lopez won two tournaments and finished second in four others. In 1988 *Golf Magazine* named her the Golfer of the Decade for the period from 1978 to 1987. She wasn't through yet. In May of 1989 Lopez won her third major—the LPGA Championship—which was her 40th Tour victory. Only a handful of women had reached that number. Wright reached it before she was 28. Whitworth reached it before she was 29. And later, in 2002, Sorenstam reached her 40th Tour victory at the age of 31 years and 11 months. That was just a few months younger than Lopez, who won her 40th at the age of 32 years and 4 months.

In July of 1989 Lopez finished second (again) at the U.S. Women's Open, this time by four shots to Betsy King. On May 5, 1991, Lopez won the Sara Lee Classic. Five months later, she gave birth to her third daughter, Torri Heather, on October 30. Phil Mickelson may have played with the pressure of awaiting his wife's imminent labor at the 1999 U.S. Open, but he didn't have any morning sickness. I can think of only two other LPGA greats who gave birth during their careers. Judy Rankin had only one child, and her son was born before she won her first LPGA tournament. Juli Inkster won the Crestar Classic on May 7, 1989—a full nine months before her daughter Hayley was born on February 4, 1990.

In the 1997 U.S. Women's Open, Lopez would yet again (her fourth time) finish in second place. In that Open, played in Oregon, the 40-year-old Lopez became the first to shoot four sub-70 rounds (69–68–69–69), and her 275 total would have been good enough to win 50 of the first 52 Opens. But Alison Nicholas shot a 274 to give Lopez her fourth runner-up (and closest) finish in an Open.

In 2002 Lopez played 14 events in a good-bye tour of sorts. She played the U.S. Women's Open for a last time, and the fans couldn't get enough of her. One of the most beloved and outstanding female athletes of all time, she had played for most of a quarter-century. Time takes a toll on even the superstars in life. Lopez's father, Domingo, passed away early in 2002. Two years later her husband would suffer a heart attack, recover, and, together with Lopez, travel on a cross-country tour to launch a "Back in Full Swing" campaign to promote life after heart disease.

In 2005 she was named captain of the U.S. Solheim Cup, which regained the Cup from the European team in September of 2005. Perhaps she picked up some tips on managing from her husband, who had managed the Cincinnati Reds in 1996 and part of 1997.

Who's Better, Who's Best
Nancy Lopez or Louise Suggs or Betsy Rawls?

Only Whitworth, Wright, and Sorenstam have more than 60 Tour victories, and they're all ranked ahead of Lopez. Among all the women ahead of Lopez on the official career wins list—the aforementioned three, plus Patty Berg, Louise Suggs, and Betsy Rawls— none ever had children.

Lopez deserves to be ahead of women like Louise Suggs and Betsy Rawls. Suggs played in an era when there were only 20 LPGA members, so her 8 majors and 58 wins as a professional compare favorably to Lopez's record. Rawls played from 1951 to 1975, and her 55 wins and 8 majors are more impressive to me than Suggs's. But Rawls was never the dominant golfer in her era, trailing first Didrikson and Berg and then Wright and Whitworth.

A Better Analogy

Nancy Lopez and Arnold Palmer Palmer and Lopez are similar. First, because of the way the fans in the gallery took to them. Second, because of the way both began their sky-rocketing careers. Both of them had remarkable staying power and both are responsible for an increased popularity in their game.

Dottie Pepper, winner of 17 LPGA Tour events and 1992 Rolex Player of the Year: "As good as Nancy has been on the golf course, she has been even better off the course. There is something very genuine about her. Nancy—like Arnold Palmer—related to the people. Nancy didn't just relate to the gallery, she related to her competitors. She beat you—but she beat you with a smile on her face."

Why do I rank Nancy Lopez so high, despite her relatively puny number of majors? After her first five years (1978–82), she had won 25 tournaments. After that, she had a period of nine years (1983–91) when she was devoting herself to being a baseball wife and a mother—but all the while her skills were still there. From 1983 to 1991 she made 140 of 146 cuts, and she won 19 times in 146 tournaments. I project that if she could have taken a different path and played full-time, she would have ended her career with 10 more victories in those nine seasons and probably a few more after 1992 (when she won only four times).

Arnold Palmer is fourth in career PGA victories. Nancy Lopez is seventh in LPGA victories. Palmer dominated for a short period of time (1960–62) when he won 24 tournaments and 5 majors in three years. Lopez had a similar period from 1978 to 1980, winning 20 times in those three years.

Yes, there are men and women with more victories, more major championships, and better stroke averages than Nancy Lopez. But not many.

38

HORTON SMITH
The Joplin Ghost

Derived from the Anglo-Saxon *smitan*, meaning "to smite or strike," Smith is a surname that was first given for a man who worked with metal (smith or blacksmith), one of the earliest jobs for which specialist skills were required. It is a craft that was practiced in all countries, making the surname and its derivations the most common in the United States.

The name Smith was even more common in 1908, when Horton Smith was born in Springfield, Missouri. One way for Smiths to stand out is to accomplish things early in life. Smith's autobiography, *The Velvet Touch* (published posthumously in 1965 with Marian Benton), is his story of a boy born in the obscurity of a southern Missouri farm who reaches the pinnacle of success before his 21st birthday.

An old proverb tells us that once you establish a reputation as an early riser, you can sleep till noon. That was true in Smith's golfing career, for he came out of the gate fast, winning many tournaments early in his professional career.

Another way for Smiths to stand out is by having an identifiable nickname. Horton was called the Missouri Rover and the Joplin Ghost. These witty nicknames were given to him because of his Missouri roots and the fact that he once was the golf pro in Joplin, Missouri.

Not only was Horton Smith a very avuncular figure, but his first and last names were connected with trustworthiness and respect. In fact, when he was 31 years old, one of the most popular films was *Mr. Smith Goes to Washington*. Starring Jimmy Stewart (the Tom Hanks of his day), the movie is about Jefferson Smith, the ultimate stand-up guy—a scout leader who is appointed to the U.S. Senate, where he refuses to get drawn into the corruption.

Dr. Seuss came out with *Horton Hatches the Egg* in 1949 and *Horton Hears a Who!* later. Horton the elephant represents kindness, trustworthiness, and perseverance. I have no concrete evidence for my theory that Theodor Geisel (Dr. Seuss), born in Springfield, Massachusetts, around the same time as Horton Smith, named his elephant after the golfer—but there weren't many Hortons in Whoville or anywhere else.

I bring up the surnames because in golf, Smith is forever linked with Jones—the second most common surname in the United States. Bobby Jones was *the man* in golf in the late 1920s. Until Horton came along.

Now Horton began to play golf at age 11 with his older brother, Ren. Horton won the Springfield City Amateur Title when he was 15 years old and reached the semis of the Western Junior Championship the next year. He turned pro at the age of 18, in 1926. By 1928 he had won a couple of tournaments. And in 1929 he had one of the greatest years in golf history.

Horton entered 19 tournaments in 1929. He won eight of them and was second in six others. He won the French Open on his 21st birthday in 1929 (Walter Hagen had a cake waiting for him when Smith holed his final putt). At 21 he became the youngest ever to play on the U.S. Ryder Cup team.

One of the first stops of the 1930 season was the Savannah Open, an event that Smith defeated the 28-year-old Jones at in the beginning of Jones's magical Grand Slam year. Jones wrote about that tournament in his autobiography, *Golf Is My Game*:

> Horton and I shared a room at the hotel during the tournament, a circumstance for which
> I have long been grateful. It was the beginning of a long and close friendship. . . . Of course,
> we two roommates had a very good time together. I think we both liked one another from
> the beginning, and we had a lot of fun talking golf, practicing swings, and exchanging point-
> ers in the room. . . . We were never paired together, even for one round, but we were at all
> times acutely aware of the other's presence on the golf course.

Jones shot a course-record 67 on the opening round. Smith bettered that with a 66 in the second round. Then Jones rebroke the record with a 65 in the third round. Smith finally won the tournament in the final round, by making birdie on the final hole. So, now, for the short remainder of Jones's professional career, we have a worthy foe ready to take the mantle. That tournament in Savannah was the last time Jones would lose, however, before winning his four Grand Slam tournaments.

In 1930 Smith entered 22 tournaments. He finished in the top three a whopping 14 times. He may not have hit a Grand Slam in 1930, but he hit a few home runs. Smith finished fourth at the 1930 British Open, falling 5 strokes back of Jones, who broke the course record at Hoylake by 10 strokes. Then Smith finished third at the 1930 U.S. Open, falling two strokes back of Jones at Interlachen. Smith blew that U.S. Open in the third round, when he shot a 76 and Jones had a blistering 68. Smith (a professional in 1930, he didn't enter the British or U.S. Amateurs that were part of Jones's run) was the first player to defeat Jones after the Grand Slam was completed.

Smith is believed to be the first golfer to use a sand wedge in tournaments. He used a model invented by a cotton farmer named Edward Kerr McClain. Smith used it in 1930, before it was banned for having a concave face. Smith gave one to Bobby Jones, who used it to make a crucial birdie at Hoylake in the British Open.

Smith's game was marked by his uncanny ability to make both long and short putts. His putting was not to be believed. Byron Nelson rated Smith the finest putter and chipper of his era. Paul Runyan had this to say about Smith:

> Horton was the best putter I've ever seen. To mention anyone else in the same breath is a travesty. He planted himself parallel to the intended line and was sound technically. But what made him a great putter was his attitude. He had a dogged determination to do it the same way, week after week and year after year. He made up more strokes on the greens than anybody I've ever seen.

Smith didn't smoke or drink. A famous story often told about him goes something like this: About the time of the 1929 season when he was winning everything in sight, Smith was introduced to a young, attractive lady by a hostess at a party. The young lady asked Smith if he wanted a cigarette.

"Thanks, but I don't smoke."

She offered him a drink.

"Thanks, but I don't drink."

"But," she said, "haven't you any bad habits?"

"Yes," he answered, "I'm short with too many putts."

Smith cooled down some after his early success, but his biggest tournament victories were yet to come, in 1934 and 1936, when he won two of the first three Masters Tournaments, which, at the time, were called the Augusta National Invitations. In the first Masters it seemed that Craig Wood might win or at least tie for first, but Smith sank a 20-foot putt on the 17th for a birdie, got his par-4 on the 18th, and won by a stroke.

In 1936 Smith won again by an incredible subpar finish, this time under rainy conditions that made par golf next to impossible. His 50-foot chip into the cup, across the rain-soaked 14th hole, started his successful march to a second Masters.

In 1940 he finished one stroke back of Lawson Little and Gene Sarazen at the U.S. Open. Strangely, he never won other major tournaments. His record of 32 tournament wins gets him into the top 50 of all time, especially since two of the victories were Masters.

Smith married Susan Singer in the late 1930s. Her family were founding members of the Augusta club, and she was an heiress to the Singer family fortune. He left golf for the

Army in 1941, when he was 33 years old. He served as a U.S. Army Air Corps officer in the Special Services in the European theater of operations during World War II. Horton divorced Susan in 1945 and never remarried. He became an administrator and spent several years as president of the PGA.

After suffering with Hodgkin's disease for six years, Smith died on October 15, 1963. He passed away at age 55 while driving to see his physician, one day after collapsing while watching Ryder Cup matches on television.

OK, so maybe Mr. Smith and Mr. Jones weren't as dynamic as the modern-day *Men in Black* pairing of Will Smith and Tommy Lee Jones, but Horton Smith and Bobby Jones were captivating and compelling in their own right.

Bobby Jones said of his friend, "Horton has the fiercest and most belligerent dedication to golf of anyone I've ever known. There is no way to measure what he has done for the game." He meant what he said, and he said what he meant: his friend Horton from Joplin was faithful to golf 100 percent.

Who's Better, Who's Best
Horton Smith or Johnny Miller?

Smith broke through early in his pro career, challenging the established Bobby Jones; Miller broke through early in his career, challenging Nicklaus. Horton Smith's 1929 season (eight wins) is very comparable to Miller's 1974 season (eight wins). Both won a pair of impressive major championships and then stopped winning at a relatively young age.

Miller, who also didn't smoke or drink, had the same vice that Smith had—he left too many of his putts short. Miller and Smith are ranked closely, but Miller gets placed higher based on a competitive field in the early '70s that was tougher than the one four decades earlier.

39

VIJAY SINGH
The Underdog

Vijay Singh has almost 13 years on Tiger Woods. When Singh turned 30 years old, he didn't have 10 major championships or 46 PGA Tour victories like Woods had at that age. And he had not won a single major or a single PGA Tour tournament. Singh was a veteran of the Asian Tour and the European Tour and had merely 11 international victories. At the end of 1992, Singh's official World Golf Ranking was 156. At the end of 1994, when he was 32 years old, he was 52nd in the world.

Would anyone have thought that Singh would—through sheer determination and grit—become the top player in the world in 2004, bumping off Tiger Woods (at least, temporarily), and have one of the greatest seasons ever in golf history? Would anyone have guessed that this 6'2" golfer from Fiji would win three majors (one each in 1998, 2000, and 2004) and 19 PGA Tour events in a three-year period (2003–05)?

Thus far, Vijay Singh has won 16 official PGA Tour events since his 40th birthday. The record is held by Sam Snead, who won 17. Singh keeps himself in marvelous shape, so Snead's record of being the oldest winner—at nearly 53 years of age—is in real jeopardy. In fact, Singh is getting better with age.

Singh was born on February 22, 1963, in Lautoka, Fiji. Fiji is located on an island about 2,000 miles east of Australia. Singh is the only world-class golfer from Fiji. He learned the game from his father, Mohan, an airplane technician who also taught golf. One of six children, Vijay started the game at the age of eight, caddying for his dad. This wasn't a rich family. This was a family where the six children shared one bedroom, with Vijay sharing a bed with one of his brothers.

His father did not teach him the finer points of the game. Mohan was a disciplinarian who wasn't particularly close to his son. He just told him about the grip and occasionally pointed out mistakes. Mohan had a friend who was a Pan Am pilot who sometimes flew in golf equipment and magazines. That was quite important to Singh's career, as 14-year-old Vijay modeled his swing after pictures of Tom Weiskopf's swing in a magazine that his father's friend gave him. But he did not have a proper coach, and his father was always too busy to spend a lot of time with his son.

Even at this early age, Singh was a tireless worker on the golf range, and soon he was down to a scratch golfer at the age of 17. He turned pro the following year. He left for Australia, where he made the grade at the Australian Tour school in 1983.

Although he earned a victory on the Asian Tour in 1984 at the Malaysian PGA Championship, he soon was banned from the Asian Tour. At a 1985 tournament in Jakarta, Indonesia, Singh signed an incorrect scorecard that improved his score by a stroke. When the discrepancy was discovered, he was immediately banned from the Tour, which has a zero-tolerance policy for cheating. Singh says that it was an honest mistake. Critics have said that he was caught committing an unpardonable sin.

He was literally banished to a golf club job in Borneo and again worked endlessly on his game. He was joined by his supportive wife, Ardena, who had been with him since he was a teenager first leaving Fiji.

It took two years, but by 1987 he had saved enough money to get to Britain and attempt to play in the British Open. He went there with £3,000, practiced for four weeks, and then missed the cut. He tried to get his card to play the European Tour but failed at that as well. He did have a bit of luck, however, that would push his career in the right direction. He signed a sponsorship from the Red Baron oil company, and on the strength of his performance at the European qualifying school, he was able to fill a spot in 1988 on the Safari Tour (the African Tour), funded by Red Baron.

He won his first event, the Nigerian Open, in Lagos, and the crowd adored him. They were not used to seeing a person of color win a golf event. Four top-10 finishes followed.

The Singhs went to Sweden, where he earned his European playing card. He joined the European Tour at the end of 1988. After he broke through with a win at the Volvo Open in France, he decided it was time for his first golf lesson. After his 1989 victory at the Volvo (where he recorded a hole in one), Singh spent two days with golf pro Bob Torrance in Ayrshire. This helped his confidence, especially with his putting. He was always a long hitter, accurate from the hours and hours spent on the driving range. The weakest part of his game always was his putting. Singh had a singular ambition. It was to establish himself in Europe and then win a place on the U.S. Tour.

His wife, Ardena, is the real hero in this story. At times, in the late 1980s, she carried her husband's clubs and served as his caddie. She traveled all over the world with her husband, as he played in Malaysia, France, Nigeria, the Ivory Coast, Morocco, Zimbabwe, Singapore, Spain, Germany, England, South Africa, Sweden, Taiwan, and Canada. This was all before he joined the PGA Tour in the United States in 1993, in a quest to "settle down." Ardena gave birth to their son, Qass, in June of 1990.

In 1993 the golfer whose name in Hindi means "victory" won the Buick Classic for his first PGA Tour win. He was PGA Tour Rookie of the Year and earned $657,831. Playing in 14 events, he had six top 10s. He had his first top 10 at a major championship, finishing fourth at the 1993 PGA Championship. Then after a winless 1994 season due to neck and back problems, he won the Phoenix Thunderbird Open and the Buick Classic in 1995.

He hired a personal trainer, Randy Warren, to further push him. The hard work began paying off, even as the Tour welcomed in the impossible-to-stop Tiger Woods. Beginning in 1997, when Singh was 34, on through 2005—a nine-year stretch in the Tiger Woods era—Singh won 27 times.

Top Players During the Tiger Era (1997–2005)

	Wins	Majors
Tiger Woods	44	10
Vijay Singh	27	3
Phil Mickelson	18	2

Singh hasn't won the popularity contests that go to the wildly popular Woods and the fan-friendly Phil Mickelson. He carries a chip on his shoulder, perhaps because of his background. He faced prejudice growing up in Fiji, because of his Indian descent. He faced ostracism from his fellow pros, because of the incorrect scorecard. He felt slighted by the media and has had his bad moments with them.

He won his first major in 1998, at the PGA Championship. He was 35 years old and had a gritty performance, surviving a two-putt par on the 18th hole to finish two strokes ahead of Steve Stricker. He birdied the 11th hole, when his second shot ricocheted off a tree and settled 50 feet from the hole. Sometimes you get lucky.

In 2000 Singh won the Masters Tournament. In the four rounds, he played the 12th hole (par-3) at Augusta to 1-under par. Tiger Woods played the same hole 3-over. Aside from that hole, and one other shot he would have needed to catch Singh, Woods could have had all four majors in the one year.

In 2004 Singh—in the middle of one of the greatest years anyone has ever had in golf—won the PGA Championship. At the age of 41 years, 5 months, and 23 days, he was the fourth oldest to win a PGA Championship. It wasn't pretty. His closing round of

4-over par 76 was the highest final-day score by a major championship winner since 1938 British Open champ Red Whitcombe shot a 78.

Singh, after shooting 67–68–69 in the first three rounds, had nothing to apologize for. He couldn't make a birdie in regulation and then refound his stroke in the three-hole play-off with Chris DiMarco.

In 2003 Singh came down on the side against letting Annika Sorenstam play in the men's Colonial Tournament in Texas. Singh admitted that he hoped Sorenstam would miss the cut, if he missed as well. It didn't come out well in the papers.

At the Presidents Cup in 2000 (the Ryder Cup–like event where a team of U.S. golfers compete against an international field separate from Europe), Woods met Singh in a singles match at the Robert Trent Jones Country Club, in Virginia. Singh's caddie, Paul Tesori, wore a hat that read "Tiger Who?" Woods won the match 2 and 1. A lot of people were upset about that. You don't pull on Superman's cape, after all. But Singh was the 2000 Masters champ—it wasn't like he was chopped liver.

Singh can't help himself from displeasing people, even following his greatest accomplishments. In April of 2005 Singh was announced as a member of the World Golf Hall of Fame. He was elected by the PGA Tour/Champions Tour ballot voting body, which included writers, historians, and Tour golfers. What an honor! The annual induction ceremony was scheduled for November 14, 2005. This was no good for Singh. He had to play in a tournament that day. They would have to find a later date to induct him.

He plays in more tournaments than anyone. It's as if he's making up for lost time, and he deserves to. From 1995 through 2005, he has played in 288 PGA Tour events. In 2004 Singh was the Player of the Year, posting nine wins and earning $10.9 million while becoming number one in the official World Golf Ranking. He became just the sixth player to accumulate nine wins in one calendar year. He played a very heavy schedule of 28 tournaments and finished with a leading 18 top 10s. He led the Tour in scoring average (68.64).

Vijay Singh Tour Victories
2005: six
2004: nine
2003: four

That's 19 tour wins over a three-year stretch. He also had 49 top-10 finishes in those three years. He was ranked either first, second, or third in four consecutive years beginning in 2002.

He has earned the respect he had been seeking since he was a young kid on the Asian Tour in the mid-1980s. No one has come further, either literally or figuratively. He has developed a Hogan-like dedication to practice and has willed himself to the top of the golf world.

Jim Nantz, golf announcer for CBS Sports: "I do see Vijay as showing signs of fatigue. But what he's been able to accomplish—and what Phil [Mickelson] has—against Tiger is remarkable. If Vijay or Phil lived in another era, I think they would be much more appreciated."

Lanny Wadkins, CBS golf analyst and PGA pro: "I would rank [Ernie] Els slightly behind Vijay Singh. Singh plays well week in and week out, whereas Els has stretches. I would put Singh close to Raymond Floyd. He has some more majors in him, if he putts even a little bit better. He understands that the window starts closing in the early 40s."

Indian summer is a name given to a period of sunny, warm weather in autumn, not long before winter. The Indian Singh is in an extended, late prime of his career—call it this Indian's summer. It won't be long before his winter sets in, though. This ranking is a projection that Mickelson and Els will do more in the next decade than Singh. But then again, Singh has made a career out of proving people wrong.

40

PATTY BERG
The Freckled Fireplug

Patty Berg was born in February of 1918 in Minneapolis, Minnesota. Like Babe Didrikson, she loved and excelled in all sports. Like Annika Sorenstam, she was raised in a cold-weather environment with a short golf season. Like Byron Nelson, she has been a distinguished and beloved figure in the game of golf for decades after her playing career.

Berg was an athletic kid who quarterbacked a neighborhood football team that called itself the 50th Street Tigers. One of the players on her team was Bud Wilkinson (a neighbor seven doors down from Berg), who went on to play football and would become a legendary college football coach at the University of Oklahoma.

After football she took up speed skating and won the Minnesota Speed Skating Championship Junior Girls division, and at the age of 13 she took up golf under the coaching of her dad, Herman Berg. The Bergs belonged to Interlachen Club. When Patty was 12, Bobby Jones won the U.S. Open there on the way to his Grand Slam. Patty wasn't there for that, however, not able to stay home from elementary school. No doubt her father filled her in. Herman's hobby was to film the great players of his day and study their swings.

She began taking lessons from a man named Lester Bolstead, who coached the men's golf team at the University of Minnesota. He would coach her for most of her career. She would have played in college, but there was no women's team. To say she became a serious player would be an understatement. She kept a notebook in which she recorded every shot she took in a tournament and determined her weaknesses. She won the Minneapolis City Ladies' Championship in 1934, which kept her a golfer. She had vowed after losing in 1933 not to continue unless she could improve within the year.

She grew to 5′1″ and 110 pounds. Her game was marked by a concentration and intensity, although she was most described by her hair (red) and her freckles and often referred to as a fireplug.

In 1935 she was a finalist at the U.S. Women's Amateur, which was held that year at her home course at Interlachen. She lost to Glenna Collett Vare. Berg would win the U.S. Women's Amateur three years later.

The Titleholders Championship was first played in 1937. It was a designated major championship in women's golf from 1937 to 1966. Beginning in 1930, the Western Open was a major in women's golf until 1967. Berg won seven Titleholders, including the first three times it was held. She was able to enter tournaments as an amateur because, frankly, she was better off financially than others. Her father would send her to tournaments. So she was winning majors (three Titleholders) as an amateur, while still competing in the Women's Amateur. She couldn't defend her 1939 Women's Amateur title because of an appendix operation. After her mother died at the end of 1939, she finally began helping her father out with some money. In 1940 she turned pro and was able to accept a job with the Wilson Sporting Goods Company as a spokesperson. She would give a lot of clinics for Wilson.

Berg was in a serious automobile accident on December 8, 1941 (the day after Pearl Harbor was attacked), on her way to an exhibition that would raise money for the British war relief. (Let's see, among the top 40 players, Hogan, Locke, and Berg all were in serious automobile accidents.) Berg was driving with Helen Detweiler in Texas when they got into a head-on crash. Berg's knee was cracked up. She would spend the next five months in bed, and it was a full year before she could bend her leg. Even after a series of operations, it was doubtful that she would play again. It was, ironically, a second accident—this time she slipped in a locker room—that salvaged her career. The adhesions in her leg were pulled apart due to the fall. She rehabbed the knee by walking and biking and was ready to resume her career 18 months after the auto accident at the 1943 Western Open in Glen Ellyn, Illinois. In a remarkable comeback, Berg won the Western Open.

This would have made even bigger headlines but for the fact that the more popular sport of tennis had a similar script. Alice Marble was a great tennis champion who won four U.S. Opens and the Wimbledon and Australian Open Championships. If those tournaments had been played in the early 1940s, she probably would have had more tennis majors. Marble was voted the Woman Athlete of the Year in 1939 and 1940. Marble (who was born five years before Berg) grew up in San Francisco and worked out with local baseball players, including Joe DiMaggio, when she was 13. When Marble was just beginning to get her career going in 1933 (at the age of 20), she played one day in the soaring heat and collapsed with sunstroke. The following year she collapsed and was hospitalized. She was diagnosed with tuberculosis and told her tennis career was over. She spent most of the next year in a sanitarium and didn't recover her health until 1936, when she won the first of her four U.S. Opens. Berg wasn't quite as attractive as Marble, and golf wasn't quite as popular as tennis at the time. Otherwise it was a perfect match. Following Berg's personal comeback, it was off to the war. She entered the service in 1943 and came out in 1945. She served as a military lieutenant.

Her most lasting contributions to the game of golf came after the war, when she helped found and set up the LPGA. She led the Women's Professional Golf Association (WPGA), the LPGA's predecessor, with three victories in 1948 and 1949. In 1950 she was one of the LPGA's 13 founding members, and she served as president from 1950 to 1952. Between 1948 and 1962 she won 44 professional titles.

She won the 1948 Western Open by a stroke in a thrilling extra-hole battle against Didrikson. After trailing most of the way, Berg won 1-up and immediately offered her winner's check ($500) to the Western Women's Golf Association "to further interest in the game of golf among young women." It's no wonder she was as popular on the Tour with her fellow women golfers as she was.

She wasn't as popular, as crude, or as much of an attraction as Didrikson, however. Who was? But Berg was almost as good. When cancer took Didrikson from the Tour, it was Berg who was the leading money winner in 1954, 1955, and 1957. It was Berg who won the Vare Trophy for the lowest scoring average in 1953, 1955, and 1956. It was Berg who won four more Titleholders Championships, in 1948, 1953, 1955, and 1957.

Besides the seven Titleholders, Berg won seven Western Opens that were majors (plus the 1946 U.S. Women's Open). The first was in 1941. The last was in 1958, when she was 40. In addition to the 15 majors (3 won as an amateur), Berg finished second at the 1957 Women's Open, second at the 1956 LPGA Championship, and second as late as the 1959 LPGA Championship. And it was Berg who won the very first U.S. Women's Open, in 1946.

Who's Better, Who's Best
Patty Berg or Juli Inkster?

It's hard to put Berg's 15 majors in context. I have to believe that Juli Inkster, despite winning only 7 majors, deserves to be ranked nearly as high as Berg. Berg reminds me most of Bobby Jones, who was an elder statesman and goodwill ambassador for many years.

In the 1950s and '60s, she would travel to exhibitions called the Patty Berg Swing Parade. She won 83 tournaments in her life and gave countless clinics and speeches and did much promotional work.

Berg was one of the greatest fairway wood players, male or female, to ever play the game. She continued to play until 1980, when hip surgery kept her from being able to walk 18 holes. She overcame a bout with cancer and continued to give clinics into her 70s.

Juli Inkster, like Patty Berg, was one of the greatest female amateur golfers ever. Inkster won three U.S. Women's Amateur titles in a row (1980–82) and won two majors as an LPGA rookie. She won five more, completing the modern-day LPGA career Grand Slam. She came close in other majors, losing twice in 1992 alone. And, like Lopez, she missed almost two years of play because of her pregnancies.

Inkster had staying power like Berg. Berg snuck in five majors in her late 30s between 1955 and 1958, after Babe died and before the teen Mickey Wright became a force. Juli Inkster defeated Annika Sorenstam to win the 2002 U.S. Women's Open at the age of 42, becoming the second oldest woman to win a major (Babe was 43 at the 1954 U.S. Women's Open). Inkster competed in her 30s against a growing international field of younger competition and did so while raising two daughters. You better believe that her seven majors are impressive. Inkster, just three years younger than Nancy Lopez, had 18 fewer tournament victories than Lopez. She comes very close to Lopez and Berg, but ultimately winds up short of the two of them. Berg gets the nod over Inkster.

A Better Analogy

Patty Berg and George Halas Halas was one of the founders of the National Football League and the father of the Chicago Bears. He single-handedly changed the way Americans spent their Sunday. He didn't invent the game, but he took the game and made it a rich spectator sport. For 40 years he stood on the Bears sidelines, a commanding figure seen under a gray fedora, leading his team to more wins than any other coach in his lifetime.

Berg was one of the founders of the Ladies Professional Golf Association. They barnstormed the country, and no one did more for the public relations aspect of the LPGA than Berg. She gave a healthy, wholesome image to women golfers everywhere. Just like Halas was the NFL, Berg was the LPGA.

One of Berg's mantras when she taught and gave clinics was that one has to learn correct methods at the very outset. This was very important to her. The LPGA learned the correct methods from Berg at the very outset. She practiced what she preached.

41

RALPH GULDAHL
"Guldahl Comes Alive"

Even the best golfers rarely get a four-year term as the best player on the planet. Some might make it to the top for a tournament or a series of tournaments. Others may reach the pinnacle for a year or two (like Vijay Singh). In the rare circumstances that a player is head-and-shoulders above all others for a long enough time, they are known by a single name: Tiger, Jack, Annika. The reason Ralph Guldahl requires not only both names but several pages of explanation is there wasn't much more beyond the four years. He was a one-term-and-out superstar.

Guldahl was born a year before the threesome of Ben Hogan, Sam Snead, and Byron Nelson. For a time when they were in their late 20s, Guldahl was better than those three and everyone else. He didn't have a comfortable ride down the elevator. His career never entered a slow period of declining skills. No, his career was a personification of a Jimmy Durante quote: "Be nice to people you meet on the way up, because you meet them again on the way down." His career came to a halt by the time he turned 30 years old. It wasn't because of an injury. It wasn't because of a lack of desire to play. His career was over because he lost his skills.

Some say it was after he wrote a book called *Groove Your Golf* in 1939. I looked for it online and found a used copy selling for $250. It's probably a bargain. The book was an instructional, made by a golfer who had previously done very little analyzing of his own golf swing. Was it a coincidence that his game went to hell after he wrote the book?

Guldahl was born in Texas (like Nelson and Hogan) in 1911. He grew to be 6'3" and was a powerful driver who had an exceptional iron game and short game as well. He got a job as a club pro at the St. Louis Country Club in the early 1930s but was unaffiliated when he played as a 23-year-old at the 1933 U.S. Open at Glenview, Illinois.

He almost won that Open, but his putter let him down. He bogeyed the 18th hole in the final round—an easy four-foot putt—after exploding a ball out of a sand trap. Guldahl lost by one stroke to amateur Johnny Goodman but still pocketed the $1,000 that went to the professional who finished highest.

Guldahl finished eighth in 1934 at the U.S. Open but was off-the-charts bad in the 1935 U.S. Open, finishing tied for 40th at Oakmont after shooting 82–82 on the final two rounds.

Discouraged, he went home to Dallas in 1935 and began working at different jobs to get out of the depression (his) and the Depression (the country's). Several reports have him selling cars. Another newspaper report had him working as a carpenter. This carpenter would be reborn into golfing soon enough.

His young son, Buddy, developed colds for which the doctors prescribed desert air. So Guldahl moved his family to the California desert. While he was in California, he played in a few local tournaments, attracting the attention of some wealthy benefactors who staked him to play in the True Temper Open in Detroit in 1936. He earned $240 at the tournament in Detroit, finished eighth (eight strokes back) in the 1936 U.S. Open (earning $137), and was a pro golfer again.

Later in 1936 he won the Western Open, which was considered a major in those days (none of the top U.S. golfers regularly went to England for the British Open in that era). This was the first of three straight Western Opens that Guldahl would capture.

In 1937 Guldahl played three major tournaments. He won the Western Open and the U.S. Open. He won the latter in style, taking off his cap to comb his hair before he teed off on the 18th and final hole. He looked good, beating Snead by two strokes, and he looked good in all the pictures. Earlier in 1937 he had finished second in the Masters—the first time he entered the tournament in Augusta. He lost by two strokes to Byron Nelson, who shot a final-round 70 to Guldahl's 76. Guldahl also played on the Ryder Cup team in 1937. That team was the first U.S. team to win on British soil. Guldahl was undefeated in Ryder Cup competition. Remember that at this point in their careers, neither Snead nor Hogan could sniff a major.

In 1938 Guldahl was again second at the Masters, this time to Henry Picard by two strokes. He won the Western Open again. And he won the U.S. Open again, this time by being six strokes better than anyone else at Cherry Hills Country Club in Englewood, Colorado.

After finishing second at the 1937 and 1938 Masters, the tall Texan won the tournament in 1939. In that tournament, he defeated Snead by a stroke. The rest of the top 10 included Hogan, Lawson Little, Gene Sarazen, and Craig Wood.

Guldahl shot a final-nine 33 to win that Masters and set a course record 279. (The previous record was 282, set by Sarazen and Wood. The record at the time of this writing is 270, set by Tiger Woods.) Guldahl eagled the 13th hole. Bobby Jones would say afterward that it was the greatest exhibition of golf he had ever seen. The reporters wrote that Guldahl had the "appearance and poise" of a movie actor.

But, as they say, what goes up must come down. After three Western Opens, two U.S. Opens, and a Masters, the majors stopped happening for Guldahl. He played five PGA Championships in a row, beginning in 1937, and had to face the same people on the way down as he did on his way up. He was eliminated the last two times by Nelson, once (in 1940) in the semifinals. In that match Guldahl was 1-down after the 34th hole and squared the match with a five-foot birdie putt on the 35th hole. It came down to the last hole, when Nelson chipped up to within inches of the cup. That was the closest he came to another major.

He won only twice after 1939: the 1940 Milwaukee Open and the 1940 Inverness Invitational. He had 16 Tour victories and 20 runner-up finishes. Even today only Tiger and Jack have 30 wins in their 20s, so Guldahl was pretty special. Guldahl really came to a halt. Just like that.

Guldahl was back at a "real" job in the mid-1940s. He never did regain his touch. He became a club pro in Tarzana, California, and worked there from 1961 until his death in 1987. He missed out on the big money. He missed out on 20 more years on the Tour (Snead was still winning tournaments in the mid-1960s).

When Guldahl did give it a shot, he failed. In 1946, at the Masters, he finished 26 strokes above par, winding up in 48th place. At the 1948 U.S. Open, he finished tied for 32nd.

Maybe it was the book he authored. Even he didn't have the answers to that one. Perhaps this simple instructional book in which he broke down his swing was the culprit. Or maybe it had nothing to do with the book—maybe it was a deal with the devil. How many of us would sell our souls to be the best in the world at something we love, even for a short period of time?

Who's Better, Who's Best
Ralph Guldahl, Lloyd Mangrum, or Horton Smith?

Guldahl is ranked behind Lloyd Mangrum and Horton Smith. Yet Guldahl, with a Masters and a pair of U.S. Opens, has more majors. They all reached the semifinals of the PGA Championship, but never the finals. None of them ever played the British Open.

Yes, Guldahl has that four-year stretch of superiority. But Mangrum, with only a 1946 U.S. Open title (and two Western Opens), was consistently good for a long period of time. Mangrum had six top-five finishes in the U.S. Open and seven top-five finishes at the Masters. He won 36 times on the Tour and was runner-up another 28 times. Smith finishes ahead of Guldahl (but behind Mangrum) with his pair of Masters Championships and 30 Tour victories. Neither of those players had a peak like Guldahl, but they lasted much longer.

A Better Analogy

Ralph Guldahl and Peter Frampton Hmmm. An analogy for Guldahl would be the British rocker Peter Frampton. In a period of four years around Frampton's birth, three other great British rockers would be born: David Bowie (1947), Elton John (1947), and Phil Collins (1951). Frampton, like Guldahl, didn't hit it big in his early 20s. Frampton hit it big in 1976, when his *Frampton Comes Alive* album went platinum six times over. Filling arenas everywhere he went, he was the biggest attraction on both sides of the Atlantic. And yet he couldn't follow up the album with anything remotely successful. He was yesterday's news by his 30th birthday. Meanwhile, some of the arena-rock groups and performers from his era—like David Bowie and Elton John—outlasted him by decades. Elton John, who is responsible for 1 percent of the recorded music sales in the mid-2000s, is the Snead of the group.

42

PAYNE STEWART
A Major Player

Payne Stewart's father, William, was a former Missouri Amateur champion who qualified for the 1955 U.S. Open. Payne was born in Springfield, Missouri, in 1957, and began to play four years later. He picked up the game quickly and enthusiastically.

He turned pro in 1982, at the age of 25, and won his first PGA Tour event. Stewart was one of a very few regulars on the professional golf tour who dressed in plus fours, which are pants that extend four inches below the knees and are usually worn with argyle socks. He may have been noticed because he wore these knickers, but his play attracted attention on its own. In July he won the Quad Cities Open (shooting a course-record 63 on the final day) with his father watching. It would be the only tournament that Payne would be able to share with his father, who died of cancer in 1985. In 1987, when he won the Bay Hill Invitational, Stewart donated the entire first-place check to the Florida Hospital Circle of Friends in his father's memory.

Stewart didn't capture his first major until the last one of the 1980s was played: the 1989 PGA Championship. Wearing plus fours in the Chicago Bears colors, Stewart was six strokes back with five holes to play. But he birdied four of the last five holes and was in the clubhouse when leader Mike Reid double-bogeyed the 17th hole. Stewart had his first major after Reid, who had seemingly recovered on the 18th hole, missed a four-foot putt that would have tied him with Stewart. It was only Stewart's fifth victory.

By this time, Stewart had acquired a reputation for finishing second. In the 1980s he had five tournament victories and finished in second place in 15 other tournaments. That included the 1985 British Open, when he lost in a play-off. In 1985 he also was leading at Shinnecock Hills at the U.S. Open with six holes to play but lost the lead and the tournament to Ray Floyd. It was always "close, but no cigar" for Stewart, who had the tag of the best player yet to win a major.

He never quite overcame his Avis reputation (the rental car company that has to try harder because it is second). For his career, he won only 11 tournaments and finished in second place another 28 times.

Payne Stewart's Runner-Up Finishes at the Majors

1. 1985 British Open—finished one shot back of Sandy Lyle
2. 1990 British Open—shot 13-under, lost to Nick Faldo
3. 1993 U.S. Open—finished two shots back of Lee Janzen
4. 1998 U.S. Open—finished two shots back of Lee Janzen

Janzen won only eight PGA Tournaments in his career, and he defeated Stewart in a pair of U.S. Opens. Had Stewart been able to hold on to the 1998 lead, or won just once more, he would have been placed in the top 35 golfers of all time.

He had his moments. In 1991, at the U.S. Open, he beat Scott Simpson, 75 and 77, in an 18-hole play-off to capture his first U.S. Open and second major.

The victories still came few and far between. In the 1998 U.S. Open, in San Francisco, Stewart began the final round with a four-stroke lead. He hit only six fairways and hit only nine greens in regulation. On a day when 72 would have won the U.S. Open, Stewart shot 74 and lost to Lee Janzen.

Stewart can't rank any higher due to his lack of success at Augusta. He was 0–14 at the Masters. But at this tournament, he never came close. He finished as high as eighth place only once (1986). His only other top-10 finish was a tie for ninth place in 1993.

"I'm a big believer in fate," said U.S. Ryder Cup captain Ben Crenshaw before the final day of the 1999 Ryder Cup in Brookline, Massachusetts. Stewart, playing in his fifth Ryder Cup, was on the historic U.S. team that won 8.5 points on the final day to defeat the European team 14.5 to 13.5.

A few months earlier, in June of 1999, fate had a hand in the final round of the U.S. Open played at Pinehurst No. 2. Phil Mickelson led Stewart by one stroke with only three holes to play but was prepared to leave—and forfeit a chance at his first major championship—to return to his wife, Amy, who was due to give birth to the couple's first child. Phil and Amy had their baby the day after the U.S. Open. Stewart, who had blown a big lead at the 1998 U.S. Open, surely wanted to win—not be handed—a major championship, which would be his third.

Mickelson knew the pain of losing major championships—following Stewart's birdie on 17 and 15-foot par putt on 18, he now knew the pain of losing to Stewart. In a memorable exchange between the two competitors, Stewart consoled Mickelson, wishing him luck with the baby. "There's nothing like being a father," Stewart told Mickelson on that Father's Day.

Stewart had made peace with the world, becoming a deeply religious man by the fall of 1999. He was extremely popular on and off the course. He had won three major championships, the last one on a Father's Day that began with him watching a television feature on his deceased father.

One putt was enough at the end of his career to place him in the top 50 of all time. A year after blowing his lead at the U.S. Open, he rolled in his fateful 15-foot putt on the 72nd and final hole to win the 1999 U.S. Open.

Bobby Casper, radio golf analyst for Sirius and Westwood One: "Payne is close to Ernie Els and Vijay Singh. He ranks behind those guys, but not by much. Payne was a streaky player, and he played his best in major championships. As a driver, he didn't hit the ball as long as some of the top hitters, but he hit it straight. He was a course manager. When he played in a major, he got himself out of trouble immediately. He would get himself back into a lay-up position, and managed his game extremely well."

The news of any plane crash is frightening and shocking. But when the news broke about a Lear jet straying off course over Florida, it was more unsettling than most. Although none of the passengers were identified at first, some of the sports radio stations hinted that the plane carried a pro golfer.

Eventually, the plane crashed and the passengers' identities were revealed. On October 25, 1999, less than a month after being part of the victorious Ryder Cup team, Payne Stewart was killed in the crash. The gruesome details came in soon enough: Stewart's wife called his cell phone in a frantic effort to reach him; Air Force pilots reported that the cockpit windows were covered with frost and that the passengers had lost consciousness due to a lack of oxygen; the plane would have been shot down if it was on course to crash in a major metropolitan area; the jet continued flying until it ran out of gas.

Yes, Stewart had only 11 tournament victories. And yes, he won only 4 tournaments after May of 1990; however, 2 of them were U.S. Opens. Considering how close he had come in so many different tournaments, he was bound to win a few more tournaments and perhaps another major championship.

Who's Better, Who's Best
Payne Stewart or Tony Lema?

Professional golfers spend their lives traveling. In the early part of the game's history, several great golfers were involved in serious, life-threatening automobile accidents. By the late 1990s, most golfers used private planes to get from place to place. Stewart's accident ended the life of one of the most popular golfers on Tour. But Stewart wasn't the first pro golfer killed in a private plane crash.

"Champagne" Tony Lema also had a reputation as a player who often finished second. He was runner-up in 11 PGA Tournaments including the 1963 Masters, when he finished one stroke back of Jack Nicklaus. In 1965, the popular Lema became only the third golfer to surpass $100,000 in one year.

Stewart was 42 years old when he died. Lema was 32 years old when his private plane crashed in 1966, killing him. Lema won the 1964 British Open and had 10 Tour victories at the time of his death. Stewart had 11 Tour victories, but also had an additional 10 years of playing time over Lema. Stewart had three majors, but only one by the age of 32.

While Lema was on his way to a very successful career, Stewart is ranked ahead of him.

43

LAWSON LITTLE
The Little Slam

These days there is almost no reason in the world that a top amateur golfer wouldn't turn professional. After all, the prize money just cannot be ignored. Just a decade ago, in 1996, when Tiger Woods turned pro, there were only nine players on the PGA Tour who won a million dollars or more in a year. By 2005 there were 78 different players who made more than a million in that year alone. Poor Harrison Frazar finished 79th on the money list and won "only" $999,083.

But the big money hasn't always been part of the PGA Tour. It is generally thought that Bobby Jones was the greatest amateur player. Tiger Woods might have been better. And Lawson Little was the greatest amateur after Jones and before Woods. Little deserves to be ranked in the top 50 golfers of all time, amateur or not.

Born in Newport, Rhode Island, in 1911, Lawson Little grew up an Army brat, spending time on different military bases, including stints in San Antonio, Texas, the Philippines, and Tianjin, China. The cultural and geographical variety gave him the perfect background for golfing—playing on different courses all over the world.

His father, Colonel Lawson Little, was a surgeon, and while the colonel couldn't give his son golf instruction, per se, he instead gave him life lessons that Lawson made use of on the golf course. You couldn't mistake that Little came from a military background—he approached the golf course as a battleground, with the idea that the more a soldier knows about the ground he fights on, the better his chances for victory. Lawson never overlooked any detail, no matter how slight.

When the family returned to the United States, the young Lawson received lessons from club professionals, and he entered the 1927 U.S. Open at Oakmont. In the next two years, the not-so-little Little (a big hitting six-footer) won the Northern California Amateur. He entered Stanford University (like Tom Watson and Tiger Woods) in 1930 and played on the golf team. He entered his first U.S. Amateur in 1929, at Pebble Beach. That was the tournament where Bobby Jones (who had already won four Amateur titles) would be eliminated before the third round. That hadn't happened to Jones since the future Grand Slammer was 14. The brackets had Little and Jones in the same half of the draw. Jones's surprise elimination by Johnny Goodman meant that it would be Goodman who would face Little in the next round. Little beat the golfer who eliminated the great champion Jones—only for the 18-year-old Little to lose in the next round himself.

Little admired and learned from the 1927 U.S. Open champ that year, Tommy Armour, and sought out Armour's expertise over the years. Armour helped Little control his tee shots. Unlike later Stanford athletes John McEnroe and Tiger Woods, Little earned a degree from Stanford. It's not like he was passing up the opportunity to make millions of dollars by remaining in college.

Lawson Little's Approach to Golf

In August of 1935, *American Golf* magazine ran a story by Bob Davis in which Little is quoted. "Brought up in the atmosphere of Army life, where my father was a doctor, I became saturated with the military idea that the more a soldier knows about the ground he fights upon, the better his chances for victory. Very well; why not regard a golf course as a personal battleground? . . . Whenever I go into competition, my first concern is the battlefield. Or to be more explicit, the 18 battlefields."

He always could putt. Little's strength in golf was his short game, and his touch around the greens won him much praise. Following graduation from Stanford, he was selected to play in the 1934 Walker Cup for the United States.

The Walker Cup is held every two years, played alternatively in Britain and America between male amateur golfers of Great Britain and Ireland and the United States. The match was first played in 1922. This was a big deal. In 1934 the Walker Cup was played at St. Andrews. Little won his singles match, 6 and 5, over Cyril Tolley and won his foursomes match, 8 and 6, with Johnny Goodman as his partner.

He became one of the leading contenders to win the British Amateur at Prestwick. He played seven matches in the British Amateur and stormed through them with little difficulty. In the final, Little's victory was record-breaking. He closed out the match, 14 and 13, against Jimmy Wallace, the largest margin of victory in a British Amateur final. In that final match, Little shot a 66 in his first 18 holes, which put him 12-up with 18 holes to play. He needed just five more holes to win the British Amateur, and when he did win, he became the first American ever to win the British Amateur in his first visit. The U.S. papers went crazy about the performance, with sportswriter T. C. Watson writing the following:

> Lawson Little, rated by critics just weeks ago as "just another Stanford student," today won
> the British Amateur by shooting some of the greatest golf ever seen in competition. . . .

Only Bobby Jones's decisive swamping of Al Espinosa in the American Open at Winged Foot in New York could compare with it.

The U.S. Amateur was next, at Brookline, Massachusetts, later that summer. There would be six rounds of 18-hole matches and two rounds of 36-hole matches to determine a champion.

Grantland Rice, a famed sportswriter of the early part of the century, covered the U.S. Amateur. In one article he wrote prior to Little's final match against David "Spec" Goldman, he described Little as follows:

- "The far-hitting Little, with steel wrists, a powerful body and the putting stroke of a southern breeze . . ."
- "The curly-headed, barrel-chested son of Stanford . . ."
- "Little, the mighty hitter, cold as frosted granite, with a putting touch as sure as death and taxes . . ."
- "He can out hit his opponents from 20 to 30 yards. He can match him with the long irons, the shorter pitches around the slippery, sloping surfaces of the greens. In addition to this, Little has the flare, the so-called 'it,' the vital spark which Goldman lacks."

Rice was correct. Little was 5-up over Goldman after 18 holes and defeated him, 7 and 6. He joined Harold Hilton (from 1911) and Bobby Jones as the only golfers to win two major amateur championships in one year—which, according to Grantland Rice, was "as close to a miracle as sport can show."

In 1935 Little returned to Great Britain to defend his British Amateur title at Royal Lytham and St. Annes. He shot 80 in his first match but got lucky and won, 1-up. In the final he won 1-up again, as Dr. William Tweddell missed a putt that would have squared the match on the final hole.

Little then returned to the United States and successfully defended his U.S. Amateur title in September. That made him the first to win both major amateur titles in successive years.

In the first half of the 1900s, there were three great golf achievements. First would have to be Jones's Grand Slam in 1930 and his run at the U.S. Open in the 1920s (eight out of nine years he finished first, second, or third). Another is Walter Hagen winning 23 consecutive PGA Championship matches and winning that tournament five straight times. And the third is Lawson Little's "Little Slam," in which he won 31 consecutive matches to win two U.S. Amateur and two British Amateur titles. Making those 31 consecutive matches even more impressive was that they were usually one-sided affairs. Only three times did they have to go the distance. And only once was he pushed to extra holes.

In 1936 Little got married, turned pro, and won the Canadian Open. Three years later, he finished in a tie for third at the U.S. Open. In 1940 Little played the U.S. Open, which was at Canterbury Golf Club in Cleveland, where he was caught at the end by Gene Sarazen. Sarazen and Little played an 18-hole play-off, and Little won by three strokes. After the match, just before Little was to receive his $1,000 prize money, Sarazen put his hands on the championship cup and said, "I had dates with this graceful lady in 1922 and 1932, and had hoped to keep another with her today. She led me on for three days, but today she said, 'I'm sorry, Gene, but I'm going home with Mr. Little. He's younger than you are.'"

Little didn't have much more success following that. He won only eight times on the Tour. It was said (because of the 31 consecutive match-play wins in the four Amateur titles and the 18-hole play-off against Sarazen) that Little was much better suited for match-play than for stroke-play competition. Fair enough. But that doesn't explain Little's 2–5 mark in five years of match-play competition at the PGA Championships. He ranks among the greatest ever because of his Little Slam. He didn't live up to expectations on the professional circuit. The cup that went home with Little for winning the U.S. Open was nothing more than a one-night stand. He didn't have the long-term relationship with the majors like Sarazen and other golfers had.

He had heart trouble beginning in 1957 (at the age of 46) and had brain surgery in 1963. He didn't have a long career, and he didn't have a long life. He died early in 1968, in Pebble Beach, where he had lived for the last 15 years of his life.

A Better Analogy

Lawson Little and Herschel Walker I wanted to find an athlete who was as dominant in his sport as any amateur ever and had a good (but not great) professional career. I thought of Herschel Walker in an instant.

Herschel Walker was a consensus All-American from 1980 to 1982 with the University of Georgia and established 11 NCAA records. He rushed for 5,259 yards in his three years, which was a three-year record. He had the third most rushing yards in college football history when he left after his junior season.

In Herschel's freshman season, he was third in the Heisman Trophy balloting. As a sophomore in 1981, he finished second to Marcus Allen. As a junior in 1982, Walker won the Heisman Trophy, in a landslide over runner-up John Elway.

Walker was a very, very good professional, but aside from his cashing Donald Trump's checks in the USFL, he never led the NFL in rushing yards. No one would consider him one of the top-10 running backs of all time in his professional career. Everyone would consider him one of the very best from his amateur days.

Lawson Little had a career similar to Herschel Walker's. Little would not be ranked among the greatest golfers of all time based solely on his professional career, which began in 1936. Little won the Walker Cup, while Walker won a little. They both should have done more.

44

TOM KITE
The $6 Million Man

Tom Kite was born on December 9, 1949, in McKinney, Texas. He started playing golf at the age of 6 and won his first tournament at 11.

As Kite explained in his 1997 book, *A Fairway to Heaven: My Lessons from Harvey Penick on Golf and Life*, he owes a lot to the Internal Revenue Service, which transferred his dad from its office in Dallas to Austin. Because of that move, he came into contact with golf instructor Harvey Penick and his pupil Ben Crenshaw.

When he was 13 years old, Kite met Penick. Penick was the golf coach at the University of Texas for 33 years, taking no salary, while teaching at the Austin Country Club, a position he held for 48 years. Beginning in 1963 and continuing through his graduation from Texas in 1972, Kite soaked up everything from the Yoda of golf.

In 1973 Kite was the PGA Rookie of the Year. He entered 34 tournaments and had three top-10 finishes. The next year, he had eight top-10 finishes, and it continued a trend throughout his career. He would wind up with 209 top-10 finishes. Kite outworked nearly everyone on the Tour. There was a definite contrast between Kite and Crenshaw, with whom he's forever been compared. Crenshaw had more natural ability. Kite was characterized as the one who worked harder. As Kite put it, "No one would deny Ben is more of a showman. I'm a guy laying bricks."

That didn't mean they didn't have a friendly competition. They did. They weren't Bird and Magic—Larry Bird and Magic Johnson were more dominant in their sports than Kite and Crenshaw in theirs—but there was a similarity in two athletes the same age who were constantly competing against each other from college on to the pros. Plus in the golfers' case, they were coached by the same man, Penick. Usually, the great rivalries (think Bird vs. Magic or Martina vs. Chrissie) feature two contrasting styles. White vs. black. City vs. country. Baseline player vs. serve-and-volleyer. But in the case of Kite vs. Crenshaw, it was . . . what? Ben was more polished looking and popular with the fans? They even branched from the same coaching tree.

Both won 19 times on the PGA Tour. Crenshaw won two Masters and Kite won the 1992 U.S. Open. In the same time period—with a similar number of tournaments played—Kite had 65 more top 10s than Crenshaw did.

I think that Greg Norman, Hale Irwin, and Lee Trevino are the best players never to win the Masters (not counting the founder, Bobby Jones, who played the first few in a semiretirement stage of his career). But if you said that Kite was the best never to win at Augusta, I wouldn't argue too hard.

Tom Kite at the Masters
1976 fifth place (tie)
1977 third place (tie)
1979 fifth place
1980 sixth place (tie)
1981 fifth place (tie)
1982 fifth place (tie)
1983 second place (tie)
1984 sixth place (tie)
1986 second place (tie)
1994 fourth place
1997 second place

That's 11 years he finished among the top-six finishers at the Masters. Add to that a pair of top-five finishes at the British Open in 1976 and 1978 and a pair of top-five finishes at the PGA Championship in 1981 and 1984, and you have the makings of a very strange career.

Entering the 1992 U.S. Open at Pebble Beach, Kite had finished in the top six in 13 different majors, without winning any. To say he had the biggest victory of his career at the 1992 Open, when he shot even-par 72 in tough Sunday conditions to give him a two-stroke victory over Jeff Sluman, would be an understatement.

Because he had another commitment after the U.S. Open, it was left to Kite's wife, Christy, to make the following gesture. She took the U.S. Open trophy to the Austin Country Club, found Penick, and said, "I have something here you own a part of," and put it on the old man's lap.

Now Kite didn't have the Greg Norman type of talent or frustration. Kite's frustration was that he played his absolute best in the biggest tournaments in the world and came up just short against the greatest golfers of all time.

Kite's Runner-Up Finishes at the Majors

1978 British Open: two shots back of Jack Nicklaus

1983 Masters: four shots back of Seve Ballesteros

1986 Masters: one shot back of Jack Nicklaus

1997 Masters: twelve shots back of Tiger Woods

Add to that list one of his two third-place finishes at the majors, when he finished tied for third at the 1977 Masters, trailing only Tom Watson by four strokes and Jack Nicklaus by two.

He didn't lose in play-offs or to miracle shots. He lost to the greatest golfers of all time, but he was first among all golfers in money earnings. By 1989 he became the first ever to earn more than $6 million for his career. By the end of 1996, when Kite was 47, his career earnings were just under $10 million. That's less than Tiger Woods made in 2005 or Vijay Singh made in 2004.

He didn't play for the history books. He played for his family, for Christy and his children. He took great pride in winning tournaments on Mother's Day (1992 Bell South Classic) and on Father's Day (1992 U.S. Open). He played for his father, who was his best friend and each year walked the course at Augusta with him. He played for his coach, the great Harvey Penick, who taught him so much before dying in 1995. And he played for the IRS. For without them, Kite might never have fallen under the tutelage of Penick's wisdom and advice.

Who's Better, Who's Best
Tom Kite or Bernhard Langer?

It's not so easy judging European golfers—Langer is the best ever from Germany—with U.S. Tour players like Kite. Langer won two Masters, in 1985 and 1993, and Kite didn't win any. But Kite did have those 11 top-six finishes at Augusta.

Langer was all over the place. He was capable of shooting wonderful golf there, with 68s on a daily basis. Or he was capable of not making the cut, even in the prime of his career. Langer had only two top-six finishes besides his two Masters victories.

In the 1985 tournament, he made a remarkable shot. In the third round, on the 13th hole, he found himself by the trees in a bad lie. He played a 3-wood, with 215 yards to carry the creek. The ball took a big bounce right over the water and stopped 18 feet from the hole. Langer made his 2-under eagle and went on to win the Masters by two shots.

In 1993 Langer was, again, all over the place at the Masters. In the final round, he shot an even-par 72. But how many holes did he make par on that day? Just four times would he par the hole. On the other 14 holes, he had seven birdies and seven bogeys.

I prefer the consistent Kite over Langer. And then, of course, it was decided in a 1993 singles match played between the U.S. team member Kite and European team member Langer. The U.S. Ryder Cup team, down by one point after two days of competition, mounted a memorable comeback by winning six singles matches. One of those singles matches saw Kite defeat Langer, 5 and 3, to win a much-needed point for the United States. That point wins Kite a spot over Langer in this book.

Who's Better, Who's Best
Tom Kite or Tom Watson?

Tom Watson was born on September 4, 1949; Tom Kite was born on December 9, 1949. Watson had 218 top-10 finishes in his PGA Tour career; Kite had 209 top-10 finishes in his PGA Tour career. Kite has one more Champions Tour victory (7–6) than Watson does. Watson has one more international victory (4–3) than Kite does.

Kite won more money because he played in more Tour events in his career—698, compared to Watson's 585. But the difference in their place in history is that while Kite was close a lot, Watson won a lot more. Watson won 39 times on the Tour to Kite's 19 wins, and Watson won eight majors to Kite's one.

45

BEN CRENSHAW
Gentle Ben

Gentle Ben is a nickname that was given to Ben Crenshaw out of sarcasm due to his bouts of temper tantrums. He was anything but gentle. Some also felt that the nickname fit because of the way in which he handled himself after losing major championships. Look, if it weren't for the 1960s television show about a docile bear with the same name, it is doubtful Crenshaw would be known as Gentle Ben.

Most athletes have little appreciation for those who have come before them. There are too many baseball players who don't know about Jackie Robinson; there are NFL players who know nothing of the players who played in the 1950s who draw no pension. NBA players who played under head coach Lenny Wilkens didn't know that he played in the league much less that he is a Hall of Famer.

There are golfers who are like that, too. Not Ben Crenshaw. Crenshaw is a golf historian who revels in the history of the game. He has collected hundreds of golf books, many of them collectors' items. He has memorabilia, paintings, prints, and sculptures. He knows what happened in the game and how it evolved. It helped him as a student. It helped him as a player. It helped him as a course designer. He did more than appreciate the history of the game. He made some of his own.

Ben was introduced to the game by his father and won his first tournament as a fourth-grader. He used clubs that his father had bought him when he was 10. When he was 15 his father gave him a putter, which he used throughout his life. He called the putter Little Ben, and it was always his strong suit. Crenshaw never was able to drive the ball as far as others on the Tour, but his short game made up for it.

There was never any doubt where he would go to college. He was a student of Harvey Penick, who was the golf coach at the University of Texas. Penick taught Crenshaw simplicity. He told his students, "Take dead aim."

While on the Texas golf team, Crenshaw won the NCAA golf championship three times, in 1971, 1972, and 1973. In 1972 he shared the title with teammate Tom Kite. He won the 1973 qualifying tournament by 12 strokes. He joined the Tour at the end of the 1973 season and won the San Antonio–Texas Open in his first professional tournament. His "golden boy" image and boyish looks led to a strong following among female fans, whose ranks were dubbed Ben's Bunnies. This was not sarcastic.

Perhaps at this point in his career, Crenshaw stopped into one of the flea markets or used bookstores to pile up on some golf history, and he found a beautiful lantern. He picked it up and bought it. While rubbing the lantern clean, out popped a genie, who granted him three wishes for his golf career—but only three. "Use them wisely," the genie said. Because there would be no more golf dreams realized besides these three. Crenshaw had his trusty putter, his world-class coach, and his supportive family, and he followed the chosen path for his career.

Ben Crenshaw won his first pro tournament, but his first major championship would take 12 long years. This is what he had to endure. He shot well enough to win the Masters twice, but once he got in the way of Raymond Floyd's winning performance (1976) and the other time it was Seve Ballesteros's show (1983).

He missed a play-off at the 1975 U.S. Open when he hit into the water on the 71st hole. That shot cost him two strokes, and that is what he lost by.

He lost a play-off for the PGA Championship in 1979 after he shot a 272 (69–67–69–67) at Oakland Hills—the second lowest 72-hole score since the PGA went to stroke play in 1957. It wasn't good enough, as Australian David Graham matched the 272, despite a double-bogey on the final hole. In the excruciating play-off, Graham nailed an 18-foot putt on the first extra hole, made a 10-foot putt on the second extra hole, and birdied the third hole to defeat Crenshaw.

In 1978, he finished two strokes back of Jack Nicklaus, who had 14 majors in hand by that point. The next year, Crenshaw tied Nicklaus, but they finished in a tie for second behind Seve Ballesteros. Crenshaw might have had Seve, but he double-bogeyed the 71st hole.

It was time for the genie to grant wish number one. In the 1984 Masters, Crenshaw came to the 13th hole leading the tournament and faced a decision on his second shot—whether to risk going for the green and risk seeing his ball drop into the creek or to lay up and hope to pitch it close enough for par. Crenshaw knew that at the same spot, in the 1954 Masters, Billy Joe Patton went for it from the same spot, the ball went into the water, and Patton failed to win the tournament. Crenshaw was going to go for the green, when he looked up at the gallery and saw Patton. At that point he decided against going for the green and laid up. He won the tournament. Patton said later, "He must have had visions. I wasn't there."

Nice work, genie. Crenshaw was two strokes off the lead going into the final round, but his 68 on the last round defeated Tom Watson by two strokes.

The next year there were no visions, miracles, or wishes granted. Crenshaw began losing weight. His game went into the tank. He had only two top-25 finishes in his 22 tournaments and earned only $25,000 in 1985. He had Graves' disease, an autoimmune disease that causes a common form of hyperthyroidism, which he successfully battled.

He didn't win too much, though. After two victories in 1986, he never won more than once in a year. He wasn't playing well in the months before the 1995 Masters either.

Just before the Masters Tournament, his golf teacher, Harvey Penick, passed away from cancer at the age of 90. Crenshaw, who was a pupil and friend of Penick for more than 35 years, helped with the funeral arrangements, served as a pallbearer, and then went out and was granted his second golfing wish. The wish was, once again, a supernatural force.

He won the Masters for Penick, telling the world afterward, "I felt a hand on my shoulder. Harvey's. I believe in fate." There are some golf tournaments throughout history (Crenshaw's Masters, Payne Stewart's 1999 U.S. Open, Ben Hogan's 1950 U.S. Open) that had seemingly implausible Hollywood endings. Crenshaw would never win another tournament. He barely had any top-10 finishes. From 1998 through 2001, he entered 52 tournaments and made four cuts.

You are probably wondering now about the third wish. Didn't the genie grant the third golfing wish? In 1999 Crenshaw (who had played on the U.S. Ryder Cup team four times) was selected as the nonplaying captain. Just one month before the Europe vs. America battle was to take place in Brookline, Massachusetts, Crenshaw had to call out several members of his team. "It burns the hell out of me to listen to some of their viewpoints. Every fine player who's worth his salt has given his heart and soul to the Ryder Cup on both sides of the Atlantic. I'm personally disappointed in a couple of people." The next day he singled out the four players on his team—Tiger Woods, Phil Mickelson, David Duval, and Mark O'Meara—who had openly expressed the view that they should be paid more than an honorarium to play in the Ryder Cup. There was a couple of million dollars in profit for the Cup that the players didn't share in. Crenshaw went nuts at this attitude.

The U.S. team mounted a final-day comeback, winning 8.5 points of a possible 12, to win the Ryder Cup for the first time since 1993. The U.S. team, captained by Ben Crenshaw, won 14.5 to 13.5.

"I truly believe there's an aura across the 17th green," Crenshaw said afterward. "When you see a putt of that diabolical nature go in, that's a little spooky." The fact that Justin Leonard made his putt on the same hole where Francis Ouimet clinched the 1913 U.S. Open over Ted Ray and Harry Vardon convinced Crenshaw there were supernatural forces beyond anyone's control. Nice work, genie.

By the way, in keeping with a plan established in 1999, the PGA distributes millions of dollars to charities and universities throughout the nation on behalf of the American participants in the Ryder Cup matches. The captain and 12 players each designate money to be distributed to the charities of their choice. It's a great compromise.

A Better Analogy

Ben Crenshaw and Phil Jackson While many people scratch their heads at this one, hear me out. Crenshaw had a deep respect for his longtime coach, Penick. Phil Jackson has a similar respect for the coach of his young days, Red Holzman. Crenshaw had a deep sense of his game's history. So does Phil Jackson, who knows all about Lester Harrison (an NBA coach from the early 1950s who coached Holzman) and everyone else from the league's inception.

Jackson won two championships as a good, but not great, player. Crenshaw won two majors as a player. Jackson's greatest success has come as a head coach, leading the Chicago Bulls and Los Angeles Lakers to nine NBA titles. His greatest strength is standing up to superstars like Michael Jordan and Kobe Bryant. Crenshaw was the coach for the 1999 Ryder Cup team, and his greatest strength was standing up to superstars like Tiger Woods and Phil Mickelson.

46

NICK PRICE
The Price Is Right

Nick Price was born January 28, 1957, in Durban, South Africa. He was the youngest of three brothers by seven years. His father, Ray, was a big sports fan, and cricket matches were popular in the Price house. Nick's parents were British, having met in India when Ray was serving as a major in the Indian Army.

His father, much older than fathers of most of his peers, passed away in 1967, when Nick was only 10 years old. By 1961, the family moved to what is now Zimbabwe, then still under British rule. The fact that Zimbabwe was still under British rule in 1961 is very important in the Nick Price story because he grew up during the Unilateral Declaration of Independence era, when the government declared independence from Britain. A period of unrest followed, along with a civil war into which Price was drafted. As Price writes in his 1997 book, *The Swing*, "Clearly, as a white person I had advantages that black people did not have. I was never comfortable with these conditions nor did I understand them."

He had advantages that athletes from cold-weather areas didn't have, too. The climate in South Africa was perfect to play outdoor sports 12 months a year. His older brothers got him into golf when he was eight years old, and he was hooked immediately.

Price was basically self-taught. He traveled outside Africa for the first time at age 17, when he was invited to participate in the Junior World Championship at Torrey Pines in San Diego. He, along with his mother, took a flight to Johannesburg, then took an 18-hour flight to New York, and then flew to San Diego—with a stop in Chicago first. Nothing like a nice, relaxing 24 hours of flying to get you ready for the best golf of your life. Price actually defeated the other 255 golfers from 28 countries in the 15- to 17-year-old age group.

By 1975, at an age when some of his peers were conscripted into the Army, Nick Price made it to the semis of the British Amateur. He started on the European Tour in 1978. After improving for three years, he had a terrible 1981 and became discouraged. He sought out his friend David Leadbetter, who had come from Europe to America. Price knew Leadbetter from Zimbabwe and had played a lot of golf with him. Leadbetter was the one teacher that an unknown from Africa named Nick Price could call up and seek help from. He spent five weeks working on his swing with Leadbetter.

Did it help? Well, in 1981, Price was 23rd in the British Open, and his career was floundering. In 1982 he tied for second at the British Open. In November of 1982, Price qualified for the PGA Tour by finishing third in the qualifying school tournament.

He won his first PGA Tournament, the World Series of Golf, in 1983. He had rounds of 66–68–69–67 to defeat Jack Nicklaus by four shots. Twenty years later Price recounted how that day was one of the two greatest days in his golfing career (the other being the final round of the 1994 British Open):

> Every time you look at the leader board, you see the names Nicklaus, Floyd, Watson. And these guys who were idols of mine, and here I was, 25 or 26 years old, probably four of the most distinguished players of my generation ahead of me breathing down my neck. And that was staring me in the face at every leader board. But I proved to myself that day that if I just focused on what I was trying to do, I could achieve.

That win gave him a lucky ticket to be exempt from qualifying for tournaments.

Not that Price needed much help qualifying, although he didn't win again on the PGA Tour until 1991. He did win overseas. But he just couldn't win in the United States in the 1980s.

Nick Price in PGA Tour Events
1984: 0 victories in 19 tournaments
1985: 0 victories in 20 tournaments
1986: 0 victories in 25 tournaments
1987: 0 victories in 25 tournaments
1988: 0 victories in 24 tournaments
1989: 0 victories in 27 tournaments
1990: 0 victories in 28 tournaments

And then Price became the biggest winner of the early 1990s. Only Woods had as many PGA Tour wins (15) as Price in the 1990s. Price was the 1993 and 1994 Player of the Year. He won the PGA Championship in 1992 and 1994. He won the British Open in 1994. He's one of only seven players since 1945 to win consecutive majors (Ben Hogan, Jack Nicklaus, Arnold Palmer, Lee Trevino, Tom Watson, and Tiger Woods).

His first major came in 1992 at the PGA Championship at Bellerive Country Club, in St. Louis. Price, who had come within three strokes of winning two majors (the 1982 and the 1988 British Opens), made nine straight pars on the front nine holes of the final round. He made three birdie putts on the back nine. He won by three strokes over four different golfers.

At the British Open in 1994 at Turnberry, he played the final three holes eagle-birdie-par to make up a two-stroke deficit over Jesper Parnevik. He took a five-stroke lead at the PGA Championship at Southern Hills with a second-round 65 and then cruised to a six-stroke victory.

Price said in Bob McCullough's 2001 *My Greatest Day in Golf* that you have to look at a career over a lifetime. "You don't measure a person's career by a three-or-four year stretch." Price had a steady progression, peaked in the early '90s, and then continued to play at a high level for a number of years. Two dozen international victories and 18 PGA Tour victories, including three majors, earn him a spot in the top 50.

Who's Better, Who's Best
Nick Price, Larry Nelson, Henry Cotton, or Retief Goosen?

Three of these four golfers have won three majors in their careers. Henry Cotton was a European golfer who won three British Opens and might have won more. He won two before World War II, and he won in 1948. Six British Opens were canceled due to wartime conditions, and a person would have to figure that Cotton would have won at least one or two more but for the cancelations. Of course, even fewer American stars competed in the British Open in the late 1930s. The cost of traveling to Britain prohibited the trips by Nelson, Hogan, Snead, and others.

Cotton played an important part in golf history. In the years between 1922 and 1933, only one Brit had won the British Open. Cotton, who won for the first time in 1934, changed that. No American would win the British Open again until Sam Snead in 1946.

Larry Nelson was a Vietnam veteran who turned pro after he returned from Vietnam in 1971. He won the PGA Championship in 1981 and then repeated in 1987 by defeating Lanny Wadkins in a play-off. Nelson also won the 1983 U.S. Open at Oakmont. But Nelson won only 10 PGA Tour events total. Even if you think he deserves extra points for his success on the Seniors Tour (yes) and for his time in Vietnam (yes, yes), he still comes up a little short of the more dominating Price.

Cotton didn't have the competition that Nelson and Price had, while Price just had a longer and more productive career—worldwide—than Nelson had.

One modern player that can challenge Price's spot is fellow South African Retief Goosen. The Goose, born in February of 1959, is two years younger than Price. Retief won the U.S. Open in both 2001 and 2004 and was second at the 2002 Masters. He is so consistent that it is easy to overlook him. In 2005, he tied for 3rd at the Masters, tied for 11th at the U.S. Open, tied for 5th at the British Open, and tied for 6th at the PGA Championship. His strength is in his long irons; he can reach almost any fairway and will probably add to his two major championships. As of this writing, however, he still trails Price.

47

YOUNG TOM MORRIS
The First Great Champ

There will be plenty of skeptics who question my placement of Tom Morris Jr. among the top 50 golfers of all time. But I think this one is a no-brainer. Only two golfers ever won four professional majors in a row. One is Tom Morris Jr., the first great champion. The other one is Tiger Woods, the latest great champion. I know, I know. When Morris competed there were only about a dozen golfers, mostly local, in the field. All you can do is beat the competition. But yes, that's why Tiger is ranked 1st and Morris merely 47th.

Just as is true in the case of many great champions, including Tiger, one has to learn first about the father. Old Tom Morris, born in 1821 in St. Andrews, Scotland, was a professional golfer, and a good one at that. His first job was as an apprentice to Allan Robertson, probably the best golfer of his era. Robertson had a pretty good business making feather golf balls in the mid-1840s. When the new gutta-percha balls were introduced, Robertson stuck with the feather balls. Morris opened his own shop, making the new gutta-percha balls as well as golf clubs.

In 1851 Morris moved to Prestwick, and that same year, his son, the great Young Tom Morris, was born. It was six years after that when the Prestwick Golf Club sent letters to other golf clubs in Scotland, inviting them to play in a match. At first it was a team competition. The timing was perfect for a championship, and the Prestwick Golf Club—with Old Tom Morris's help—set up the British Open (meaning that it was open to amateurs and professionals alike). Tom Morris Sr. finished second to Willie Park Sr. in the inaugural event of 1860. It was the first of four British Championships that he would win.

So Young Tom Morris was born into golf the way Prince Andrew, son of Queen Elizabeth II, was born into the royal British family. Consider the Morrises the royal golf family. Was Tom Morris Sr. the Earl Woods of his day, pushing his son into golf as soon as possible? Quite probably, yes. The sun never set on the Morrises' empire. The father won four of the first eight British Opens, and his son followed by winning four in a row.

Young Tom won his first match at the age of 13. Three years later he was beating the top players in Scotland (a.k.a. the top golfers in the world). Morris set the standards that the Great Triumvirate would have to live up to years later. When Harry Vardon, James Braid, and J. H. Taylor were battling, the mark was Young Tom's four consecutive Opens. Or the record of four victories, held by both father and son Morris. The junior Morris was a powerful striker who was also great at recovery shots. His iron play was considered revolutionary. It was rumored that Young Tom was the first to put backspin on the ball. His short game was his strength, despite the conditions of the greens.

He won his first British Open in 1868, when he was 17, toppling the previous year's winner—his father, Old Tom Morris. Young Tom beat the scoring record by five strokes. In 1869 he shot 154, which bettered his own record by three more strokes. He defended his title the following year, lowering the scoring record once again. When he won the 1870 British Open, Young Tom began with a 3 on the first hole. He played the first 12 holes in 47 strokes. He won by 12 strokes over Bob Kirk and David Strath.

OK, I know it's not the same thing as Tiger winning in Pebble Beach by 15 strokes, but that a 19-year-old won "the Championship" by 12 strokes is impressive. Morris's score was not broken for 34 years—and was never broken with the gutta-percha ball.

The rules of the British Open at the time awarded a belt to the champion, with the champion keeping it if he won for three straight years. There was no Open in 1871, because Morris had won the darn thing three straight years. They didn't have a trophy to award, so they canceled the event.

Prestwick members, who had hosted the Open the first 11 years, then came up with the idea of sharing the Open Championship with the Royal & Ancient Golf Club of St. Andrews and the Honourable Company of Edinburgh Golfers. Prestwick proposed that the three clubs take turns staging the Open and chip in equally toward the creation of a new trophy. When the new trophy wasn't ready in 1872, they awarded a Claret Jug.

Claret is a dry red wine produced in the famous French wine-making region of Bordeaux. The British Open trophy was made in the style of silver jugs used to serve claret at nineteenth-century gatherings.

Young Tom won his fourth Open in 1872 and received the very first Claret Jug. It was his fourth championship in a row. He won those four Opens by almost eight strokes per year, so it wasn't even close.

The Morrises were playing golf at North Berwick in 1875 when a telegraph messenger pushed through the crowd and approached Old Tom with a message. The message said that his daughter-in-law had given birth but was gravely ill. It is believed that the match was stopped at this point. Young Tom couldn't get back before his wife died while giving birth to their stillborn child. Three months later Young Tom, at the age of 24, was dead himself. He died of a hemorrhage, which may have been the result of too much drinking.

Leslie Balfour Melville, a Scot born in 1854 who was a great tennis, golf, and rugby champion, saw both Young Tom and Harry Vardon play. Melville told writer Bernard Darwin that he couldn't imagine anyone playing better than Young Tommy.

Young Tom Morris hadn't anything to prove and didn't play in the Open the last few years of his life, so even if he hadn't died so young, it is doubtful that he would have added to his golf legacy.

The Best Father-Son Combination in Golf History?

There aren't many father-son winners in golf history. Willie Park Jr. won two British Opens after his dad won four early ones. They were the second-best father-son combo in golf next to the Morrises. In the remaining golf pairs, the fathers were clearly better than their sons, who did well to win a tournament or two.

Father-Son Winners in Golf

Tom Morris Sr.	Tom Morris Jr.
Willie Park Sr.	Willie Park Jr.
Joe Kirkwood Sr.	Joe Kirkwood Jr.
Clayton Heafner	Vance Heafner
Julius Boros	Guy Boros
Al Geiberger	Brent Geiberger

Who's Better, Who's Best
Young Tom Morris or Willie Anderson?

It's startling to see the similarities between Young Tom and Willie Anderson. Young Tom won 4 British Opens in a five-year stretch and won 4 of the first 12 British Opens played. Anderson won 4 U.S. Opens (1901, 1903, 1904, and 1905) in a five-year stretch and won 4 of the first 11 played. He had seven other top-five finishes. Very little is known about Anderson personally.

Anderson was born in Scotland (as was Young Tom) in 1880 and came to the United States when Frank Slazenger went from the United States to Scotland and paid for golfers to come across to America and work for him (to build up interest in golf and to benefit Slazenger's sporting goods company). Willie was just a kid at 15 when he immigrated to this country. He was a hired gun, working for 10 different golf courses over the next 14 years. Anderson was among the first Scottish professionals to come to America and the first dominant figure in U.S. Open history. Anderson not only won the four U.S. Opens, but he won four Western Opens between 1902 and 1909.

Asked many years ago how Anderson would have compared to Walter Hagen and Bobby Jones, 1908 U.S. Open champ Fred McLeod said without hesitation, "As good as either one."

Both died young—Young Tom at the age of 24 and Anderson at the age of 30. Bill Fields, writing in 2005 in *Golf World*, says that it was epilepsy that killed Anderson. Like Morris's, his death was rumored to be from drinking.

Young Tom played "home games" at the British Open, so he had it easier than Anderson, who spent the last half of his life in a strange country, exposing people to the game of golf. A match play between these two would have been fascinating. Anderson was the first golfer to break 300 in a 72-hole event. Young Tom regularly destroyed his competition.

I'm giving the nod to Young Tom Morris, but I'm fascinated with Willie Anderson. Only four men have won the U.S. Open as many as four times. Besides Anderson, they are Bobby Jones, Ben Hogan, and Jack Nicklaus. None of the other three will be forgotten. Anderson shouldn't be either.

48

LANNY WADKINS
Ryder Cup Counts!

Lanny Wadkins was born on December 5, 1949, in Richmond, Virginia, the son of a truck driver father and schoolteacher mother. He was 10 years old when Arnold Palmer, in 1960, won both the Masters and the U.S. Open. Wadkins copied his game and even went on to capture an Arnold Palmer scholarship to his alma mater, Wake Forest University.

Sixteen years after Palmer captured the U.S. Amateur title, Wadkins did the same. Lanny started the final round two shots back of another collegian, Tom Kite, but after two early birdies, Wadkins took the lead. He sealed the victory with a 20-foot putt on the 18th hole.

The 5'9" 175-pound golfer was one of the most heralded golfers to begin his PGA Tour career. In October of 1972 at the Sahara Invitational, 43-year-old Palmer, who hadn't won a tournament in 15 months, was defeated by a 22-year-old rookie named Lanny Wadkins.

If Lanny modeled his game after Arnold, people were noticing. Palmer played a reckless, go-for-broke game that Wadkins enjoyed himself. Wadkins played the game that Phil Mickelson frequently played, thrilling the crowd by never laying up.

Roger Maltbie, PGA member and winner of five PGA Tournaments: "His style of game was very similar to Arnold, but he didn't have the power that Arnold had. When Arnold was younger, he could really knock that ball."

Wadkins had to feel almost embarrassed at winning the tournament over the beloved Palmer. Heck, Palmer was his hero. There's a reason that athletes shouldn't get too sentimental toward the outgoing players. No one knows how much time they have to win, and they can't give up on a tournament thinking that they have time on their side. In 1972 Wadkins had the world at his command. There was no reason for anyone to begrudge Wadkins his victory. Palmer's time as a dominant golfer had passed.

In 1977 the 27-year-old Wadkins captured his first major at the PGA Championship, held at Pebble Beach. Wadkins began the final round six shots behind Gene Littler but caught him on the 18th hole with a birdie. Littler was not only 20 years older and enjoy-ing a last hurrah at a major, but he was a cancer survivor. For the first time ever, a major was decided in a sudden-death play-off. Wadkins, the fiercest of competitors, defeated Littler on the third play-off hole.

The victory would turn out to be the highlight of Wadkins's pro career. It represented his only major. If Littler was the obvious sentimental choice, then Wadkins wouldn't have been a bad second sentimental pick. He had not fulfilled the high expectations since turning pro, in part because of surgery to remove his gall bladder and appendix at the end of 1974. But at the time, Wadkins had time, and Littler did not, to win more golf majors.

- **1982 PGA Championship:** Raymond Floyd shot a 63 in the first round, and the great front-runner was not going to lose this tournament. Wadkins beat everyone else, finishing three strokes back (after being eight strokes back after the first 18 holes).
- **1984 PGA Championship:** Wadkins tied for the first-day lead with a 4-under par 68. He had a share of the lead with Lee Trevino and Gary Player after round two. Wadkins was only one shot back of Trevino on the par-three 16th hole, needing to make up one stroke over three holes. Wadkins missed a 12-foot putt for birdie, and Trevino made his 15-foot putt for par. Wadkins then bogeyed the 17th and 18th holes, while Trevino added a birdie on the final hole for victory. But if Wadkins had made his birdie on 16, then that one shot might have made the difference between winning and losing a major.
- **1986 U.S. Open:** Greg Norman led after 54 holes but fell apart in the last round. Wadkins shot a 65 to finish at 281, and it forced Floyd to shoot a 66 to finish with 279 and the title.
- **1987 PGA Championship:** Wadkins was caught by Larry Nelson, who came from three strokes off the pace. Nelson won with a par-4 on the first extra hole, as Wadkins missed a four-foot putt for his par.

Wadkins was third at the Masters in 1990, 1991, and 1993, never closer than the tie for third in 1991, just two shots behind winner Ian Woosnam.

But aside from his win at Pebble Beach at the PGA, his most memorable professional golf victory had to come at the Ryder Cup.

At the 1983 Ryder Cup, Europe came within inches of pulling off a Ryder Cup vic-tory in the United States. The teams were deadlocked after two days and 10 singles matches. On the third day, Seve Ballesteros halved with Fuzzy Zoeller after one of the great shots in Ryder Cup history. Meanwhile, Wadkins fell one hole down to Jose Maria Canizares going into the 18th hole, a par-5 dogleg left into the wind. Wadkins salvaged his team by hitting a 60-yard pitching wedge approach to within a foot of the hole to halve the match. If Wadkins hadn't won the hole, Europe would "halve" the Ryder Cup. After Wadkins took his shot, captain Jack Nicklaus felt such relief that he dropped to his knees and kissed Wadkins's divot.

Roger Maltbie: "It was so clear how emotional he was, and how much the Ryder Cup meant to him. We wish some of the younger players had the same passion for it now, like Lanny had."

Lanny Wadkins at the Ryder Cup

No one played more foursome matches than Wadkins for the United States (15, same as Casper). No one but Casper played more than Wadkins's 34 matches. Wadkins played for the United States in 1977, 1979, 1983, 1985, 1987, 1989, 1991, and 1993 and captained the 1995 team. His Ryder Cup record was 20–11–3.

Most Points Won for the United States
1. 23.5 Billy Casper
2. 23.0 Arnold Palmer
3. 21.5 Lanny Wadkins

Wadkins was the third leading money winner in 1977 and 1983. In 1985 he had his greatest year. He won three tournaments and had top-10 finishes in 12 of his 24 events. He was named PGA Player of the Year in 1985, when he finished second to Curtis Strange in the money list.

Wadkins gets the nod over Strange, who won 2 U.S. Opens, in 1988 and 1989, but not much else. He won 17 times, including the two majors. Larry Nelson's two PGA Championships and his U.S. Open gave him three majors, but he had only seven other victories (unless you want to count his 19 Champions Tour wins).

Who's Better, Who's Best
Lanny Wadkins or Johnny Miller?

Jim Nantz, who shares a broadcast booth at CBS Sports with Wadkins, was persuasive when he suggested that Wadkins wasn't far from Miller. In fact, look at the numbers:

> Miller: 25 PGA Tour wins, 2 majors, 4 runner-up finishes in majors
> Wadkins: 21 PGA Tour wins, 1 major, 4 runner-up finishes in majors

Miller, though, put his numbers together in a much shorter time period than Wadkins. Miller led the money list in 1974, becoming the only person to head the money list besides Jack Nicklaus from 1971 to 1976. Miller not only led the money list in 1974, but he was second in 1975.

Miller with eight wins dominated the Tour in 1974. Wadkins never won even four times in one year. Still, if you factor in the U.S. Amateur title and the Ryder Cup, then Wadkins earns a place in the top 50 of all time.

Miller, born a few years before Wadkins, was through by the age of 35. He won 22 of his 25 events before he turned 35. Wadkins, though, had only won 12 events by December of 1984, his 35th birthday. Though Wadkins didn't quite catch Miller's numbers, he made it close enough to warrant the discussion and earn a place in this book.

Who's Better, Who's Best
Lanny Wadkins or Davis Love III?

Let's compare Wadkins's numbers with those of Love.

> Lanny Wadkins: 21 PGA Tour wins, 1 major, 4 runner-up finishes in majors
> Davis Love III: 18 PGA Tour wins, 1 major, 3 runner-up finishes in majors

This is pretty close, especially in light of the fact that Davis Love III was born in April of 1964 and still has time to add to his Tour victories. Love has been a part of six Ryder Cup teams and won the Players Championship in 1992. In 2005, he finished in the top six at both the U.S. Open and the PGA Championship. If he does well in the remaining majors on the back end of his career, he could take Wadkins's spot in the top 50 of all time.

49

GENE LITTLER
Gene the Machine

Gene Littler was born on July 21, 1930, in San Diego, California. In high school he competed in track and baseball and played the violin. He attended San Diego State University beginning in 1949 and left school two years later to enlist in the Navy. (This was during the Korean War.) For three years he was assigned to Special Services, where he stayed far from the trouble spots and actually improved his golf game. I guess he was lucky, stationed where he could play golf a lot and work on his game.

He would be known for having a beautiful swing, and it was little wonder that his model was Sam Snead. Littler's swing appeared effortless, similar to Snead's. His nickname, Gene the Machine, came from the rhyme in his name and the fact that he was very even tempered, never rattled, and never seemed to make costly mistakes. He was as dependable as a machine. But Littler wasn't that little. He was 5'9" and weighed 160 pounds.

Just as Byron Nelson and Ben Hogan were both from Texas and knew about each other from an early age, Littler and Billy Casper were similarly linked. Littler was less than a year older than Casper, and the two of them both grew up in the San Diego area. Casper grew up 15 miles south of San Diego, and Littler grew up about 15 miles north. They even faced each other a few times in high school and in junior golf matches. Littler almost always won. For a short time they were teammates on the San Diego Naval Training Station golf team.

It was Littler who won the U.S. Amateur in 1953, the year before Arnold Palmer won it. Still with his amateur standing, he won the 1954 San Diego Open. Later in 1954 he turned professional and joined the PGA Tour. After a superb rookie season, Littler was destined for great things.

Remember, Palmer, Casper, and Littler all turned pro in 1954. Littler was not even 24 years old in the summer of 1954, when he came within one stroke of winning the U.S. Open at Baltusrol. He had a bad third round, shooting 76. He lost by a stroke to Ed Furgol, whose win was his only top-three finish in any major ever.

Gene the Machine was on his way to a Hall of Fame career. He started winning regularly in 1955.

1955	Championships	Top 10s
Gene Littler	4	10
Arnold Palmer	1	8
Billy Casper	0	2

Littler, at the age of 26, won three more tournaments in 1956 and now was opening a sizable lead on Palmer and Casper.

Career Through 1956	Championships	Top 10s
Gene Littler	8	43
Arnold Palmer	3	18
Billy Casper	1	12

Those three rookies were quite formidable. Look at how they dominated the U.S. Open beginning in 1959:

U.S. Open Champions
1959 Billy Casper
1960 Arnold Palmer
1961 Gene Littler

Littler was quiet and calm compared with Casper, who was bigger and more demonstrative. Even early in his career, before he became a Mormon, Casper was known to have a temper. Palmer was anything but quiet himself, drawing in fans with his stylish play. Littler was the perfectionist who valued each and every shot. He was one of the most respected—if not the most respected—golfer on the Tour.

Through the end of the 1963 season, it was still a close call between the San Diego members of the Class of '54. But Palmer pulled away.

Career Through 1963	Championships	Majors	Top 10s
Arnold Palmer	40	4	131
Billy Casper	21	1	112
Gene Littler	19	1	125

After 1963 Casper found a way to combat personal demons and allergic reactions. His play improved with the years, and he would get many more victories than Palmer or Littler after the 1963 season. Casper passed Palmer with the whole world watching on the final round of a U.S. Open. You want to know why Casper is ranked so much higher than Littler? In the years from 1964 to 1969, Casper won 23 times, while Littler won only three tournaments. Littler had other interests, including his collection of antique cars. He had a 1914 Model T as well as 1919 and 1924 Rolls-Royces.

Maybe Littler's game was like one of his vintage cars, which increased in value with age. Maybe Littler's game never changed, but Palmer's game had gone into decline, while Jack Nicklaus was in his three-year slump—and they left some tournaments for others to win.

In 1969 Littler took the Phoenix Thunderbird Open and the Greater Greensboro Open. In April of 1970 he tied Casper through 72 holes of the Masters. They played an 18-hole play-off the next day for the major championship. Littler blew the championship on Sunday's 16th hole.

The three vets from the Class of '54 were Ryder Cup teammates on many occasions. Casper played on the Ryder Cup team in 1961, 1963, 1965, 1967, 1969, 1971, 1973, and 1975. Palmer played on six of those eight teams, missing 1969 and 1975. Littler also played on six of those teams, missing 1973 and 1975.

There was a good reason that Littler didn't play on the 1973 or 1975 Ryder Cup teams. He was battling cancer. At the age of 42 he underwent surgery to remove malignant growths underneath his left shoulder in 1972. There was doubt whether he would survive five years.

What he did was return to golf, and five years later, in 1977, he nearly won another major title. In fact, he had it in his pocket. At Pebble Beach for the 1977 PGA Championship, Littler didn't bogey any of the first 42 holes. Through 54 holes he had shot a 206, which was good for 10-under par and a four-stroke lead on Nicklaus.

Lanny Wadkins started the final day six shots behind Littler and was still five behind with nine holes to play. Littler bogeyed five of the first six holes on the back nine. Wadkins finished in a tie with Littler, who shot a final-round 76. For the first time, a major championship was decided in a sudden-death play-off, and Lanny made his six-foot par putt to edge the 47-year-old Littler.

Littler won eight Seniors titles, though, and is a member of the PGA Hall of Fame. Littler finished with 29 Tour wins and the one major championship. Palmer and Casper would prove more dominating throughout the prime of their careers. Wadkins is just a little ahead of Gene the Machine, although Littler had eight more Tour victories (29 to Wadkins's 21).

Who's Better, Who's Best
Gene Littler or Curtis Strange?

This is an interesting comparison, between the volatile Curtis Strange, who was born in 1955, and the calm, cool Littler, who was a rookie on the Tour then. Strange is not ranked in the top 50 in this book, and Littler is. Here's the reasoning:

Curtis Strange: 17 PGA Tour victories
Gene Littler: 29 PGA Tour victories
Edge: Littler

Curtis Strange: Won the 1988 U.S. Open; won the 1989 U.S. Open
Gene Littler: Won the 1961 U.S. Open
Edge: Strange

But it's not a big edge. Strange was second at two other majors (the 1989 PGA Championship and the 1985 Masters). Littler, however, was second at three other majors (1954 U.S. Open, the 1970 Masters, and the 1977 PGA Championship). Considering that Littler lost two of those majors in play-offs, you can see that Strange's edge is not much here. I also think that the contemporaries of Strange (Greg Norman and Nick Faldo chief among them) were not as formidable as Arnold Palmer, Jack Nicklaus, Gary Player, and Billy Casper were to Littler.

Finally, a big edge goes to Littler, who contended for major championships in the mid-1950s and also in the mid-1970s. His career may not have had the peak that Strange's did, when Curtis was the best player in the game. But Strange's stay at the top was too short to be of great consequence. Littler had a much longer period when he was among the best. So it's Littler who wins this matchup.

50

PAUL RUNYAN
Little Poison

I end the book with Littler and Littlest. Gene Littler is ranked number 49. Paul Runyan, the golfer who was nicknamed Little Poison, weighed only 130 pounds. The "Poison" part of the nickname came about because many athletes who stood 5'7" or less were called Little Poison (like baseball's Lloyd Waner). I could have ended the book with Lawson Little, Gene Littler, and Paul Runyan (little, littler, littlest), but I am sparing you (at least in this chapter) my odd sense of humor.

Speaking of little, Runyan even titled his own instructional book *The Short Way to Lower Scoring*. He had a devastating short game—one of the best. It made up for the fact that he couldn't drive the ball more than 230 yards.

In almost every article and interview from his playing days, his size is mentioned. A famous sportswriter of the day, Henry McLemore, wrote in 1940, "Runyan has an inability to hit the ball very far. Slight in build, with hands and almost girlish wrists, he gets none of the tremendous drive of his rivals."

McLemore used Runyan's "little-man" status to hold him up as a shining example to the armchair quarterbacks (or golfers) who lacked the size or strength of the people they played against. Generations later the sports and the athletes changed, but the tone of the stories did not. Great athletes find a way, even if they're quarterbacks who can't see over their linemen or point guards who shoot over much taller players. Runyan found a way, despite not being able to drive the ball as far.

Runyan was born on July 12, 1908, in Hot Springs, Arkansas, and began his golf career as a caddie. In 1925, at the age of 17, he became an assistant to Craig Wood at Forest Hills Golf Course, in White Plains, New York. Wood became his teacher as well as his boss.

Runyan's first PGA win came in 1930, when he was a 118-pound unknown at the North and South Open Championship. He would add more tournament victories than pounds in the following years. In 1933 he had one of the very best years any golfer has had before or since.

Most Tournament Victories in a Calendar Year
1. 18 Byron Nelson, 1945
2. 13 Ben Hogan, 1946
3. 11 Sam Snead, 1950
4. 10 Ben Hogan, 1948
5. 9 Paul Runyan, 1933; Tiger Woods, 2000; Vijay Singh, 2004

Runyan followed that up in 1934 with a season that was almost as good. He went from nine wins to six. He played in two majors, winning the PGA and finishing two strokes back at the inaugural Masters. How did the only other five golfers to win as many as nine times in a single year fare the following year? Not as well as Runyan.

Nelson went from 18 wins to 6.

Hogan went from 13 wins to 7.

Snead went from 11 wins to 2.

(Hogan went from 10 in 1948 to a terrible auto accident in 1949.)

Woods went from 9 wins to 5.

Singh went from 9 wins to 4.

The point here isn't to take away from Nelson or Hogan. The point here is to show how difficult it is to come close to a career season.

Runyan's greatest year, 1933, was the year prior to the first Masters Tournament. In the first Masters the front-page headlines were that Bobby Jones returned to competitive golf for the first time after four years. He was paired for the first-ever round of the Masters with Runyan. Although Jones outdrove him, Runyan had a lower score. Jones was smart enough to limit his competitive golf to the one tournament each year in Augusta. He knew that it was Runyan's time, and although Runyan wasn't old, he wasn't the Bobby Jones–caliber player that the world was accustomed to seeing.

The pupil Runyan would defeat Craig Wood, his one-time teacher, in the finals of the PGA Championship nine years after Runyan worked as Wood's assistant. It was Runyan's first major victory. They were as different as golfers could be. Wood was a long hitter, while Runyan was the putting master. At the 35th hole Wood almost holed his second shot, making birdie and bringing the match all square going into the last hole. Both players managed to miss the final green and chipped within 12 feet. Runyan was able to make his putt and put the pressure on Wood. Wood responded, and they needed extra holes. Finally, at the 37th hole, Runyan made another 12-foot putt and won the PGA.

In the 1938 PGA Championship, Runyan was a bogey-free machine, making just one bogey in his final 70 holes. Despite Snead outdriving him by 40 yards off every tee, Runyan had his short game working. He had a 5-up lead halfway through. He closed out the match with a half on the 29th.

Runyan was one very good match player. He was 2–0 in match play against Byron Nelson, Walter Hagen, and Ben Hogan. He split two matches with Gene Sarazen. He enjoyed beating bigger players, and perhaps he got himself psyched up to play the top players long before it was fashionable to have a "mental coach."

After his career he became a great teacher, giving golf instruction for many years in the San Diego area. He taught two of the greats ranked ahead of him: Mickey Wright and Gene Littler. He played or taught for 78 years. By his last years he wasn't just shooting his age—often he was shooting 14 shots under his age!

Who's Better, Who's Best
Paul Runyan, Harry Cooper, or Leo Diegel?

One can't simply just list the top 50 all-time PGA Tour winners and call them the greatest golfers of all time. This book has fit in the top women players, the top international players, and even the top amateurs, like Bobby Jones and Lawson Little. Still, every golfer who won 29 or more times on the PGA Tour appears in this book, with two exceptions. Harry Cooper had 31 victories and Leo Diegel had 30. Littler and Runyan get the final two spots over Cooper and Diegel, despite their 29 Tour victories apiece.

Cooper won 31 times, but he never did win a major championship. It's hard to put him ahead of Runyan, who won nine times in one year (more than Cooper ever did) and won two majors, in one of them kicking the crap out of Snead.

But it's a real debate over who's better between Diegel and Runyan. Let's take a look at their career numbers. Diegel is ahead 30–29 in Tour victories. Not much to go on. Both had the two PGA Championships. Runyan beat a 26-year-old Snead, 8 and 7, in the 1938 finals—the biggest winning margin of victory in the history of the PGA Championship match-play records. But Diegel was the winner taking the fewest holes to win, with 154. He did that twice, tying in 1929 the record he set in 1928.

Runyan beat a deep field. In 1938 Little Poison defeated Horton Smith and Snead on his way to the PGA Championship. Diegel also beat a deep field. In the 1928 PGA Championship, Diegel defeated George Christ in the second round, Walter Hagen in the quarterfinals (the Anti–George Christ), Gene Sarazen in the semifinals, and Al Espinosa in the finals. It would have been great to see him play Bobby Jones, but that wasn't going to happen in the PGA Championship.

In their PGA Tournament careers, Runyan was 25–10 in his matches. Diegel was 19–11, a clear advantage for Little Poison. Runyan had four top-four finishes at the Masters, finishing third in 1934 and 1942. The closest Diegel came to capturing a major title aside from the pair he won was the U.S. Open in 1920.

I'm going with Runyan—but just by a "little." I'm also sharing a quote by Runyan, who passed away on March 17, 2002, at the age of 93. When asked in 1967 why golf is a great game, he replied:

Because you can play it from childhood until you have one foot in the grave. It's a great game because it possesses more of the variables of suspense, and because you are completely responsible for success or failure.

THE 19TH HOLE
Breaking Down the Rankings

For people who don't want to go through the book and count up the various breakdowns, I include the following. The year 1960 seemed like the beginning of the modern age in golf, with the world becoming smaller because of easier airplane travel. Arnold Palmer was the father of the modern-day golfers. It seems to me that the golfers of the 1950s, like Sam Snead and Ben Hogan, had more in common with the golfers from the 1920s than the ones from the 1980s.

10 Best Male Golfers Pre-1960
1. Ben Hogan
2. Sam Snead
3. Harry Vardon
4. Bobby Jones
5. Walter Hagen
6. Byron Nelson
7. Gene Sarazen
8. Jim Barnes
9. Peter Thomson
10. Bobby Locke

Jones and Nelson had nothing left to prove and retired young. Snead and Sarazen get extra credit for attendance records. The easiest choice in this book is Hogan at the top of this list. Prior to Tiger and Jack, Hogan was clearly the best of all time.

10 Best Male Golfers 1960 to the Present
1. Tiger Woods
2. Jack Nicklaus
3. Gary Player
4. Arnold Palmer
5. Tom Watson
6. Billy Casper
7. Lee Trevino
8. Nick Faldo
9. Hale Irwin
10. Seve Ballesteros

In time the number of majors won will be almost a roll call of this list. Tiger will be in the 20s, followed by Jack's 18. Casper and Irwin don't have as many majors as Ray Floyd, yet they got on this list over him.

10 Best Female Golfers

1. Mickey Wright
2. Babe Didrikson Zaharias
3. Annika Sorenstam
4. Kathy Whitworth
5. Nancy Lopez
6. Patty Berg
7. Louise Suggs
8. Betsy Rawls
9. Juli Inkster
10. Karrie Webb
    Patty Sheehan (tie)

My apologies to JoAnne Carner for not finding a spot on this list for her. Suggs had 10 majors, fewer than Berg's 14 in a similar time period. Not only did Rawls have 8 majors, but they included 4 U.S. Women's Opens and 2 LPGA Championships.

10 Best International Golfers

1. Harry Vardon
2. Gary Player
3. Nick Faldo
4. Seve Ballesteros
5. Greg Norman
6. Peter Thomson
7. Bobby Locke
8. J. H. Taylor
9. Ernie Els
10. Tommy Armour

Looking at this list, one can see that there sure have been some great golfers from South Africa. It's too bad Locke and Thomson didn't compete more against the best U.S. golfers in their primes. Retief Goosen would make this list if it were expanded just a bit.

10 Best Golfers Who Never Won the Masters Tournament
1. Bobby Jones
2. Walter Hagen
3. Lee Trevino
4. Hale Irwin
5. Greg Norman
6. Peter Thomson
7. Bobby Locke
8. Ernie Els
9. Tommy Armour
10. Tom Kite

Jones and Hagen were past their prime when the first tournament was held at Augusta in 1934. Jones finished tied for 13th in 1934, and Hagen finished tied for 11th in 1936.

Trevino never did like playing at Augusta and even skipped a few years. He did finish as high as 10th in 1975 and 1985. Irwin had four consecutive top-five finishes. Don't ask about Norman's Masters history. He finished second three times in painful fashion.

Thomson finished fifth in 1957, in one of his only seven trips. Right off the plane from South Africa, Locke finished tied for 10th in 1948. Els finished second to Tiger in 2000 and second to Phil in 2004.

Johnny Miller finished second, or tied for second, three times (1971, 1975, and 1981). Julius Boros tied for third in 1963. Tom Kite finished second at Augusta to Tiger Woods, Jack Nicklaus, and Seve Ballesteros.

Please feel free to e-mail your choices and comments to me at talkto@elliottkalb.com.

INDEX